POMPEII

GUIDE TO THE LOST CITY

SALVATORE
NAPPO

To my wife Ela

WEIDENFELD & NICOLSON
LONDON

POMPEII
GUIDE TO THE LOST CITY

Text
Salvatore Ciro Nappo

Photographs
Alfredo and Pio Foglia

Editors
Valeria Manferto De Fabianis
Laura Accomazzo

Graphic design
Anna Galliani
Clara Zanotti

Colour drawings
Fabio Bourbon
Monica Falcone
Roberta Vigone

Translation
A.B.A., Milan

CONTENTS

1 This flying cherub, portrayed with the attributes of Mercury, is wearing the winged petasus (wide-brimmed hat) and holding the caduceus (a staff with two entwined serpents) which symbolised health.

2-3 This aerial view of Pompeii, seen from the north-west, shows its intricate road network and the layout of the buildings, which emphasise the size of the town. The districts which have not yet been explored can be seen at the top left.

4 This magnificent gold ring with a figured gem is particularly interesting because the setting portrays a head, shown in left profile, with such realistic features, suggesting that it depicts the owner.

5 This portrait of Terentius Neo and his wife comes from the tablinum in the house named after him (VII-2-6). The characters were painted by a specialist who played on the contrast between the intellectual appearance of the couple (the man is holding a book, and the woman a stylus and a diptych) and their obvious working-class background.

ISBN 0-297-82467-8

Colour separations Fotomec Turin
Printed in Italy by Milanostampa 1998

4

INTRODUCTION

The discovery of the ancient towns and territories, whose life was cut short by the eruption of Vesuvius on August 24, AD 79 represented a crucial and decisive stage in our acquisition of knowledge about the Ancient Roman world. In fact, until that time, what glimpses we did have of the ancient world – in the monumental remains of Imperial Rome and the ruins scattered over the Roman countryside and Campanian coast – appear now to have been misleading. The fact that various structures had been preserved only in part, and then extensively modified over the centuries, prevented researchers from being able to take the correct approach and gaining sufficient knowledge of what the Roman world was really like. Ancient Greek and Roman texts often appeared obscure and enigmatic, because they talked about things which the writer considered to be obvious, but which were totally obscure to most readers, unable to see what was being described.

What the excavations in the Vesuvius area produced was an intact image of ancient life, almost as if in suspended animation, undamaged by the passing of the centuries. They not only unearthed the treasures desired by a collective imagination, but also a vivid picture of everyday life in all its manifold aspects and a wealth of architecture, from the noblest to the simplest forms. After years of oblivion, the ancient world appeared in all its complexity and recounted the dramatic story of its fate.

The progress of the archaeological excavations and the continual finds caused such a sensation and such interest, that enlightened, cosmopolitan eighteenth-century society began to reinterpret the ancient world in their own. The city of Pompeii was taken as a model, giving rise to the neoclassicism which

characterised the arts and literature of Western Europe for over 50 years in the late eighteenth and early nineteenth centuries. The excavations around Vesuvius led to a shift from the study and collection of antiques uprooted from their context, to the philological study of the ancient world. For the first time, decorations could be seen in their real architectural setting; objects in their natural domestic context; monuments in their natural urban configuration, and the town itself in relationship with the surrounding area.

Yet Pompeii is important, not only for the representation of life it preserved, nor for the treasure trove of decoration and artefacts found, but because it constitutes a tangible example of the Roman culture that civilised the western and eastern Mediterranean and left such an indelible imprint upon it. It was not just Rome that made the Empire great, but the thousands of Roman towns like Pompeii, scattered all over the world, from the Atlantic Ocean to the Black Sea, from the cold North Sea moorlands to the hot shores of the Red Sea; towns which enjoyed a healthy economy, civilised customs and the stability of a population whose strength lay in its shared culture.

Discovering Pompeii is like opening a window on the ancient world. Although archaeologists and historians have always taken the wider picture into account, with Pompeii, even the least knowledgeable visitor is gripped by a sense of genuine adventure upon entering the old town. The paved roads, the ruins of the monumental forum, the different houses and shops, tradesmen's workshops, the paintings of the noblemen – still in their original colours, mosaics and various artefacts are all there, in situ, for the visitor to see. Just around every corner you almost expect to encounter a servant

girl on her way to a nearby fountain to fill her *hydria* (urn) with drinking water; or a *cliens*, perhaps about to knock on his patron's door; a group of enterprising youths in a heated debate on forthcoming elections or, in a doorway, an innkeeper complaining that business is not doing too well.

Why publish this volume now? Two hundred and fifty years ago, the blow

of a pickaxe first brought back to life a town sleeping under a thick blanket of ash and lapilli, yet, at the same time, it initiated that town's slow but sure deterioration. It has been unanimously agreed that the 23 hectares of the town still buried, must remain buried in order to allow future generations to enjoy this immense store of ancient civilisation and culture. Contemporary sensitive attitudes demand the preservation of this unique site. This volume is intended to bear witness to what the 42-hectare excavation site of Pompeii represents, in the hope that knowledge will lead to greater consideration and respect by modern man for the relics of his past.

HISTORICAL CONTEXT

Pompeii stands on a plateau, which was originally formed by a volcanic lava flow, whose outermost limits run from the south-east to south-west of the site covered by the town. This plateau, which covers an area of over 60 hectares, occupied an enviable position prior to the town's construction: it dominated the surrounding plain from varying heights, and descended naturally from north to south. To the north were the gentle slopes of the foot of Vesuvius, which offered fertile land, suitable for growing vines and certainly not known to be a volcano.

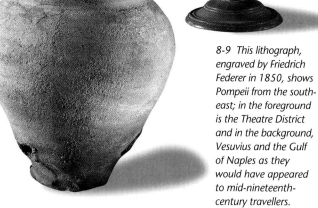

8 left This type of earthenware lamp (which has a semi-circular spout, round disc and vertical handle) was very common in the first half of the first century BC, and was made by local potters.

8 centre This earthenware vase (olla pertusa), used for flowers and plants, had three holes in the bottom so that water could drain out.

8 right This tall-stemmed goblet is decorated with winged figures, separated by plant compositions and ribbons. Its print decoration, orange colour and brightness identify it as Arezzo pottery, a type of tableware made mainly in Arezzo from the first century AD in imitation of bronze vases.

8-9 This lithograph, engraved by Friedrich Federer in 1850, shows Pompeii from the south-east; in the foreground is the Theatre District and in the background, Vesuvius and the Gulf of Naples as they would have appeared to mid-nineteenth-century travellers.

To the south, the plateau overlooked the River Sarnus, which originates in Mount Torrenone, one of the last spurs of the Campanian Apennines, about 20 kilometres to the east of the town. The river made a wide curve to the north, ran south of the plateau on which the future city was to stand, and slowly made its way to the Gulf of Naples. The River Sarnus, crucial to the history and economic life of Pompeii, crossed a large, fertile valley and was entirely navigable, allowing the import and export of goods to and from the towns of inland Campania. Its central position meant that the plateau overlooked the gulf, making it a good place to keep watch on ships rounding Cape Campanella (Sorrento) and headed north, or vice versa. It appeared to be the ideal place to build a town.

The first settlements in the area, dating from the middle Bronze Age, were not far away, but further south, on the right bank of the River Sarnus, on the site where S. Abbondio (Pompeii) now stands. The life of this town was interrupted at the end of the second millennium BC by an eruption

which represents the last evident activity of Vesuvius before the disaster of AD 79. During the Iron Age (900–600 BC), large settlements were concentrated along the middle reaches of the Sarnus in the areas of Striano, San Marzano and San Valentino Torio. These towns are mainly known for their necropolises, and the goods unearthed from some of the graves there show that there was healthy trade with the maritime centres active at that time, especially the Greek centre of Pithecusa (Ischia). The decline of these inland towns in the sixth century BC coincided with increasing interest in the Pompeii plateau, and from then on it became a place of permanent settlement rather than a sporadically inhabited area. The plateau area was surrounded by a boundary wall made of soft lava called *pappamonte*, which has been identified at a number of points in the Pompeii excavations, alongside the most recent fortifications. This boundary wall shows that the people who settled in this area had ambitious plans, designed to meet future urban space requirements.

At about the same time, two characteristic buildings were erected on two of the most prominent terraces of the plateau: the Temple of Apollo to the west, in an ideal position to be seen from the sea, and the Temple of Hercules and Minerva to the south-west, which dominates the lower reaches of the river. A third religious area, consisting of a sacred building in

a beech grove, was recently identified in the middle of Regio VI, but no structural elements survive. No specifically urban elements have been found, and archaeological investigations failed to confirm the theory that the small area corresponding to the *insulae* (blocks of buildings, surrounded by four roads) around the Civil Forum was the original site of the ancient settlement. It may be assumed, however, that at this time, the buildings, largely made of wood and unfired brick, were ruthlessly demolished to make way for more modern constructions.

Who occupied the town during this period? For a long time, it was believed to have been either the Greeks, who had dominated the coast and sea trade for over a century, or the Etruscans, who controlled the inland routes and were firmly entrenched in towns like Capua, Nola and Pontecagnano in the area to the north of the River Sele (the Paestum Valley). A third, more interesting theory, which was recently put forward, is that the occupants were Ausonians. This indigenous population – having contact with both the Greeks and the Etruscans – would thus have acquired all the knowledge needed to build a permanent settlement and a suitable trading base for imports and exports between inland Campania and the towns of the Mediterranean. As such, it would have been used by both the Greeks and the Etruscans, it was therefore left in peace. In other words, it was a kind of free port with shrines to meet the needs of all those who used it, and with no need for solid defence walls. Indeed, the boundary wall, of *pappamonte* blocks, can certainly not be considered a true defence system because, in view of the nature of the material and the characteristics of the surviving sections, it would have been impossible to lay more than three courses of blocks. That would have meant a maximum height of around 1.2 metres: not sufficient to withstand an armed attack.

Events associated with the power struggle between the Greeks and the Etruscans (525–474 BC) over the domination of Campania may well have been the reason why the Pompeiians replaced the fragile *pappamonte* wall with a proper city wall. The earlier defence system was supplanted by the later one, when the former proved

inadequate, in view of developments in the rivalry between the populations. The new wall, which had a double curtain of square Sarnus stone blocks, presented the same layout as the previous one and surrounded the same area. It was adapted to current *polyorcetic* techniques by using a material that enabled it to be built to a greater height and to absorb impacts more effectively. For various reasons, the construction of this new defence system is believed to date from the first quarter of the fifth century BC.

The final victory of the Greeks over the Etruscans, at the naval battle of Cumae in 474 BC, marked the beginning of the gradual decline of Pompeii as a trading centre, as demonstrated by the gradual impoverishment of votive offerings to the shrines inside the walls and a Temple dedicated to Poseidon, which stood outside the town, near the Sarnus estuary. In the late fifth or early fourth century BC, the Samnite populations of the Campanian Apennines probably began to move downhill and settle as far afield as the coastal towns. This also happened in Pompeii, where Osco-Samnite settlers seem to have totally supplanted the previous population.

On the occasion of the inevitable battle between the Samnites and the Romans for supremacy in Campania, the new Pompeiians constructed a new city wall, again made of Sarnus stone blocks, but consisting of a single curtain with an *agger* (rampart) behind it and a vallum on the outside. This wall followed almost exactly the same line as the previous one, which had fallen into disrepair and its blocks used to build the new settlement. With the defeat of the Samnites, Pompeii came under the influence of Rome as one of its Italic allies, and a long period of peace commenced.

It is not known what kind of urban organisation existed during this period. A theory may be advanced, however, based on the results of the latest archaeological research conducted in various parts of the town, and which provide an insight into the latter half of the period. It was during this time that the town acquired its appearance as we

know it today: the town gates were built on the main roads and the nucleus of the town was concentrated in the upper part to the west, near the Temple of Apollo, around an open space, perhaps a market place, later occupied by the Civil Forum.

The eastern part was divided into plots of farm land, although the town was later extended into this area. A new military crisis caused by the Second Punic War, with the consequent invasion of southern Italy by Hannibal, led to further reinforcement of the walls, now consisting of a double curtain with an *agger* and vallum. Pompeii, which had been left unharmed by Hannibal's raids, never betrayed its allegiance with Rome, and willingly accepted the influx of peoples from towns destroyed by Hannibal, such as Capua, Nuceria and Praeneste. It is likely that these newcomers received sites in the eastern part of the town, which had already been divided into regular *insulae* for residential purpose, as well as a plot of agricultural

land outside the town. By the middle of the second century BC, the whole area within the city walls was probably occupied by dwellings systematically distributed between regular *insulae*.

Outside the city walls, the fertile land began to be cultivated intensively, and was soon covered, not only with farms, but also with luxurious villas exploiting the land's panoramic position near the coast. The new markets in the east opened up to trade with the Italic towns after the Roman conquest, bringing Pompeii new wealth, which was invested mainly in residential and urban renovation employing the architectural and decorative scheme of Hellenistic towns.

The Civil Forum was built and the main political and religious buildings erected; the whole district around the ancient Temple of Hercules and Minerva was reorganised, and the Triangular Forum, the Large Theatre, and the Quadriporticus were constructed. The roads leading to the main venues in the town were monumentalised with

10-11 This painting, a characteristic example of 'popular painting', depicts the fierce battle between citizens of Pompeii and Nuceria in Pompeii's amphi-theatre in AD 59, also recounted by the historian Tacitus (Annals, XIV, 17). The fresco is particularly important because it shows the Palaestra on the right, and the Amphitheatre shaded by the velarium.

magnificent façades of grey tuff, a new material which met the needs of the town's architects, and was especially popular during this period. The houses were decorated in the 1st style, which imitated isodomic marble construction.

This long period of prosperity came to an abrupt end when the Italic allies, including Pompeii, waged war on Rome to obtain the status of Roman citizens (89–80 BC). The town was prepared for a war that seemed likely to be long and hard. Defences were fortified with the addition of 12 stout towers incorporated into the city walls. The dictator Lucius Cornelius Sulla brought an end to the war by defeating the rebels, led by Lucius Cluentius, on several occasions. Sulla sacked and laid waste to several of those towns which had been most hostile to him, including Stabiae. In Pompeii, he founded a colony of some 2,000 veterans under the name Colonia Cornelia Veneria Pompeianorum. These veterans soon took over the running of the town, but continued the programme of Hellenisation initiated by previous generations, building the Temple of Venus, the Odeon, the Forum Baths and the Amphitheatre. It was not until the second half of the first century BC that magistrates were appointed from old, noble Samnite families. The town seemed practically untouched by the fierce power struggle which preceded the reign of Augustus. The years that followed were years of prosperity and well-being, and gradually the city walls lost their significance and other structures were built over them.

In AD 62, Pompeii, like many other towns around Vesuvius, suffered the effects of a severe earthquake, and many of its structures were left in ruins. Restoration work commenced immediately, and much was completed within a very short space of time, especially that undertaken in private homes. However, there followed a new sequence of earth tremors (a seismic swarm, thought to have taken place around AD 70), which brought Pompeii to the verge of collapse, and some of its citizens, especially the wealthier ones, left town for safer havens. Many

were forced to sell property at extremely low prices, and the brave souls who remained and had money, soon became the owners of large properties. Urban land cost so little that it was actually advantageous to buy a house, demolish it and turn the site into a vegetable garden. This was a period of serious social unrest; in some years it actually proved impossible to elect the annual magistrates.

When this period of emergency was over, Pompeii gradually recovered, and the Emperor Vespasian sent one of his magistrates, Suedius Clemens, from Rome to restore order to the town's

property register and to punish those who had occupied public property unlawfully. Pompeii became a huge building site: tradesmen, builders, decorators and technicians worked non-stop to restore essential services and make homes habitable again. The new-found dynamism of the Pompeiians was cut short, however, by the terrible eruption of Vesuvius on August 24, AD 79. The town was shrouded in a six-metre layer of volcanic debris, never to recover.

11 top This small painting depicts a seaside shrine with a small tetrastyle temple on the left and a huge unroofed area with a portico at the end. A fisherman with rod and line can be seen in the foreground. This type of painting was particularly fashionable in the age of Augustus.

11 bottom This small painting portrays a seaside landing stage with a double-fronted, T-shaped portico. There is a round tower at the right-hand end and a square tower at the left-hand end. Behind the portico there is a wood and other buildings. Some fishermen sit on the edge of benches, while a boat is rowed in the foreground.

THE EARTHQUAKE OF AD 62

On February 5, AD 62 , Pompeii and the area surrounding Mount Vesuvius were hit by a violent earthquake, causing terrible destruction over a huge area. On the basis of recent studies, seismologists believe that the intensity of the earthquake was equivalent to the 8th magnitude on the Mercalli scale, with the epicentre in the Pompeii area. Seneca, in his treatise *Naturales Quaestiones*, accurately described the effects of the earthquake of AD 62, emphasising the frequency of such events in Campania. In the case of Pompeii, exceptional iconographic documentation of the AD 62 earthquake exists, namely a bas-relief on two *lararium* slabs found in the house of Lucius Caecilius Jucundus, portraying some of the town's monuments damaged by the earthquake. Recent studies based on archaeological documentation prove the existence of other earthquakes which occurred in Pompeii and around Vesuvius in the period AD 62-79. Experts believe that the occurrence of a series of seismic events in the period preceding the violent explosive eruption of AD 79 is typical of the natural phenomena which precede the resumption of a volcano's eruptive behaviour after a long period of inactivity.

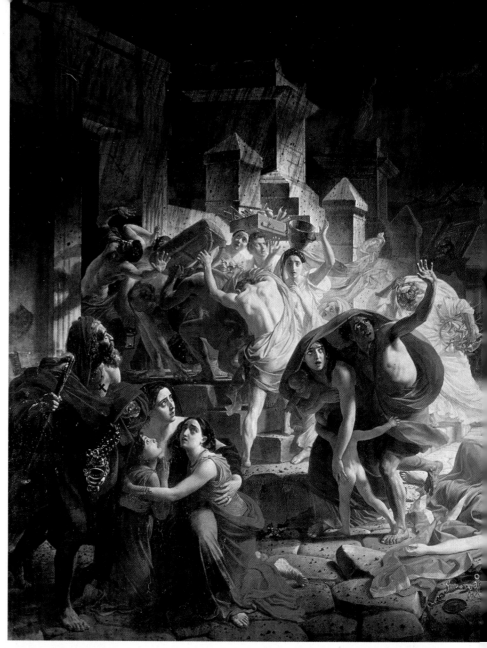

VESUVIUS

Originally, Vesuvius had the classic cone shape, but a series of eruptions in prehistoric times, in particular, ones which took place between 15,000 and 3,800 years ago, modified its shape. These violent eruptions caused the collapse of the summit of the mountain. Within the summit area, a new volcanic cone formed inside a larger caldera, created by eruptions which took place circa 1800–1000 BC. The outer caldera, with its semi-circular shape, is Mount Somma, which represents the remains of the ancient volcano.

Invaluable evidence of what Vesuvius looked like before the eruption is provided by Strabo (64 BC–AD 24) in his *Geographica*. He describes it thus: 'Above these places, towers Mount Vesuvius, wholly occupied by beautiful fields all around, except on the summit; the summit itself is mainly flat but wholly sterile, with an ashy appearance; it has cavities with cracks opening in the rocks, which are sooty on the surface, as if devoured by flames. Thus some may suppose that this place once burned and had craters of fire that later died out when the combustible material was used up. This may be the reason for the fertility

12-13 The tragic eruption of Vesuvius in AD 79 touched many artists who visited Pompeii in the nineteenth century. An oil on canvas by K. Brullow (1799–1852) is shown here.

12 bottom This relief slab decorating the lararium in the House of Caecilius Jucundus (V-I-26) portrays the buildings on the north side of the Civil Forum during the earthquake; the Temple of Jupiter is collapsing in the middle, while a sacrificial scene is shown on the right, as if to ward off a repetition of the event.

of the surrounding land, as in the case of Catania, where it is said that the soil covered with ash thrown out by the fire of Etna is particularly suitable for vine growing' (V-4-8).

A different kind of documentary evidence demonstrates how the Pompeiians themselves perceived Mount Vesuvius. In the House of the Centenary (IX-8-5), a *lararium* fresco found in the servants' quarters portrays Bacchus, represented with a bunch of grapes, a thyrsus and a panther, in front of a mountain (possibly Vesuvius) entirely covered in vineyards. The mountain was viewed as the home of this god of festivity and prosperity, and the Pompeiians never considered it to be dangerous.

THE ERUPTION

At about 10am on August 24, AD 79, Vesuvius awoke after 1,000 years of inactivity, and its terrible eruption wiped out towns for miles around, including Pompeii and Herculaneum.

First there was a violent explosion, and shortly afterwards an eruptive column formed, over 20 kilometres high. It took on the typical 'mushroom' or 'Mediterranean pine' shape, and was filled with ash, gas and pumice. The material thrown up from the crater then began to fall, and was blown to the south-west by a strong wind at a higher altitude. Pompeii, which lay in that direction, was immediately exposed to a shower of lapilli and stone fragments which continued almost non-stop until the next morning. By the early afternoon, the accumulation of pumice had caused the first roof

collapses and the first deaths. Fires caused by lanterns falling began to illuminate the town, otherwise oppressed by an unnatural darkness caused by atmospheric dust impenetrable by sunlight. At about 7.30am on August 25, Pompeii was hit by a violent discharge of hot gases and ash – a *nuée ardente*. Its effects were devastating; some 2,000 people – 15 per cent of the town's entire population – suffocated or were burned to death. In the town, people had to walk on a layer of pumice that was now over two metres deep. Victims were often found close together, parents embracing their children and brothers and sisters clutching one another. Many died in groups, taken by surprise, or killed as they fled. Another volcanic discharge followed, and another shortly afterwards. The last discharge was the most disastrous of all for Pompeii: it took the form of a thick stream of pyroclastic material which engulfed the walls and totally buried the victims of the two previous *nuées ardentes*, as well as the uppermost sections of buildings. Pliny the Elder, a great scientist and admiral of the Roman fleet, seems to have been a famous victim of this last lethal discharge – the most widespread of all; he suffocated on the beach of nearby Stabiae, to which he had hurried to organise a rescue party and study the phenomenon first hand. A few days after the eruption, Pompeii and the entire Sarnus Valley had been completely transformed; the whole district was covered by a vast, white shroud. The River Sarnus, obstructed by volcanic debris, made its way to the sea with great difficulty. As it approached Pompeii, it no longer followed its original wide curve, but flowed straight on. Even the sea appeared to have receded somewhat, as a result of the sudden growth of the coastline. The town was covered with a layer of debris some six metres deep, from which only the tallest and strongest buildings emerged. Although non-residents were prohibited from entering the site, in order to protect the survivors' property, raiders found their way in over the years – sometimes by digging tunnels – and looted much of the town. In time, nature gained the upper hand, and the white shroud covering the area was replaced by a thick pine wood.

THE LETTERS OF PLINY THE YOUNGER

Pliny the Younger, at the behest of the great historian Tacitus, wrote two letters, in which he recounted the death of his uncle Pliny the Elder – a brilliant scientist and attentive observer of natural phenomena, who sailed immediately to Pompeii to bring help to the victims and to witness for himself the terrifying volcanic explosion and the consequences. Although this account of the tragedy is based on reports by a few who escaped, Pliny the Younger watched it from Cape Misenum to the north, on the other side of the Gulf of Naples, and his letter represents an accurate record of great scientific and documentary value.

This is the text of Pliny the Younger's first letter, in which he recounts what happened to his uncle (letter VI-16): 'My dear Tacitus, You ask me to write and tell you about the death of my uncle, so that the account you set down for posterity is as reliable as possible. I am grateful to you, for I know that his death will be remembered forever if it is commemorated by you. Like the people and towns of the area, he was involved in a catastrophe that struck the loveliest lands in the world, and the memory of the event will ensure an eternal life for him. Although he wrote a great number of enduring works himself, your eternal writings will make a decisive contribution to the survival of his name. Happy are they whom the gods have allowed to do something worth writing about or to write something worth reading, and the happiest of all, in my opinion, are those who have done both. As a result of his own books and yours, my uncle will be counted among the latter. So I have great pleasure in accepting the task you have entrusted to me; indeed, I insist on it.

'My uncle was in Misenum where he commanded the fleet. It was about an hour after midday on August 24, when my mother pointed out to him a cloud that had appeared, of a size and shape never seen before. He had been out in the sun, taken a cold bath and eaten a light meal lying on a couch, and was now studying. He called for his sandals and climbed a hill – an

excellent position from which to observe the phenomenon. The cloud was rising from a mountain; we could not be sure which, because we were watching it from so far away. I only discovered later that it was Vesuvius. The shape of the cloud was more like a pine tree than anything else.

'The cloud rose into the sky as if from a huge trunk, expanded, and almost put out branches. The cloud spread out into a wide umbrella, perhaps because it was pushed upwards, intact, by a sudden blast, which then weakened, leaving the cloud unsupported. Some of the cloud was snow white, while in other parts it was opaque, mottled with patches caused by the ash and earth lifted with it. My uncle was a man of science, and he determined to see it at first hand.

'He ordered a *liburna* to be made ready. He said to me, "You can come with me if you like," but I replied, "I'd rather stay here and study" (as it happened he had set me an essay). Just as he was leaving the house, a letter was delivered from Tascius' wife Rectina, who was terrified by the imminent danger. Her villa stood at the foot of Vesuvius, and there was no way out except for by sea. She begged my uncle to save her. He changed his plans, and the scientist's thirst for knowledge was replaced by a hero's spirit. He had the *quadriremis* [boat with four banks of oars] launched, and embarked himself. He intended to rescue many people besides Rectina, because that delightful district was densely inhabited. He hastened to a place, from which others were escaping, and steered his course directly towards the danger. He showed no sign of fear; indeed, he dictated or wrote down every variation of that evil cloud, and everything else that he saw.

'Ash was falling onto the ships now, and the closer they sailed, the hotter and thicker the cloud became. Pieces of pumice fell too, and stones that were blackened, burned and shattered by the fire. The ships unexpectedly sailed into shallow water, and debris from the mountain prevented the party from disembarking. My uncle

14-15 This attractive 1813 oil painting, by Pierre-Henri de Valenciennes, immortalises the last dramatic moments in the life of Pliny the Elder.

14 bottom Pliny the Elder, shown here in a portrait by Bollinger, died on the beach between Stabiae and Pompeii in AD 79 during the eruption of Vesuvius, in a vain attempt to rescue some of the inhabitants of Pompeii.

hesitated for a moment, wondering whether to turn back as the helmsman advised, but then said, "Fortune favours the brave. Make for Pomponianus!"

'Pomponianus' villa was separated from the centre of the gulf; the Stabian coastline forms a gently curving shore. The danger was not yet close, but it was quite evident, that it became greater, the closer it got. Pomponianus

had loaded his possessions onto ships there, and planned to escape as soon as the contrary wind dropped. That same wind proved favourable to my uncle, who managed to disembark. He embraced his frightened friend, and gave him comfort and courage. In order to calm his friend's fears by showing his own lack of concern, he asked to be taken to the baths. After his bath he sat down to dinner. He was quite happy, or appeared to be (which amounts to the same thing).

'Meanwhile, sheets of flame and columns of fire were illuminating many parts of Vesuvius, and their brightness stood out vividly against the darkness of the night. To alleviate people's fears, my uncle kept saying that farmers who had fled in a panic had left fires burning in the open and in their abandoned homes. Then he went to bed, and actually fell into a deep sleep.

'Those walking up and down outside his door could hear the snores that issued from his heavy body. However, the courtyard leading to his room was by now piled so high with ash and stones that if he had stayed there any longer, he would have been unable to leave, so he was woken up. He came

out and joined Pomponianus and the others, who had not yielded to sleep. They debated whether it was best to stay in the house or wander about outside. The buildings were being shaken by a series of violent earth tremors; as if torn from their foundations they seemed to sway, then come to rest again. Outside, however, there was danger from the shower of lapilli, light and corroded though they were. After weighing up the risks, they decided to go outside. In my uncle's case sense prevailed, but in the case of the others, one fear prevailed over another. They put pillows on their heads and bound them tightly with cloths to protect themselves against the hail of lapilli.

'By now it was daylight elsewhere, but there, the darkness was thicker and blacker than ever before. However, the darkness was illuminated by many fires and various lights. They decided to go down to the shore, to see close up whether it was now possible to attempt an escape by sea. However, the sea was still too rough. My uncle spread out a tarpaulin and lay down on it. Once or twice he called for cold water, and drank it down straight away. Then he was awoken by flames, and a smell of

sulphur heralding more flames, which put the others to flight. He stood up, supported by two slaves, but immediately collapsed – as far as I can gather because his breathing was obstructed by the dust-laden air, and his throat, which had always been weak and narrow and was often inflamed, closed up. When daylight came again on the third day, his body was found intact and unharmed, still wearing the last tunic he had put on. He looked more like a sleeper than a dead man.

'Meanwhile at Misenum, my mother and I… but our affairs have nothing to do with history, and you only asked for information about my uncle's death, so I'll close here. I will say one more thing, namely that this account is based on my own personal experience and everything I heard immediately after the disaster, while memories of the events were still fresh. I leave it to you to select the most important facts, because writing a letter is not the same as writing history, and writing for a friend is not the same as writing for the public. Farewell.'

HISTORY OF THE EXCAVATIONS

In 1748, ten years after the start of explorations in Herculaneum, excavations began in Pompeii, wrongly believed by the first explorers to be Stabiae. At this stage their digging was random; explorations were performed at the crossroads between Via Stabia and Via di Nola, in the Amphitheatre,

which was already recognisable, and in what is known as the Villa of Cicero outside the Herculaneum Gate. The first results did not seem encouraging, and it was decided to move on to the more promising Gragnano (Castellammare di Stabia) and Herculaneum. The excavators returned to Pompeii in 1755. Operations were directed by military engineer R.J. de Alcubierre, aided by two more engineers, C. Weber and later F. la Vega, who were responsible for the documentation, drawing the buildings and writing the excavation journals.

During this first phase, the excavations were mainly designed to recover objets d'art, such as figure paintings, statues and certain articles, and the documentation produced was intended more for tax than for scientific purposes. Once the rooms had been excavated, it was the task of C. Paderni, the curator of the Portici museum, to select the items considered worthy of the King's private collection and destroy the remainder, to prevent them from falling into the wrong hands. The chosen paintings were detached by the sculptor Canart

using a special process and then taken away, framed and hung on the walls as if in an art gallery. After being stripped, the buildings were buried again. This method of excavation aroused great controversy. Strong accusations made by J. Winckelmann, and protests by numerous experts eventually forced King Carlo III to call a halt to the destructive practice.

In 1765, F. la Vega became director of excavations in Pompeii. His practice was to leave the excavated monuments in full view, especially after the magnificent Villa of Diomedes and Via delle Tombe were found. La Vega was undoubtedly the best and most far-sighted of the eighteenth-century excavators: he strenuously defended the system of uncovering each building in its entirety and preparing maintenance works in order to preserve in situ the architectural structures and everything that had not been removed to the Royal Museum. La Vega also removed the earth dug from the archaeological area so as not to hinder further excavations, but the digging was still scattered rather than performed in adjacent areas. Two areas were explored: the Theatre District to the south, and Via delle Tombe to the north.

With the advent of French rule in Naples (1799–1815), procedures changed radically. Primarily as a result of the interest of Caroline Bonaparte, the wife of Joachim Murat, King of Naples, it was planned to expropriate all areas on which the ancient town stood, and then to join the excavated sectors to create a continuous itinerary for visitors. Later, the entire city wall

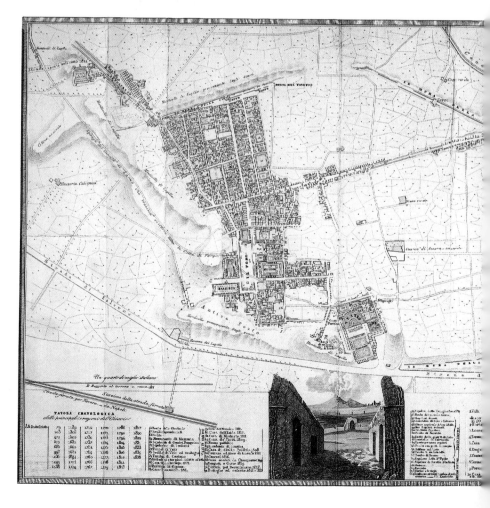

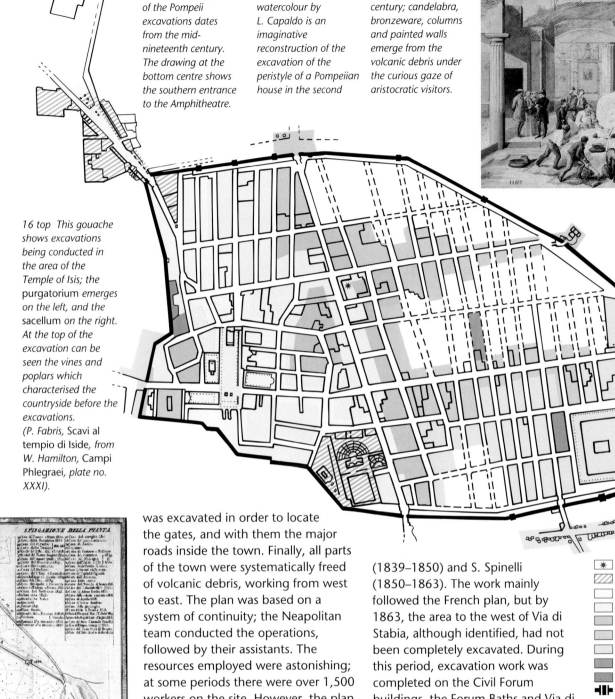

16 bottom This plan of the Pompeii excavations dates from the mid-nineteenth century. The drawing at the bottom centre shows the southern entrance to the Amphitheatre.

17 top This watercolour by L. Capaldo is an imaginative reconstruction of the excavation of the peristyle of a Pompeiian house in the second half of the nineteenth century; candelabra, bronzeware, columns and painted walls emerge from the volcanic debris under the curious gaze of aristocratic visitors.

16 top This gouache shows excavations being conducted in the area of the Temple of Isis; the purgatorium emerges on the left, and the sacellum on the right. At the top of the excavation can be seen the vines and poplars which characterised the countryside before the excavations. (P. Fabris, Scavi al tempio di Iside, from W. Hamilton, Campi Phlegraei, plate no. XXXI).

was excavated in order to locate the gates, and with them the major roads inside the town. Finally, all parts of the town were systematically freed of volcanic debris, working from west to east. The plan was based on a system of continuity; the Neapolitan team conducted the operations, followed by their assistants. The resources employed were astonishing; at some periods there were over 1,500 workers on the site. However, the plan proved over-ambitious, and when the Bourbon dynasty returned to power in 1815, only part of it had been completed: the land had been expropriated and the Theatre District joined up with the adjacent area to the north, along Via Consolare and Via delle Tombe, by means of excavations carried out in the Forum area.

Compared with the feverish activity of the French period, work slowed down considerably under Bourbon rule (1815–1863), mainly due to lack of funds and adequate resources, although the small workforce was led by expert directors such as M. Arditi (1807–1838), F.M. Avellino

(1839–1850) and S. Spinelli (1850–1863). The work mainly followed the French plan, but by 1863, the area to the west of Via di Stabia, although identified, had not been completely excavated. During this period, excavation work was completed on the Civil Forum buildings, the Forum Baths and Via di Nola as far as the Nola Gate; houses fully excavated included the House of the Tragic Poet, the House of the Canal, the House of Castor and Pollux, the Houses of the Mosaic Fountains and the House of Meleager, to name the most important.

G. Fiorelli, who directed the excavations from 1863 to 1875, was a prominent figure in Pompeii. He eliminated discontinuity and random digging and introduced a new method: instead of excavating the roads first and then penetrating into the houses from below, he had the excavations carried out from above in order to recover all elements

✳	The first pick stroke
▨	1748–1798
☐	1806–1815
☐	1815–1860
☐	1860–1878
▨	1879–1923
▨	1924–1961
▨	1961–1983
▨	1983–present day
▄▋▄	The city walls

Excavation directors:
1748–1780 R.J. de Alcubierre
1765–1804 F. la Vega
1804–1806 P. la Vega
1807–1838 M. Arditi
1839–1850 F.M. Avellino
1850–1863 S. Spinelli
1863–1875 G. Fiorelli
1875–1893 M. Ruggero
1893–1900 G. de Petra
1901–1904 E. Pais
1905–1910 A. Sogliano
1911–1923 V. Spinazzola
1924–1961 A. Maiuri
1961–1976 A. de Franciscis
1976–1977 L. d'Amore
1977–1982 F. Zevi
1982–1984 G. Cerulli Irelli
1984–1994 B. Conticello
1994–present day P.G. Guzzo

constituting a house. He aimed to use this information to restore as much as possible of the ancient architecture, although the most important paintings and mosaics had already been removed.

Fiorelli also brought order to the topography of the districts excavated, by dividing the town into Regiones, Insulae and Houses. He also invented the plaster casts which not only reveal the shape of the bodies of the eruption's victims, but also the roots of trees and all the organic elements which left a mould in the volcanic ash after their decomposition. As a result of his excellent work in Pompeii, G. Fiorelli was appointed Director-General of Antiquities and Fine Arts.

His successors, M. Ruggero (1875–1893), G. de Petra (1893–1900), E. Pais (1901–1904) and A. Sogliano (1905–1910) continued along the same lines. In accordance with the system introduced by Fiorelli, the houses excavated in the last 20 years of the nineteenth century, like the House of Lucretius Fronto, the House of the Vettii and the House of the Golden Cherubs, were no longer roofed with unrelated materials, but philologically; that is, with the same characteristics and elements as the original building. Finally, all paintings and mosaics were left in situ.

By 1910, the whole sector to the west of Via di Stabia, and many of the houses fronting onto that road from the east, had been excavated. V. Spinazzola (1911–1923) excavated the lower *decumanus* (Via dell' Abbondanza) as far as its eastern limit at the Sarnus Gate. He carefully restored the façade of this diversified street – featuring balconies, lean-to roofs and upper floors – demonstrating

that, with careful excavation, the dynamics of the burial and collapse of the structural elements of the house can be reconstructed and precise and global restoration work performed. He also excavated the House of Loreius Tiburtinus, the House of the Ephebe and the House of Trebius Valens.

After Spinazzola, began the long tenure of one of the most dynamic but also most controversial directors in the excavations' history: A. Maiuri (1924–1961). This great archaeologist, with his intensive activity, completely excavated the city walls, and discovered the largest necropolis ever known in Pompeii

along the southern front. The removal of the lapilli from Via di Nocera allowed for the exploration of Regiones I and II, but the work was conducted hastily and with inadequate resources, so that most of the excavated areas were restored in a makeshift manner and then practically abandoned. Consequently, these areas, despite being the most recently excavated, have deteriorated the most. However, in addition to the magnificent excavation of the House of Menander and the Villa of the Mysteries, Maiuri must take the credit for introducing stratigraphic surveys below the AD 79 levels to investigate

18 top This picture shows the excavation of a thermopolium in Via dell'Abbondanza (II-2-1). The excavation of the road was directed by Spinazzola (1911-1923), who attempted to recover the upper floors and façades of houses with balconies and lean-to roofs.

18 centre One of the most exciting moments was the discovery of the bronze objects and statues which, more than any other item, demonstrated the wealth

of a household. This picture depicts the finding of a lamp-bearing Ephebe in a house in Via dell'Abbondanza.

18 bottom The tragic death of the town's inhabitants is witnessed by the plaster casts first made by G. Fiorelli in 1870. This victim was found on the road separating Insulae 20 and 21 of Regio I; the cast is now on display in the 'Fugitives' Garden' (I-21-1).

19 top The controversial late-nineteenth-century excavations were followed by careful restoration: walls were strengthened and wooden beams reinstalled to roof those rooms with paintings. This picture shows the restoration of the House of the Vettii.

19 bottom The excavation of a house in the late nineteenth century. As will be seen, the whole block was not uncovered uniformly from above; the excavators penetrated into one house, dug down to the floor, and widened the exploration from

there. All digging was performed by hand, and the lapilli were carried on the excavators' backs in wooden boxes. Little damage was caused, especially to the paintings. A magnificent 2nd-style fresco can be seen in the foreground.

the more ancient history of Pompeii.

A. Maiuri was succeeded by A. de Franciscis (1961–1976), who concentrated mainly on restoration work. The only excavation he conducted in Pompeii was that of the magnificent House of Polybius. F. Zevi (1977–1982) and G. Cerulli Irelli (1982–1984) mainly tackled problems associated with the serious damage caused to the town by the earthquake of 1980. When a large amount of funding became available, B. Conticello, Superintendent of Pompeii from 1984–1994, initiated the systematic philological restoration of all the finds, starting with the insulae in Regiones I and II, where the excavations left unfinished by Maiuri were completed. Excavation of the Complex of the Chaste Lovers also began.

The rest is recent history. The current superintendent, P.G. Guzzo (1994) is concentrating on finding a solution to management and financial problems, without which it is impossible to plan the total restoration of Pompeii and completion of the excavations. Of the 66 hectares covered by the town, only 44 have been freed of volcanic debris. It has been unanimously agreed, however, that the courageous step should be taken to leave for posterity all that remains under the layer of debris, so that future generations will also be able to enjoy this important relic of our past.

TOWN PLANNING

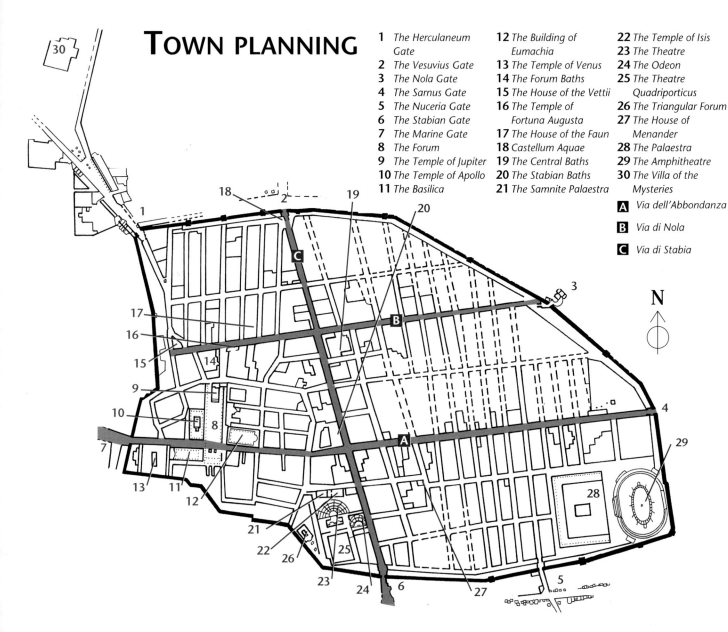

THE TOWN'S STRUCTURE

The first area of the town to be completely uncovered was more heterogeneous from a geomorphological standpoint than it appears today. The area corresponds to the last spur of a lava flow that issued from Vesuvius in ancient times. The terrain sloped from a height of 40 to 10 metres above sea level. The highest area to the north-west, later occupied by Regio VI, descended fairly regularly down to the south-eastern area, where the gentle slope was interrupted by a steep drop marking the end of the lava flow. This regularity was interrupted firstly by a deep depression running north-south which was to be occupied in historical times by Via Stabiana, and secondly by two hills, later occupied by the Temple of Apollo to the west and the architectural complex of the Triangular Forum (the Temple of Hercules and Minerva) to the south. The whole area covered by this lava flow, a total of 66 hectares, was enclosed as early as the sixth century BC with a wall of *pappamonte*.

The temples are of an earlier date than the town, and the road leading from the north skirts them both: the Temple of Apollo to the east and that of the Triangular Forum to the north. A market place, which later became the Forum, soon developed as a flattish area between the two sanctuaries, and served both. The north-south depression became an alternative route for those wishing to head south without going through the sacred areas; in this case, the route followed was Via Consolare, Via delle Terme, Via della Fortuna and Via Stabiana.

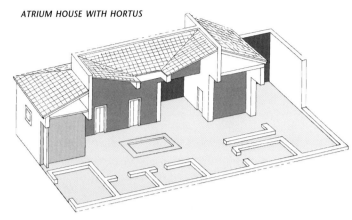

ATRIUM HOUSE WITH HORTUS

20 This aerial photo shows the southern part of the Civil Forum, that could be reached from Via dell'Abbondanza to the east and Via Marina to the west. The insulae situated round the Forum have a nearly quadrangular shape, and represent the oldest settlements in the town.

21 left This aerial view shows Insulae 7, 8, 9, 11, 12 and 23 of Regio I, which give onto Via dell'Abbondanza. Note the regular division of the Insulae, separated by roads which cross at right angles.

21 right From the Holconius crossroads to the Civil Forum is the western part of Via dell'Abbondanza, that is shown in the picture. This slightly uphill section of the road was closed to vehicle traffic.

Drawings – The main characteristic of the Italic house was the sequence of the same rooms on the same axis: *the* vestibulum, *the* atrium *with* compluvium, *the* tablinum *flanked by the* alae *and the unroofed area behind it, which, in the oldest designs, took the form of a* hortus, *but was later turned into a porticoed area. When larger sites were available, there were sometimes two porticoed areas. Simpler houses had an unroofed small court perpendicular to the entrance instead of the* atrium *with* compluvium.

It seems fairly certain that relatively regular urban blocks (*insulae*) developed around the market place and in Via Stabiana, to some extent determining the layout of the town. Four quite separate nuclei can be identified: the Forum area, the *insulae* fronting onto Via Stabiana, Regio VI and the eastern area. The first two appear to be earlier, but fierce controversy exists between historians and archaeologists over their dating. The areas of Regio VI and the eastern part of the town appear to have been designed on paper; the first is built around Via di Mercurio and the second, much larger area, around Via di Nola, Via dell'Abbondanza and Via di Nocera.

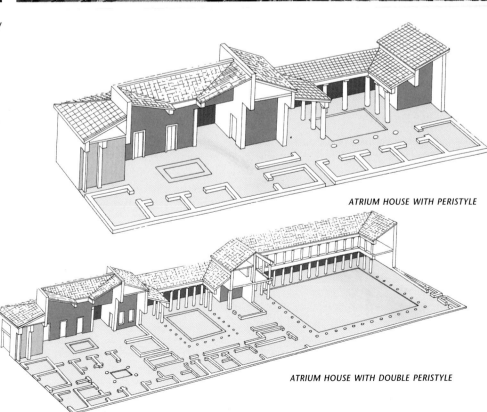

ATRIUM HOUSE WITH PERISTYLE

ATRIUM HOUSE WITH DOUBLE PERISTYLE

THE DEFENCE SYSTEM

Pompeii's defence system reached the height of its efficacy early in the first century BC, immediately before the War of the Allies, which Pompeii fought with the Italic allies against Rome to win the privileges granted to Roman citizens. The defence system consisted of a double curtain city wall made of large

oldest defence system, which dated from the sixth century BC and followed the same perimeter, consisted of a fairly low wall made of square *pappamonte* stones. This was followed by a defence system with a double curtain made of square blocks of Sarnus stone, later replaced by a single wall with a vallum and *agger*; finally, the wall took on its present form. With the advent of the Pax Romana in the age of Augustus, the city walls lost their importance to such an extent that structures such as the Imperial Villa, the Sarnus Baths and the Suburban Baths were built onto them, and the square blocks from the curtain walls were used to restore houses damaged in the earthquake of AD 62. The edict of Suedius Clemens put a stop to this devastation.

THE DEFENCE TOWERS

The towers, built between the late second and early first century BC, before the War of the Allies, certainly made Pompeii's defence system more effective. Twelve towers were built at irregular distances apart, concentrated more in the northern sector, where the flatter terrain made the town more vulnerable. The towers were constructed on three levels: the first was built within the thickness of the city walls, the second was on the same level as the sentry walk, and the third, which surmounted the rest, acted as a lookout. The towers were reached via a small door at the base leading to internal flights of stairs which served the different levels, or

square blocks which enclosed the whole of the ancient town for a length of over 3,200 metres. A huge trench (for the vallum) ran along the outer curtain, and ramparts (*agger*), reinforced at the foot by a low retaining wall, also made of square blocks, ran along the inner curtain. A road, which allowed soldiers quick access to the spots where they were most needed, ran between the retaining wall and the wall adjacent to the *insulae*.

On the top, a sentry walk ran between the walls, protected by the crenellated outer curtain. The town was made even safer by the construction of 12 towers, most of which were concentrated where attack was most likely and defence most difficult. The

22 top A section of the defence system between the Nuceria Gate and Tower II. The opus incertum *structures of stables built onto the city walls after the earthquake of AD 62 can be seen in the foreground. They were probably demolished when Imperial magistrate Suedius Clemens reorganised the town's public properties.*

22 centre left A section of the southern defence system between Tower II and the Nuceria Gate. The outer curtain of the city walls presents some irregularity in the lower part corresponding to

the oldest stage of the Samnite period, while the upper part, far more regular and made with perfect square blocks, dates from the wall restoration, between the late third and early second centuries BC.

22 centre right In Tower X of the northern defence system, the slits in the middle floor, the wider openings in the top floor and the crenellations on the terrace are clearly visible. The tower still retains part of the stucco relief decoration which imitates the marble blocks of an isodomic construction.

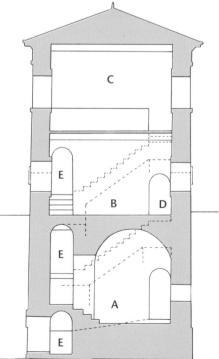

from an external staircase which allowed access as far as the middle storey. The towers constituted veritable fortresses, and were self-sufficient in the event of a siege or penetration of the enemy into the town, as they contained quarters for the troops, food stores, and water reserves in tanks built into the walls. After the conquest of Pompeii by Sulla, the towers, like the rest of the city walls, fell into disuse – although in the painting of the battle fought in the Amphitheatre between the citizens of Nuceria and Pompeii, towers II and III of the southern defence system can still be seen, intact, in the background.

THE CITY GATES

The city gates were built at the end of the roads (*decumani* and *cardines*), which marked the urban layout of the town. The Marine Gate stands at the western end of Via dell'Abbondanza, and the Sarnus Gate to the east. Marine Gate, which led to the harbour, consists of a single large barrel-vaulted area divided into a large section for goods traffic and a smaller one for pedestrians. Sarnus Gate had a single archway and led to the fields and villages near the River Sarnus. The Nola Gate to the east and the Herculaneum Gate to the west stood at either end of the upper *decumanus*, namely Via di Nola and Via della Fortuna Augusta, with its continuation, Via Consolare. Nola Gate has a single, very

23 top right The relationship between the town, situated at a higher level, and the low-lying countryside outside the walls can be seen from the Nuceria Gate – shown here from outside. The ruins of the ramparts which defended the east side of the road that climbs up to the gate can be seen in the foreground.

23 centre right The Marine Gate had two archways: the narrower one was designed for pedestrians, and the

wider one for vehicles. The gate constituted the eastern end of Via dell'Abbondanza, and the usual entrance to the town for goods arriving from the sea.

23 bottom right The Herculaneum Gate had three archways: the widest one, in the centre, was used for vehicles, and the smaller ones on either side for pedestrians. The Gate had opus vittatum mixtum *pillars, and was somewhat anachronistically decorated in the 1st style.*

22 bottom All 12 of Pompeii's towers are quadrangular, and built on three levels: the first two correspond to the core of the city walls, and the third emerges above the sentry walk. The towers ended in a crenellated terrace or a pinnacled roof.

23 left Tower XI, the Tower of Mercury, which forms part of the northern defence system, is one of the best-preserved in Pompeii. It closes the road of the same name to the north, and was built over an older gate that led out of town.

23 centre The keystone of the single-arch Nola Gate – seen here from inside – was decorated with the head of Minerva; the gate, which is the eastern end of the north decumanus running east-west, was built in the late third century BC.

A First level
B Intermediate level
C Top level
D Exit to sentry walk on city walls
E Stairwell

tall archway, while the Herculaneum Gate has three archways, the wider middle arch being designed for vehicular traffic, and the side ones for pedestrians. Via Stabiana, which represents the main *cardo* of the town, ends at the Vesuvius Gate to the north and the Stabian Gate to the south, both of which have a single archway. Via di Nocera, which is the east *cardo*, ends to the south at the Nuceria Gate, while the north section, where some experts believe the Capua Gate stood, is unknown. Of the seven known gates in Pompeii, the most impressive are the Herculaneum Gate, with its three archways, and the Marine Gate, in the form of a rampart. The city gates were manned by police officers and had two barricades (an internal and an external one), as proved by the hinges found.

BUILDING TECHNIQUES

From the first settlement in the sixth century BC to its burial in AD 79, Pompeii gradually expanded. The first expansion took place from the centre towards the outskirts. Then, when all the space available inside the city walls had been occupied, the town grew in on itself; the architectural volumes were modified and the ancient masonry was partly or wholly replaced. As a result, close inspection of the town's walls reveals at least six centuries of its history. The history of Pompeii used to be divided according to the different materials and building techniques used, for example, the 'limestone period', or the 'tuff period'. There were periods when one technique or material was employed more frequently than any other, but building materials and techniques were often used continuously, depending on the traditions and skills of the building workers and the raw materials available.

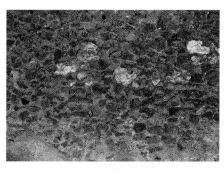

Various construction materials were employed. Sarnus stone – a travertine stone deposited in the Sarnus valley, often incorrectly called limestone – was a pale beige colour, highly porous and difficult to dress, but excellent for construction. Vesuvius lava stone, quarried from the mount's slopes, originated from the effusive flows of the volcano; it was dark grey, heavy, and basaltic in character. Lava foam from the upper part of lava flows is very light and totally porous, and was mainly used for partition walls and the upper part of walls. Grey tuff, which was quarried in the foothills between Nuceria and Sarnus, was strong and easy to cut, while yellow tuff from the Phlegraean fields to the north of Naples was soft and liable to wear. Rectangular terracotta bricks were made in different measurements and thicknesses. Travertine was mainly used for floors, thresholds and columns.

The following are the construction techniques used in Pompeii.

Opus quadratum was made of Sarnus stone or grey tuff; the parallelepiped-shaped blocks were laid lengthways in staggered courses. This technique was used not only in fortifications but also on the façades of houses, giving them an austere, impressive appearance. Mortar was not needed in the joints. This was one of the oldest techniques used in Pompeii, especially in the form using Sarnus stone.

Opus africanum consisted of vertical chains of blocks of Sarnus stone, laid

24 top left Opus quadratum *made of regular blocks of Sarnus stone.*

24 bottom left Opus quadratum *made of squared blocks of grey tuff.*

24 bottom left Opus africanum *faced with blocks of Sarnus stone, and filled with a core of lava stone.*

24 top right Opus incertum *made of lava stone with inserts of Sarnus stone.*

alternately horizontally and vertically, at some distance apart, with a filling of Sarnus stone, lava stone or a mixture of the two. There was little mortar in the joints, and the wall between the chains was the faced type with a core of rubble and mortar (*caementum*). This technique was introduced into Pompeii in the late third century BC.

Opus incertum walls had a facing of medium-sized stones, of either a single type or mixed, with a core of rubble and mortar. Lava stone, which is the heaviest type, was usually laid at the bottom, and lava foam blocks, which are lighter, on top. *Opus incertum* walls were often made with recycled materials, in which case they sometimes contained fragments of brick and roof tiles.

Opus quasi reticulatum was a type of faced wall made of lava stones and tuff, consisting of small stones approximately 10-12 square centimetres , laid in a rough lattice pattern. It was introduced into Pompeii in the first half of the first century BC.

Opus reticulatum was a type of faced wall consisting of blocks

perfectly cut into a truncated pyramid shape and laid diagonally in a lattice pattern. It was introduced into Pompeii in the middle of the first century BC.

Opus latericium was a type of faced wall consisting of blocks of baked clay of various sizes and thicknesses, laid lengthways in staggered courses. Bricks made from crushed roof tiles were often used in walls of this kind instead of

specially made bricks. *Opus latericium* was introduced into Pompeii in the second half of the first century BC.

Opus vittatum was a type of faced wall made of tuff or Sarnus stones neatly squared into a parallelepiped shape 9-13 centimetres thick, laid in staggered courses. It was introduced into Pompeii in the first half of the first century AD.

Opus vittatum mixtum, also known as *opus listatum*, was a faced wall consisting of a course of squared stones alternated with at least two courses of bricks. It was used mainly after the earthquake of AD 62.

The mortar was nearly always made of slaked lime, pozzolana and river sand, and was very strong.

24-25 *This fresco, in the 'popular painting' style, represents a procession of carpenters in honour of a deceased colleague. The carpenters, who formed a guild, were closely associated with the building workers, as their job was essential for house building.*

25 top left Opus quasi reticulatum *made of blocks of lava stone.*

25 bottom left Opus reticulatum *made of a variety of elements: grey tuff, Sarnus stone and lava stone.*

25 top right Opus reticulatum *made of a variety of elements: the door jambs seen in the foreground are made of* opus vittatum mixtum.

25 bottom right Opus latericium *made of blocks of terracotta laid in staggered rows.*

The water supply

As Pompeii was situated on a high plateau of volcanic origin, the water supply presented a problem before the construction of the public aqueduct; water could only be obtained from wells, and in much of the area, groundwater could only be reached at a depth of over 20 metres. As a result, nearly all the houses were fitted with a system which conveyed rainwater for domestic use into huge tanks, mainly installed in the atrium and the peristyle. There were also a number of wells, which may be classified as public and private; the public wells, which were available to all, tended to be distributed in the busiest areas. Less than a dozen wells are now known; the major ones were situated in Via Consolare at the corner with Vico di Narciso, two in Via del Foro in the areas later occupied by *tabernae* 7 and

15, in the Forum Baths and the Stabian Baths, in the south-eastern corner of the Basilica, in the Triangular Forum and in the open space near the Vesuvius Gate.

Several private wells have been discovered in houses; when public fountains were installed all over the town, many of these were sealed with amphoras in case an unexpected water shortage required their use. Many other wells, especially in Regiones I and II, served to irrigate the fields cultivated inside the city walls before the urbanisation in the second century BC. When the area was developed, these wells were also sealed with amphoras. Water was brought up from the wells by pulleys or by a water wheel turned by hand or by animals, generally mules.

Many of the problems associated with the water supply were solved by the construction of Augustus' aqueduct, which conveyed water to Pompeii from the springs of the River Acquarus near M. Serinus (Avellino) in the early first century AD. After following a long route, the aqueduct branched off at Palma Campania, where large parts of the ruined structure have been found; one branch led to Naples, and a smaller one ran to

a point near Pompeii's Vesuvius Gate, which is the highest point in the town. A *castellum aquae* (water tower) was built there to receive the water, which was then channelled through a series of barriers that trapped impurities, and divided between three pipes installed at different heights, so that it could be distributed on a priority basis.

The first pipe supplied a public fountain built onto the *castellum aquae*; the marble lion's head that contained the lead spout of this fountain still survives. The other two pipes ran at ground level along the pavements of Via di Stabia and Via dei Vetti, and branched off along the major town roads. The water flowed through lead pipes (*fistulae*), typically pear-shaped with a closing strip at the top; undoubtedly, they could not withstand high pressures and would have required frequent maintenance, which was why they were covered with only a few centimetres of soil. Originally, the public installation probably served all the fountains, the public baths and a few public buildings. To ensure equal pressure throughout the town, the water pipes were first connected to a *castellum plumbeum*, a kind of lead pillar roughly 1-1.5 square metres and 6 metres tall, containing a small

26 top left This bronze hydraulic valve served to turn the water on or off. It consists of two lateral tubes welded to the water pipes, separated by a cylinder into which another perfectly matching cylinder was inserted; a hole

in the inner cylinder allowed or prevented the flow of water when the hole was on the same axis as the tubes. The valve was turned with a key inserted in the upper part of the castellum plumbeum.

lead tank at the top, which acted as pressure taps.

Fountains were distributed fairly evenly all over the town, so that nearly all private homes could reach them without any difficulty; 42 have been found so far. The fountains were all served by a network of lead water pipes which ran along the pavements. The water pipes were individually connected to the *castellum plumbeum* which supplied them; no case has ever been found of a water pipe supplying two fountains. Most of the fountains have a quadrangular basin consisting of monolithic blocks secured by cramps; only one is hemispherical. One of those found is made of marble, two are of tuff, three of travertine, and all the others are of basalt lava stone. In one case the basin of the fountain is made of masonry lined with waterproof *opus signinum*.

One side of the basin, usually the one parallel to the pavement, was surmounted by a parallelepiped-shaped post; the surface of the post

which faced the basin was decorated with a gargoyle portraying various subjects, generally associated in some way with water or sacrifices. The spout, attached to the water pipe which led up from the pavement, protruded from a hole in the centre of the gargoyle. The posts were fixed to the basin with two lead cramps at the sides. The water pipe which conveyed the water up to the gargoyle was protected by a pillar almost as tall as the entire fountain; the pipe was housed in a channel which ran along its whole length. This protective pillar was fixed to the gargoyle post with lead cramps.

The base of the fountain, which had rounded edges, was sometimes made of good-quality, fine-textured *opus signinum*, and sometimes of roof

tiles embedded in mortar. The base always sloped slightly down towards the drainage hole, which was situated on the side of the basin coinciding with the slope of the road. This hole was usually plugged so that the basin could be filled, and was normally opened when the fountain was maintained and cleaned. A second water drainage channel, situated in the centre, on the edge of the slab opposite the gargoyle, acted as an overflow. Evidently, these ancient fountains had a continuous supply of water, and the water in the basin was always clean because of the overflow system, which suggests that water would have run along the streets. That part of the fountain which projected into the roadway was generally protected against vehicular traffic by kerbstones, usually made of basalt lava stone, sometimes roughly hewn and sometimes quadrangular.

The earthquake of AD 62 badly damaged the water supply system, which appears to have been rapidly

repaired. However, the earth tremors which took place in the period immediately before the eruption must have caused permanent damage, as the town's water system was completely reconstructed and the water pipes were laid at a much deeper level. Archaeological surveys have recently revealed that there were deep trenches in nearly all the main pavements when the eruption took place. The few individuals whose houses were connected to the public water system exploited the period of social unrest following the earthquake by connecting private pipes to the *castella plumbea*. Around half of the *castella plumbea* are now working as they would have in ancient times.

26 bottom left Fountains were distributed along the main roads of the town, and almost all the posts surmounting them bore an image on the front; this one portrays the head of an ox, symbolising offerings to the gods.

26-27 The Water Tower at the Vesuvius Gate was the terminal of the Claudian aqueduct which brought water from the River Serinus (in the Campanian Apennines) to Pompeii. The construction, built into the embankment of the city walls, has a magnificent opus latericium façade which was divided into three by arches with projecting pilaster strips and had three holes through which three lead pipes passed to distribute water through the town (bottom centre); kerbstones were installed at the front.

27 top This lead water pipe with a relief inscription has a roughly ovoid cross-section, and is closed at the top by a metal strip welded with a lead and tin alloy.

27 bottom This water distribution tank with valves was found in the West Insula; it has a roughly cylindrical shape, and was the terminal of a lead water pipe. Three valves which distributed water in other directions through water pipes of a smaller diameter led out of the tank. These objects, almost always found in houses, regulated the flow of water to fountains and basins.

THE WORLD OF PAINTING AND MOSAIC

29 top A 2nd-style wall decoration portrayed a rather naive architectural trompe l'oeil; on this wall in the Villa of the Mysteries (room 16, east wall), two columns on a tall podium can be seen in the foreground between antae surmounted by round arches, and a wall with orthostates, cornices and courses of rusticated ashlar is visible in the background.

28 left A wall of oecus no. 22 in the House of Sallust (VI-2-4), decorated in the 1st style. The relief decoration, which imitates an isodomic structure, presents a tall black wainscot, a series of white orthostates, three bands of coloured rusticated ashlar, a smooth frieze and a projecting stucco cornice.

28-29 On the east wall of hall 'q' of the House of the Vettii (VI-15-1), a magnificent example of the 4th style, Apollo is portrayed with his lyre and Artemis with her bow and quiver; on the ground a serpent coils round the omphalos, while a bull is led from the left for sacrifice; at the top a bacchante dances to the sound of drums.

In 1882 A. Mau wrote *Geschichte der Wandmalerei in Pompeji* (History of Wall Painting in Pompeii), a fundamental work, in which he attempted the first ever classification of Pompeii's wall paintings. As a result of his research and later studies, Roman wall frescoes up to AD 79 are now identified and classified under four decorative systems, incorrectly referred to as 'styles'.

The first system, called the 'encrustation' or 'structural style', is the oldest for which chronological evidence exists in Pompeii (200–80 BC). It imitated architectural features (cornices, pilaster strips, rustication, columns), which were made of stucco and decorated to resemble marble. This style endowed houses with a noble, austere appearance. In some of the most representative houses of Pompeii, such as the House of the Faun and the House of Sallust, it was never changed; the owners continued to use and restore it even when other types of decoration were in vogue. This style was certainly not invented in Pompeii, but probably imported from the Orient, where those decorative characteristics often corresponded to real marble features.

The second system, called the 'architectural style', seems to have been popular in the age of Sulla (80–25 BC). It used the same decorative features as the first style, but they were now painted, rather than modelled in

29 centre Walls frescoed in the 3rd style often feature large mythological scenes in the central panel. A painting of 'Hercules in the garden of the Hesperides' stands out on this wall of room 'b' in the House of Amandus the Priest (I-7-7).

29 bottom The 3rd-style wall decoration system used in the tablinum of the house of Lucretius Fronto (V-4-11) is more complex than the earlier ones. The architectural elements lose their functional aspect to become decorative motifs; the columns are so slender as to become floral candelabra, the cornices turn into magnificent arabesques, the architectural views anticipate the imaginary structures of the 4th style, and paintings fill the panels in the middle section.

stucco. The painting portrayed perspective planes on the walls, usually characterised by a foreground with a tall podium on which two or four columns stood. These columns divided the middle part of the wall into three sections and supported architraves, arches and coffered ceilings. As this 'style' developed, the central section would include a door, which was later made to 'stand open' to give a glimpse of gardens, rows of colonnades and circular temples beyond. There were also small pictures and landscapes, together with characters portrayed above the podium and behind the columns, as in the wall paintings in the Villa of the Mysteries and the Villa of Publius Fannius Sinistor at Boscoreale.

The third system, known as the 'ornamental style' (25 BC–AD 35), seems to imitate the second style to a certain extent. The structure of the wall remained unchanged, but the columns that divided the wall into three parts became slender, resembling carved ivory columns. The architectural structures acquired ornamental (rather than real) forms, the decorations were painted in miniature and bright colours predominated, standing out against a black or white background. The decorative bands featured Egyptian motifs, and the friezes resembled marble inlays. The central *aedicule*-shaped panel was dominated by the main, often large, painting, which was almost always of excellent quality, and portrayed mythological subjects that demonstrated the assimilation of Greek culture. Some good examples are preserved in the House of Lucretius Fronto, the 'Imperial' Villa and the Villa of the Mysteries.

The fourth system, called the 'illusionist style', was already present in Pompeii in the second quarter of the first century AD, but only became widely popular after the earthquake of AD 62, when many homes were restored and redecorated. This decorative system seems to follow on partly from the 2nd style, exaggerating the orderly structures portrayed in it, and partly from the 3rd style, disproportionately multiplying its ornamental and decorative tone. The structures thus appear unreal and the decoration fussy and exuberant, although the system maintained the structure consisting of a wainscot, a middle area divided into three by compartments with multi-storey porticoes instead of columns, and an upper area with sometimes illogical architectural figures. Wall decoration that combined paintings and stucco reliefs also came into vogue in this period, as can be seen in the Stabian Baths and the Forum Baths. Some excellent examples of 4th-style painting can be seen in the House of Loreius Tiburtinus, the House of the Vettii and the House of the Tragic Poet. Another type of wall painting in Pompeii, known as 'popular painting', was very important from a historical and cultural standpoint. This category includes all the portrayals of scenes from everyday life which, in a more realistic, practical way, perhaps, depict the culture and society of the lower classes in ancient Pompeii. Some good examples are the frieze in the Praedia of Julia Felix, with pictures of the Forum, the carpenters' funeral cortège, the bread stall, the riot in the Amphitheatre between the Pompeiians and the Nucerians, and the numerous propaganda and religious paintings that lined the streets. The dates given for the Pompeiian painting styles are only approximate, as painters were reluctant to depart from the contemporary decorative systems, and clients' tastes only changed gradually. There has been much debate as to whether the

ancient wall paintings used the fresco, tempera or encaustic technique. The paintings now seen on the walls of Pompeii are definitely frescoes, made by applying the colours to a freshly laid, damp coat of calcite and marble dust covering an area sufficient for one day's work. Up to seven undercoats of sand and lime, becoming gradually finer in texture toward the outer surface, were spread on a thoroughly dry wall; they served to flatten out any unevenness in the wall, and to protect the painted wall against rising damp. A layer of terracotta fragments, designed to limit the damage caused by damp, is often found between the wall and the undercoats of plaster. Before the last layer was laid, the most expert artists usually sketched the decorative system; the *parietarii* then took over, painting the walls from top to bottom, after which the *imaginarii* executed the figured paintings. A large room, which was being decorated at the time of the eruption, was recently found in the House of the Chaste Lovers, enabling all aspects of the work and equipment to be studied. Pompeii's wall frescoes are extremely important in the history of ancient art, as they give an insight into what the great art of the Greek world must have been like. They also indicate the cultural processes and interpretations it underwent when it was adopted in Italy. In fact, the art of Pompeii is merely Greek art, which travelled to Pompeii via Rome, and is therefore no more than a pale reflection of the original.

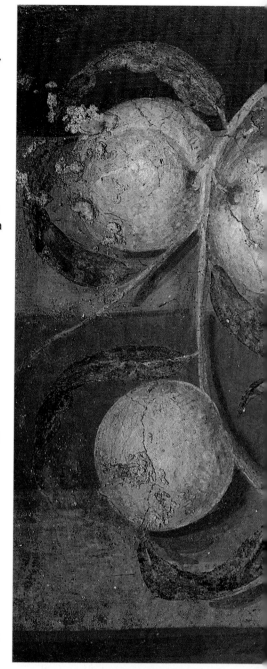

Mosaic floors were often closely related to the use of the room and the wall decoration, but they only represent a small part of the floors in Pompeii. The most common type of flooring was *opus signinum*, a layer of small fragments of tiles and amphoras embedded in mortar and sometimes covered with red paint. A very cheap but effective local variation on this technique was *lavapesta* (crushed lava), which was also employed in Pompeii. These floors were often ornamented with marble tesserae, laid to form geometrical motifs or scattered in a regular pattern; one characteristic design was a cross formed by four white tesserae with a central black one, or vice versa. Mosaic floors consisted of small pieces of stone, glass paste and especially marble, in the shape of a truncated pyramid. These tesserae were laid on a bed of cement and tamped to produce a flat surface of an almost pictorial appearance, suggesting not so much a floor as a carpet. The simplest type of mosaic, *opus tessellatum*, mainly featured geometrical patterns, and was made of larger tesserae. Mosaics portraying pictorial scenes were made of smaller tesserae, sometimes under one centimetre square; this technique was known as *opus vermiculatum* and the resulting picture, usually positioned in the middle of the floor, was known as an *emblema*. Finally, the *opus sectile* technique was a composition of coloured marble usually enclosed in a square or a circumference and used as an *emblema*.

30-31 top Still lifes, inserted in the centre of panels or in the compartments, were very common in the 4th style.
This painting, with three others, constituted the frieze occupying the upper part of the wall.

30-31 centre
This coloured opus vermiculatum *mosaic frieze edged the floor of the entrance to the House of the Faun (VI-12-2); it portrays a garland of flowers and fruit tied with a spiral ribbon and ornamented by two female tragedy masks with ringlets.*

30 left and 31 right These bowls, containing paints that had not yet been prepared, were found in house I-9-9.
In painters' studios, colours were classified as artificial or natural. Pliny the Elder gives a long list of colours in his Naturalis Historia; *he divided them into* floridi *(bright) and* austeri *(dark), and also indicated the price. The most expensive colours, such as* armenium *(blue), were usually supplied by the owner of the house to prevent imitations from being used.*

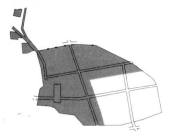

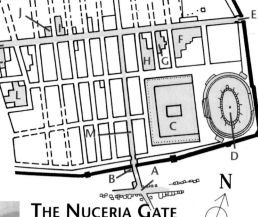

THE SOUTHERN DISTRICT OF POMPEII

THE NUCERIA GATE AND THE NECROPOLIS

The entrance to Pompeii from the Nuceria Gate is very impressive; the Necropolis, the city walls and the gate form a monumental ensemble unique to Pompeii, and every visitor, with or without any prior knowledge of Roman life, is able to gain a clear impression of being in a 'real' town. After walking along the road lined with monumental tombs, visitors see the Nuceria Gate silhouetted against the sky, its single barrel-vaulted archway made of *opus incertum* consisting of Vesuvius lava stone. A paved road follows a gradual ascent to the entrance; the route is flanked by two high walls made of *opus quadratum*, which used to end in two

crenellated towers further down. An enemy attempting to enter the town through this gate would have had to follow an uphill route under a hail of all kinds of missiles. At the sides of the gates it is still evident how impressive the high *opus quadratum* walls must have been, and what fear they must have instilled in mariners sailing up the last stretch of the slow River Sarnus, prior to reaching the sea. Yet the gate and the wall that survive

today are merely remains of the town's impressive defence system, which fell into disuse after the Civil War (89–80 BC), when Pompeii and its Italic allies were defeated by Sulla's forces. Later, after the earthquake of AD 62, the city walls were partly dismantled and the blocks of stone broken up and used to repair and reconstruct damaged houses. This and other outrages, like the occupation of the *pomoerium* (sacred public land), took place in a context of general disorder, when central control broke down and unscrupulous characters took advantage of the situation. Significant proof of these events is in evidence outside the Nuceria Gate. A travertine pillar in the middle of the crossroads where the road leading out of town crosses the road leading west from Nuceria, bears an inscription stating that Suedius

The southern district of Pompeii is the area excavated most recently (1930–1960), but also the district most seriously damaged by long years of neglect and by the 1980 earthquake. The southern district is situated around Via dell'Abbondanza and Via di Nocera, offering a comprehensive view of the main features of the town. Pompeii appears not as a heap of ruins but as a bustling town, its houses completed with rebuilt roofs, the gardens replanted as they were in Roman times, and a number of public buildings restored to their former splendour. Visitors entering Pompeii from the necropolis see the town rising above them, with its impressive Nuceria Gate and mighty walls studded with square towers. From the top of the walls, the entire southern district can be seen, with Vesuvius in the background, and blocks of houses, the colours of the ancient roofs and the greenery of the gardens in the foreground. This district was alive with the activity of shopkeepers and tradesmen, enlivened by the enthusiasm of the young men who patronised the Large Palaestra and the noisy cries of spectators on their way to watch the gladiatorial games.

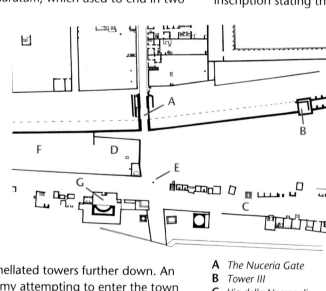

32 top This general view of the Nuceria Gate Necropolis shows the crossroads between the road leaving the town and the outer ring road, lined with tombs; the pillar with the inscription about Suedius Clemens stands in the centre.

particular rules, apart from the fact that they had to remain within the allocated area. Tombs belonging to families from different social backgrounds, from freedmen to *decurions*, were built side by side, even within the same period. Each family tried to locate its monument in the best position, hiding previously built tombs and sometimes, albeit by chance, producing some impressive scenic effects. The construction of the Nuceria Gate Necropolis began in the early first century BC, probably in the age of Sulla, and tombs were built here right up until the last years of the town's life. Members of some of the leading families of the town, like the Stronnii, Caesii, Tillii, Octavii, Herennii, Epidii and Sepunii, were laid to rest here. In Pompeii, as in almost all the Roman

Clemens, the Emperor Vespasian's envoy in Pompeii, after investigating these events and taking appropriate measures, restored the public land unlawfully occupied by private individuals to the town of Pompeii. Similar inscriptions have been found at the Herculaneum, Vesuvius and Marine Gates. The might of Suedius Clemens can be seen in this area: the *moliones* (stables) situated behind the walls and to the left of the city gate were razed to the ground, and a low *opus incertum* wall was constructed parallel to the city walls to mark the boundary of the sacred public land clearly. A number of tombs built along the road inside the public area were also destroyed and covered with soil.

All the burial monuments in the Necropolis outside the Nuceria Gate are situated along the south side of the road that connected the Stabian Gate with the Nuceria Gate, and led to the nearby town of Nuceria Alfaterna. From the Nuceria Gate onwards, tombs are also located on the north side. The Necropolis was discovered and excavated in the 1950s by A. Maiuri and, like the one outside the Herculaneum Gate, is monumental in appearance. Recent archaeological investigations have established that this Necropolis continued for several kilometres along the road that led to Nuceria. The tomb of the wealthy and influential Lucretius family was a recent discovery. The construction of the tombs does not seem to follow any

world, cremation was standard practice; the deceased was laid on a litter wearing ceremonial clothing and, if he were a magistrate, bearing his status symbols, then burnt on a pyre at an official place of cremation (*ustrinum*). The ashes, together with a coin, were collected and stored in a terracotta or glass urn, usually placed inside a lead container. The container was then buried in the sacred enclosure of the tomb, and a *columella* (a stylised lava-stone or travertine bust) was erected to mark the spot. In some cases, the tombs had chambers with a set of niches in which the cinerary urns and *columellae* were placed. The *columellae*, especially the marble ones, often bear short inscriptions indicating the name and age of the deceased. A nine-day festival of the dead (*Feralia*), which ended on February 21, was held every year, and the family celebrated rites commemorating their dead at the tomb. Private ceremonies (*Parentalia*) were carried out on the anniversary of the death.

THE ROW HOUSES IN VIA DI NOCERA

Via di Nocera represents the eastern *cardo* of the town. The paved street reveals clear signs of long usage; deep ruts have been left by cartwheels, and the edges of the pavements are worn. From the town-planning aspect, Via di Nocera represents the main axis of the south-eastern part of the town; the insulae to the east and west were designed to follow its route perfectly, giving the whole area a unified appearance. According to recent studies, this site appears to have been first developed after the Second Punic War (218–202 BC), when the devastation and destruction of many towns in central Italy by Hannibal's army led to

34 top The 'Mano Pantea', the palm of which can be seen here, was found in the Sanctuary of Magic Rites (II-1-12) and portrays the attributes of the god Sabazius, whose rites were known only to a few initiated.

34 centre left This view of Via di Nocera from the south shows the west façade of the recently restored houses, with their roofs in the original positions.

peristyles and large reception rooms decorated with 3rd- and 4th-style frescoes, they rivalled the patrician houses of Pompeii's northern *insulae* in terms of luxury and size.

This type of building underwent another radical change after the earthquake of AD 62. The large houses were split up and partly demolished to make way for the construction of shops and tradesmen's workshops. The southern district around Via di Nocera was transformed from a residential into a commercial and manufacturing area, and filled with shops, *cauponae*, *thermopolia* and vegetable gardens. Nevertheless, the first-stage structures of the row houses can still be seen in many cases. The following are some of those which can still be visited today:

The Lantern Works (I-20-3) is a varied complex in which the owner started up a number of profitable

demand for new farm land and new building areas. Pompeii offered both, so many new families arriving from Nola, Praeneste and Nuceria were allocated a plot of agricultural land and an area inside the city walls on which to build a new house.

The dwellings erected during this period were very simple, functional, cheap and easy to build. They occupied a long, narrow area measuring approximately 300 square metres, with various layouts. In some instances, they were built parallel to the width of the *insula*, while in others, they were built along both the shorter and longer sides. The houses, which always fronted onto the road, were built around an open courtyard, and there was always a small *hortus* (cultivated garden) behind them. Some of these houses were transformed when parts of them were bought and sold. During the first Imperial age (first century AD) very large houses were constructed, and with the creation of complex

businesses to exploit the large number of people who used the road overlooking the Nuceria Gate area, the Large Palaestra and the Amphitheatre. *Lucernae* (lanterns) and *fritilli* (glasses used for drinking wine and playing dice) were made in two kilns, situated in opposite corners of a large open space. Still clearly visible is the reverberating surface of the larger kiln, with bore holes at regular intervals, for the introduction of fuels used to heat the firing chamber to the right temperature. Lanterns and glasses were sold in the shop that opened onto the street, together with wine produced in the large vineyard behind the house. The same owner also had a number of rooms on the first floor and a summer triclinium in the vineyard, which was rented out to passers-by. A tuff statue of a Thracian gladiator was situated here.

The House of the Garden of Hercules is named after a statue of Hercules found near the *lararium* in the large garden used to grow roses, which constituted the basis of perfumed essences made here and sold in small, pear-shaped glass bottles. Much of the oldest part of the house's structure survives, and similar twin houses have been detected by stratigraphic tests conducted in the garden.

The House of the Floral Lararium is named after the small *lararium*, entirely frescoed with small, coloured flowers and flying cherubs, on the north wall of the small *cubiculum* overlooking the garden. The large garden represented a source of income for the owner of the house: it was given over to growing cuttings, presumably because

34 centre right The House of the Garden of Hercules (II-8-6) had a huge cultivated site, gained by demolishing some older houses.

34 bottom The House of the Garden of Hercules is separated from Via di Nocera by a tall boundary wall which sheltered the rose beds from the wind and preserved moisture.

35 top left The Lantern Works (I-20-2) was very busy in the last years of Pompeii's existence. The kiln, which was mainly used to fire lanterns and pottery, can be seen at the end of the works.

35 bottom left In house II-9-1, a pillar of the small portico that gives onto the viridarium *is decorated with a figure of Priapus displaying a huge phallus.*

35 centre This marble statuette was found in the garden of house II-9-3. Of special note are the eyes traced in black, the gold hair and the yellow drapery covering the loins.

35 right This painting in the oecus of house II-9-3 portrays a moonlit scene of two rampant deer resting against an ivy-covered tree.

garden plants were much in demand as a result of the extensive restoration work being carried out all over the town. The fact that business was flourishing is demonstrated by the magnificent 4th-style decoration of *oecus* no.8, with paintings of Europa and the Bull and Venus Fishing. The black wainscot is attractively decorated with a succession of hunting scenes and moonlit pastoral landscapes.

The building known as the Magic Rites Complex was an urban shrine devoted to the worship of an oriental deity, Sabazius, which was conducted around a peristyle. Sabazius was a sun god who protected crops and fertility; an alcoholic drink made from barley and corn was drunk and orgiastic rites were performed in his honour. There are some particularly interesting 3rd-style paintings associated with the liturgy of this cult in triclinium no.3, immediately to the north of the entrance, and in room no.6, in the north-eastern corner of the peristyle. Two *mani pantee* (bronze hands with magic symbols associated with fertility) and two magnificent vases, decorated with the attributes and images of Sabazius, represent a particularly important find.

THE PALAESTRA

The Palaestra, together with the Amphitheatre, was an important public space, which totally occupied the south-eastern boundary of the town. The space was completely closed to vehicular traffic, as demonstrated by all the side streets leading east from Via di Nocera and south from Via dell'Abbondanza. The Palaestra was built, at public expense, during the reign of Augustus (27 BC–AD 14) according to two fragments of inscriptions discovered in an area likely to have been occupied

36 left This good-quality stucco relief portrays a boxer in heroic nakedness; his hands are protected by cesti, or boxing gloves, tied with leather laces.

by regular *insulae* like those to the north and west. It was built because Augustus wished to provide the *collegia iuventum* with a campus where they could train and meet, so that they were prepared in body and mind to be called up for service in the Roman army. Every year the youth of Pompeii demonstrated their skills in the *probatio equitum* – a kind of military parade or demonstration of training and aptitude. The high priority given to these buildings and activities formed part of Octavian Augustus' plan to promote and reinforce the values of the State. It is not known what led to the expropriation of a such a densely built-up private area, but the noble purpose undoubtedly overcame any dissent.

The Palaestra is a rectangle measuring 141 x 107 metres, with three porticoed sides. The fourth (eastern) side, opposite the amphitheatre, features three monumental entrances and a crenellated wall, recalling the military

36 centre This stucco relief portrays Dionysus as a wrestler; the athlete-god rests one elbow on a hoop used for gymnastic exercises.

36 right These glass bottles of different shapes contained oils and ointments, which wrestlers used to rub on their bodies, especially before a match.

36-37 The Campus, seen from the Amphitheatre. The crenellated wall on the façade is interrupted by three monumental entrances. The swimming pool

is situated in the middle of this huge area, and Composite, colonnaded walkways can be glimpsed in the background.

37 bottom left This magnificent bronze stirrup was attached to the saddle with leather straps.

37 bottom right The bronze strigil, which had a characteristic curved blade (ligula) with a hooked end, was an essential tool for athletes; in this instance, the inner surface of the handle (capulus) is decorated with the figure of a boxer.

The strigil was used to scrape oil and sweat from the body after physical exercise.

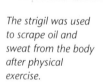

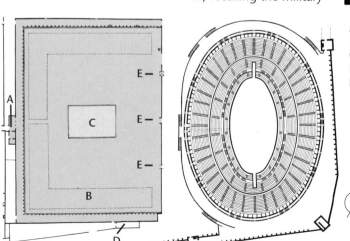

A Sacred area
B Wooded area
C Swimming pool
D Latrine
E Monumental entrances

N

nature of the building; secondary entrances were located at the ends of the south and north porticoes. The columns were of the Composite order; the moulded base rested on an *opus signinum* stylobate which rose 90 centimetres above the level of the garden, and the shaft of the column, made of *opus latericium*, was swathed in a thick undercoat of mortar, covered with a layer of calcite and marble dust, which allowed it to be decorated with bean-shaped grooves to imitate marble. The Composite capital featured acanthus leaves, volutes at the corners and a rosette in the centre.

The roof was covered with flat tiles

tympanum, and constitute the focal point of the entire construction. On the end wall of the nave there was a large altar covered with marble slabs with moulded edges and bases; here, rites associated with Augustus probably took place, and prizes were awarded to the best of the young men of Pompeii. A double row of plane trees ran parallel to the three porticoed sides; at the time of the eruption they were almost 100 years old, and the plaster casts made of the roots are still in situ.

In the middle of the Palaestra there was a swimming pool measuring 34.55 x 22.25 metres; it was lined

flushed out the large latrine in the eastern section of the southern portico. The latrine, entered through a small door under the portico, had seats of trachytic lava, probably covered with marble, on three sides. Since it also had a door opening to the outside of the Palaestra, opposite the arena, it may be ascertained that, at one time, the latrine was used when games were being held in the Amphitheatre.

The earthquake of AD 62 caused serious damage to the Palaestra, and some sectors were probably still unfit for use in AD 79. Numerous columns had to be raised, and many were still not in place at the time of the eruption. The columns of the west portico all have lead wedges at the base, inserted by casting after the columns had been replumbed, while others have a bare shaft made of *opus latericium*. The end walls of the south and west porticoes probably had to be completely rebuilt, since, when they were found, they were totally bare of the wall decorations which survive along the north wall. Unfortunately, the north wall completely collapsed during the eruption of Vesuvius, but its 3rd-style decorations survived.

The intense activity performed here, mainly by men, is demonstrated by numerous graffiti relating to military, sporting and even amorous prowess. The graffiti include the mysterious square text: '*rotas opera tenet arpo sator*' interpreted by some scholars as a cryptogram of the Lord's Prayer (*Pater Noster*).

The building recently underwent extensive restoration work; the plane trees have been replanted and the north wall rebuilt, so the Large Palaestra has been restored to its original splendour.

which terminated at the bottom in *cymae* decorated with palmettes and the face of a gorgon. Rainwater ran into a gutter at the foot of the stylobate, which conveyed it to tanks situated under the porticoes. The earth floor under the porticoes was highly suitable for athletes, who mainly trained barefoot. In the middle of the western ambulatory was an area divided into a nave and two aisles, with two pillars and half-columns at the front, which must have supported a

with waterproof cement and the surround was made of grey Nuceria tuff. At the deepest point, the pool was 2.6 metres deep. It was supplied with water from the public aqueduct, conveyed to the pool through a lead water pipe that ran from the *castellum plumbeum* in the north-western corner of the House of Loreius Tiburtinus in Via dell'Abbondanza. Water flowed continually into the pool, and the overflow ran into a small drain, which

THE AMPHITHEATRE

Pompeii's amphitheatre is the oldest known building designed for gladiatorial games. It was built around 70 BC by the two quinquennial *duumviri*, Q. Valgus and M. Porcius, as stated in two travertine inscriptions found in the *crypta* (the ring-shaped corridor below the lowest tier of steps), which reads thus: '*Quinctius C. F. Valgus M. Porcius M. f. duovir(i)*

N

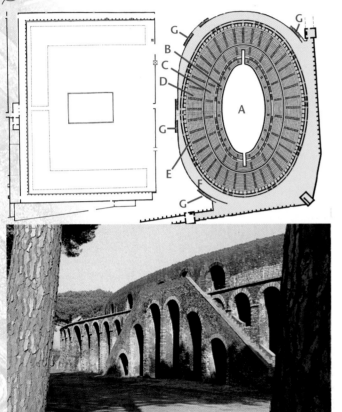

Gate), through which spectators could enter and leave. The amphitheatre was able to hold some 20,000 spectators (far more than the town's population), so it is easy to imagine the chaos that reigned when games were being held, and why it was important to close a large area to vehicular traffic and have two gates nearby.

The building stands in a large, open area, which was probably bounded by a row of plane trees. The attractive outer perimeter is divided into two tiers. The bottom tier features a continuous series of round blind arches, edged with pale blocks of local stone (Sarnus travertine), which enclose walls of *opus incertum*, mainly consisting of dark Vesuvius lava stone. Street vendors set up their stalls here, as evident from the many painted inscriptions found, one of which reads: '*Permissu aedilium Cn. Aninius Fortunatus occup(at)*' (Cnaeus Aninius Fortunatus occupies this position with the permission of the aediles). Between the upper tier and the lower tier, which had a smaller circumference, there was a large circular walkway which enabled spectators to pass all the way around the amphitheatre. The main walls also feature round arches, but they are lower than the walkway; which suggests they led either up a double flights of steps to the porticoes in the attic storey, or to the inner terraces. Two massive, double-flight staircases supported by six arches, situated to the north-west and west,

38 left The media cavea and summa cavea of the Amphitheatre were reached via a series of monumental stairways situated all round the building; this photo shows the double staircase overlooking the Palaestra, which was substructed on six round arches.

38 right As part of the arena was excavated below ground level, the corridors into it sloped downhill. The entrance, at the southern end, is paved like the roads, and flanked by pedestals for honorary statues.

quinq(uennales) coloniai honoris caussa spectacula de sua peq(unia) fac(iundia) coer(arunt) et coloneis locum in perpetuom deder(unt)' (Caius Quintus Valgus, son of Caius, and Marcus Porcius, son of Marcus, in their capacity as quinquennial *duumviri*, to demonstrate the honour of the colony, erected this sports complex at their own expense and donated it to the colonists for their perpetual use). The south-eastern corner of the town was deemed to be a suitable site; not only was it free of other buildings, but the embankment behind the town's defence walls could also be exploited for two-fifths of its circumference. The site was also ideal because of its position, close to two main town gates (the Nuceria Gate and the Sarnus

38-39 The elliptical plan of the amphitheatre is amplified by the concentric circles formed by the terraces. This photograph shows the tall parapet that protected spectators, and the three tiers of seats. Vesuvius is silhouetted in the background.

and two single-flight staircases – one to the south, the other to the north – led to the area between the lower and upper tiers, allowing access to the seats. The arena itself was on a lower level than the ground outside; it was reached through two long, wide, sloping entrance halls situated on the longer axis, both of which were paved and barrel-vaulted. The north entrance hall, which constituted the main entrance to the arena, presented two niches at the start of the slope, which still bear inscriptions relating to a father and son, both called Cuspio Pansa, who restored the amphitheatre at their own expense after the earthquake in AD 62.

Along the eastern side of the entrance hall there are a number of holes into which stakes were inserted;

these were fitted with handrails which bordered on an embankment. At the end of the two entrance halls, before reaching the arena, it was possible to enter the crypt, which ran parallel to the arena and gave access to the lower terraces, reserved for the town nobles. The arena was separated from the seats by a parapet 2.18 metres high, frescoed with various scenes, including scenes of gladiatorial combat. Sadly these have long been lost, and the only remaining evidence of them is represented by invaluable nineteenth-century drawings.

The theatre seats (*cavea*) were divided into three concentric rows called the *ima cavea* (lower terrace), *media cavea* (middle terrace) and *summa cavea* (top terrace), separated

by well-fashioned adjacent grey tuff parapets. The lower terrace was reached from the crypt, while the middle and top terraces were reached from the top, down narrow, but convenient, staircases. The auditorium was divided perpendicularly into wedges by steps or parapets. As the seats were installed by magistrates at their own expense, inscriptions naming the magistrates who had donated them always appeared on the parapet of the arena alongside the wedges. The terraces were fairly wide and shaped lengthwise, in such a way that they were higher at the front and lower at the back, so seated spectators would not be annoyed by the feet of those sitting behind. In the lower terrace, where the town nobles sat, the seats

40 top This greave is richly decorated with plant reliefs, so was probably worn for parades; greaves protected gladiators' legs, and were secured with leather laces threaded through movable rings.

were numbered and separated by a red strip. The games could also be watched from the porticoes in the attic storey, where there was standing room only, and spectators were much further away. A *velarium* system provided the eastern terraces of the Pompeii amphitheatre with some shade. The *velarium* system comprised a number of poles fixed along the upper western perimeter, to which dark linen canopies were attached.

The games held in Pompeii were well known and attracted spectators from the neighbouring towns and countryside. They were paid for by the annually elected magistrates, and lasted at least a week. Apart from these games, there were plenty of other occasions for holding games during the year. In the weeks leading up to the

occasion of the games organised by Livineius Regulus (who had already been expelled by the Senate in Rome), the citizens of Pompeii and Nuceria began with insults, proceeded to throw stones, and finally took up arms against one another. By the end of the battle some of the Nucerians had been killed, and several were injured. Nero, the patron of Nuceria, reported the matter to the Senate, which resolved to close the amphitheatre for ten years and exile the organisers. These events are realistically portrayed in a painting found in house I-3-23, which shows a bird's-eye view of the most bloodthirsty moment of the riot.

40 centre This fresco, from house VII-2-25, portrays a chariot race in which the drivers were differentiated by the colours of their tunics. It is not known if and where contests of this kind were held in Pompeii, but the discovery of this type of painting suggests that they were common.

games, the gladiators trained and resided in the Theatre Quadriporticus, where magnificent parade armour has been found. On games days, a colourful procession wound its way through the town to present the combatants to the townspeople. When the procession entered the arena through the north entrance hall, the gladiators saluted the magistrate who had paid for the games, who then received a public ovation.

The gladiators' supporters verged on the fanatical. There was great rivalry between Pompeii and Nuceria, and citizens of the two towns often came to blows when extolling the merits of one or other of the combatants. From AD 57 on, this friction was probably exacerbated by the founding of a colony in Nuceria sponsored by Nero, which may have resulted in the loss of part of Pompeii's territory. Tacitus (*Annals* XIV, 17) recounts that in AD 59, on the

40 bottom left This graffito scene, from house IX-1-12, shows an episode from the battle between two gladiators. After the sword-fight, the two confront one another unarmed. The winner was the gladiator on the right, as can be seen by the wreath he is wearing on his head.

40 bottom right The dome of this helmet, typical of Thracian gladiators, features a relief decoration representing the apotheosis of Rome.

Via dell'Abbondanza

This road is named after a relief on the pillar of the travertine fountain near the Civil Forum, which portrays the Goddess of Abundance, an allegorical deity depicted as a young woman with a cornucopia resting on her left shoulder. The road, a major traffic artery for the whole of Pompeii, constitutes the lower *decumanus*, and crosses the whole town from east to west. It can be divided into three sections, distinguished by their shape, use and date of construction. The first section starts at the Sarnus Gate to the east, and runs slightly uphill to cross the whole of Regiones I and II, before ending at the crossroads with the

other major road, Via di Stabia. This section is approximately four metres wide, and completely paved. The deep ruts left by cartwheels in the hard basalt stone demonstrate how busy the traffic was. The road was flanked by two wide pavements bounded by large blocks of Vesuvius lava or grey Nuceria tuff, which stood some 60 centimetres higher than the roadbed. The corners of these blocks, which face onto the road, often have holes in for tying up horses; these blocks are mostly situated near *tabernae* or *thermopolia*. While the maintenance of the streets was the responsibility of the aediles (public magistrates), the upkeep of the pavements, under the supervision of

the same aediles, fell to the owners of the houses fronting onto them. As a result there are frequent differences in the pavements; some are made of rough *opus signinum*, others are decorated with marble *crustae*, and others are made of lava cement. At crossroads, large, square, pavement-height blocks were placed at regular intervals between the road paving slabs. These served as pedestrian crossings, and were very useful, especially on rainy days, when the roadbed would fill with rainwater and, as it sloped downhill, became an open stream. Public fountains, constructed during the reign of Augustus, were installed at regular intervals close to the pavements, but within the roadbed.

The second section of Via dell'Abbondanza, which runs west from Via Stabia to Via dei Teatri, was wholly closed to vehicular traffic. For a distance of 50 metres this section is 80 centimetres higher than Via Stabia and steps were installed for pedestrians. This difference in levels was necessary to prevent rainwater from flowing too swiftly downhill and damaging the crossroads with Via

CIVEIVM·POLYBIVM·LIVR

Stabia. Where height difference comes to an end, water running down from the Civil Forum was channelled into a sewer leading south, out of town.

The third section of Via dell'Abbondanza, also closed to cart traffic, runs steeply uphill towards the Forum. According to recent archaeological investigations, this section must have originally been on a lower level, because the Civil Forum was entered by climbing a wide, grey tuff staircase, which probably took the form of a propylon with columns and pediment. The view of this entrance from Via di Stabia must have given the road and the Forum a monumental appearance, in view of the fact that all the houses in this section had façades made of large square blocks of grey tuff, ornamented with moulded cornices and pilaster strips.

The road was not all built at the same time. The first section appears to be the most recent (third–second century BC), and the third to be the oldest (sixth century BC), although the entire length of the pavement must have been laid during the same period: the second half of the first century BC. The road was a hive of activity, teeming with passers-by, street vendors, farmers coming into town, women drawing water from the public fountains and carts crossing town, but not without some difficulty. Shops, *thermopolia* and *tabernae* lined the road, and the entrances to private houses seem to jostle for space between the wide frontages of the business premises.

The façades of both houses and business premises had lean-to roofs and balconies, which covered nearly all the pavement, and some restored ones can be seen in Insulae 11 and 12 of Regio I. The plastered walls of the façades were the most commonly

45 bottom left
45 bottom left
Medallions or panels
with geometrical
patterns or relief figures
can often be seen on
the upper parts of walls;
the walls were plastered
around them so that
they stood out as
decorative elements
or signs.

45 bottom right
This magnificent ivory
statuette portrays the
Indian goddess Lakshmi
who, like Aphrodite,
was the goddess of
beauty and fertility.
This precious object,
which was found in
house I-8-5 on Via
dell'Abbondanza,
demonstrates that trade
took place between
Pompeii and the far
east of India.

used media for election propaganda
and business advertising; myriad
inscriptions in large red characters
sing the praises of various candidates
and advertise products and services.
Nowhere else in the town is the
sensation of everyday life in Pompeii
as vivid as in its streets.

THE PRAEDIA OF JULIA FELIX (II-4-2)

This is one of the largest and most attractive houses in Pompeii. Recent archaeological investigations have shown that it was constructed by combining two *insulae*, which were originally separated by a road that was abolished and incorporated in the property, probably after the earthquake of AD 62. The buildings are situated along Via dell'Abbondanza and have large cultivated gardens behind them. The buildings were first excavated between March 30 1757 and April 30

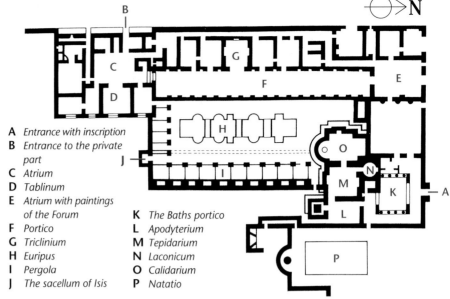

A Entrance with inscription
B Entrance to the private part
C Atrium
D Tablinum
E Atrium with paintings of the Forum
F Portico
G Triclinium
H Euripus
I Pergola
J The sacellum of Isis
K The Baths portico
L Apodyterium
M Tepidarium
N Laconicum
O Calidarium
P Natatio

1757, under the supervision of military engineer R.J. de Alcubierre and his assistant C. Weber. The excavations were only intended to recover objets d'art, and to strip the walls of those paintings considered by C. Paderni, curator of the Portici 'museum', to be suitable for the very unusual private gallery of the Bourbon royal family. As was common practice at that time, the architectural complex was buried after being despoiled. However, before that was done, in May 1757, C. Weber drew a plan of the building, on which he numbered the sites where objects had been found and removed, and listed the paintings stripped from the walls. This plan has proved an invaluable aid to discovering more about the life, activities and owner of the house. The *praedia* (estates) of Julia Felix were finally excavated between 1936 and 1953 by archaeologist A. Maiuri.

An important discovery during the first excavation established the characteristics of the property: the following inscription was found at entrance no.6 – a monumental entrance with half-columns and a pediment made of *opus latericium*: 'In praedis Iuliae Sp(urii) f(iliae) Felicis locantur balneum venerium et nongentum, tabernae, pergulae, caenacula ex idibus Aug(ustis) primis in idus Aug(ustis) sextas, annos continuos quinque. S(i) Q(uinquennium) D(ecurrerit) L(ocatio) E(rit) N(udo) C(onsensu)' (In the estate of Julia, daughter of Spurius Felix, to let: elegant baths for respectable people, shops with living quarters above, and apartments on the upper floor. From August 1 next to August 1 of the sixth

year, for five years. The lease will expire at the end of the five years).

After purchasing the large site, the owner built a multi-purpose complex, which was let out for various purposes, including business use. The large complex can be divided into four separate sections: the private house, the area around the peristyle, the baths and the garden. The entrance to the private house, which was rebuilt after AD 62, is situated at no.10, at the centre of the lane on the western side. It features an atrium with *compluvium*, and a *tablinum* on the same axis as the original entrance and the garden. The walls are still almost entirely covered with frescoes, but the central panels have been detached and removed. *Tablinum* no.92 must have looked spectacular. The 4th-style decorations consisted of wainscots with green plants on a black background; the central area was divided into three parts, with red and yellow panels containing pictures of villas, temples and flying figures in the

46 top The peristyle of the house was bounded to the west by a portico with rectangular marble columns, and to the east and south by a pergola ; the euripus in the centre was probably related to the cult of Isis.

46 centre The Praedia of Julia Felix comprised a huge area used as a garden, with square beds bounded by wooden fences; it was probably used by guests for walks after the bathing cycle.

middle, while the top part featured large still lifes. During eighteenth-century excavations, the south wall was entirely detached and removed; all that survives of the north wall is the still lifes, which can now be viewed in Naples National Museum.

The peristyle area could be reached both from the private house and from Via dell'Abbondanza, through entrance no.3. Parts of a frieze painted with a view of the Civil Forum were detached from the walls of entrance no.24 in the eighteenth century. The western part consisted of a magnificent, large portico with Corinthian marble pillars with a rectangular section and 4th-style

This entrance led to a small four-sided portico with seats for waiting customers, followed by the usual parallel rooms: the *caldarium*, the *tepidarium* with the *laconicum* on the north side, and finally, the *frigidarium*. Just outside was the swimming pool, used mainly in the summer. The baths must have been busy, because many of the public ones were closed for repair of the damages suffered in the earthquake of AD 62.

Behind the baths was a *caupona* which could be entered from Via dell'Abbondanza no.7. It was divided into compartments (pictorial sections), with stone seats and a circular table. A

small *thermopolium* annexed to the *caupona* sold food and drink directly onto the street. The large garden behind this contained large enclosures bounded by low wooden fences, which had fruit trees planted in the middle; the garden could also be reached from the southern boundary near the Amphitheatre. The various sections of the property interlinked, so that customers could reach them easily from different directions. What must once have been a luxurious mansion had been transformed into a public service business property.

decorations on the end wall, which gave onto a spectacular summer triclinium with a cascade system of ornamental fountains. The walls of the triclinium were frescoed with scenes of the Nile, and the ceiling was covered with flakes of Sarnus stone, which gave the impression of being in a cave. In the middle of the peristyle was a *euripus* (a long rectangular tank) with marble edges ornamented by apses, niches and small bridges. The eastern and southern sides were ornamented alternately with niches and apses, and both sides had grotto walls and seats shaded by a large pergola supported by *opus mixtum* pillars with a rectangular section. It is possible that the garden was laid out for religious purposes relating to the worship of Isis, as there was a small shrine dedicated to that goddess on the south side.

The baths complex could be reached from entrance no.6, made of *opus latericium*, which had a staircase leading directly to Via dell'Abbondanza.

46 bottom
An unusual triclinium at the centre of the west portico was set in a nymphaeum structure with marble steps that caused the water to descend in cascades.

46-47 This frieze, which decorated the walls of the atrium giving onto Via dell'Abbondanza (E), portrays market scenes. Fabric vendors are shown on the left and dealers in bronze

pans in the centre; in the background, on the right, a number of buyers approach a stall.

47 bottom In this fragment, a seller of metal equipment and pans can be seen in

the left foreground, and a shoe vendor on the right. The columns of the Forum portico stand in the background, with part of a pedestal for an equestrian statue on the right.

THE HOUSE OF VENUS IN THE SHELL (II-3-3)

This house, excavated by A. Maiuri in 1952, occupies the whole north-western part of the *insula* and is named after the large fresco on the south wall of the garden. The vestibule, frescoed in amaranth red, was decorated with medallions of painted busts, now barely recognisable. The Tuscan atrium was wholly frescoed with scenic 4th-style paintings, which have now faded. The marble *impluvium*, which collected rainwater from the roof through the *compluvium* and supplied the tanks

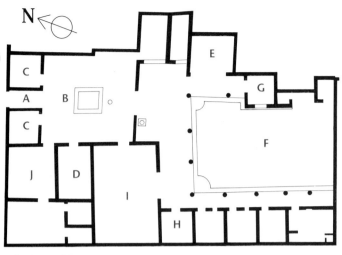

A *Vestibule*
B *Atrium*
C *Cubicula*
D *Triclinium*
E *Tablinum*
F *Peristyle*
G *Cubiculum*
H *Oecus*
I *Large drawing room*
J *Services*

below, dominates the centre of the atrium. This was badly damaged by bombing during the last war (1943).

There are two *cubiculi* on the north side of the atrium; on the right of the western side is a plaster cast of a doorway which allowed access to service rooms, which had an independent entrance on Via dell'Abbondanza; there is a triclinium exquisitely frescoed in the 4th style in the centre. Some particularly interesting features are the stucco cornice which surrounds the barrel vaults and the fresco along the architectural components which imitates a pair of balconies supported by warship prows with peacocks above the parapets. A large drawing room with a black and white mosaic floor, which was about to be given a new wall decoration in AD 79, gives onto the west side of the atrium, to the south. The *tablinum* of the house was not in the normal position (on the same axis as the vestibule, atrium and peristyle), but on the eastern side, under the east ambulatory of the peristyle. The wall decoration, which is in a very poor state of repair, suggests a decorative scheme associated with the myth of Apollo. The central picture on the north wall represents Apollo and Daphne, while individual figures in the compartments are portrayed in positions associated with the deity: one is playing a *cithara* (a stringed instrument), a woman is using a spindle, and a proffering figure seems to be turning back to look at Apollo.

However, the most attractive part of the house is the peristyle. The garden is divided into two splendid flower beds,

48 top In the north portico of the peristyle, the builders used a truss to support the wide aperture between the columns and the back wall. The walls are decorated in the 4th style, and adorned with small paintings of maritime villas.

48 centre The peristyle of the house was built round a three-sided portico formed by Composite brick columns; the lower third is yellow and the upper section is white and fluted. The west wall is wholly frescoed with 4th-style paintings.

48 bottom The fresco on the left-hand side of the back wall of the peristyle features a marble statue of Mars in the foreground, separated from an imaginary garden (paradeisos) by a trelliswork fence.

48-49 The architect who designed the house created an internal route enabling visitors to discover the peristyle area gradually, so that the real garden merged with the imaginary garden frescoed on the back wall. A large window in the centre of the fresco opens onto the sea, and Venus passes by in a shell drawn by dolphins ridden by cherubs.

49 top The central part of the back wall of the peristyle is occupied by the large fresco with Venus lying on her side in a shell pulled like a boat by a dolphin ridden by a cherub, while another cherub seems to be pushing it.

which appear to lead into the wall painting on the south side, where imaginary creatures roam among statues (Mars) and marble fountains. In the middle of the painting, beyond the garden, a large *trompe l'oeil* window opens onto the sea, where a pink shell, drawn by dolphins, bearing a recumbent Venus, adorned with frontlet, necklace, earrings and bracelets, sails past. This fresco was meaningful only if seen from the atrium or the north ambulatory of the peristyle; at close quarters, it betrays all the incongruities of a work painted by several artists, and the naive proportions of the body contrast with the splendid portrait of a woman's head, which bears a hairstyle fashionable during Nero's reign.

Another attempt was made to conceal the real architecture on the east side of the peristyle: the fresco on the outer walls of room 11 portrays a garden with marble fountains on whose edges doves perch. The west and north sides of the peristyle are wholly porticoed; the narrow walkway of the west portico, decorated with 4th-style paintings, accessed the garden rooms, which also had an upper floor. The north portico is very wide, and contains pictures of sanctuaries and seaside villas in an almost impressionistic style.

Rooms 11 and 14 are interesting. Room 11, located south of the east portico, has pale blue panels and a central *aedicule* seen in perspective. At the centre of the *aedicule* there is a picture which is thought to be a rare portrayal of the birth of Hermaphroditus, although this is not at all certain. Room 14, at the end of the west section of the north walkway, features some elegant 4th-style frescoes portraying imaginary buildings, populated by winged cherubs.

The house, badly damaged in the Second World War, was clumsily restored in the 1950s. It recently underwent complete restoration, in which the original volumes and architectural characteristics were philologically observed, so that the freshness of the colours, the splendour of the decorations and the atmosphere of an ancient Pompeiian house have been recovered.

THE HOUSE OF LOREIUS TIBURTINUS (II-2-2)

A *Entrance*
B *The oecus of Justile*
C *Atrium*
D *Viridarium*
E *Upper euripus*

F *4th-style oecus*
G *Lower euripus*
H *Oecus with Trojan cycle*
I *Fountain*
J *Summer triclinium*

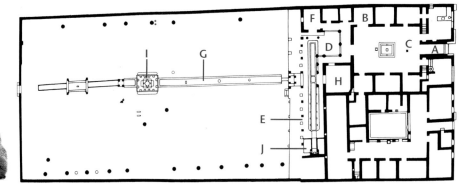

50 top The marble statue that decorated the central fountain of the lower euripus *portrays a cherub sitting on a low rock, holding a tragedy mask. This statuette is a Roman copy of a Hellenistic model, of which numerous versions exist in Pompeii.*

The House of Loreius Tiburtinus, excavated by V. Spinazzola between 1916 and 1921, gives onto Via dell'Abbondanza to the north, and occupies much of the *insula*. The house was named after the numerous electoral inscriptions on its façade and those of the houses opposite, some of which invite voters to vote for Loreius, and others for Tiburtinus. In addition, the centre of a panel on the south wall of *oecus* (reception room) 'f' depicts a priest of Isis, dressed in white, with a shaven head and bearing the *patera* (saucer), *situla* (jar) and sistrum, whose name, written below the portrait, was Amulius Faventinus Tiburs. The last owner was probably Octavius Quartio, whose bronze seal has been found; he converted the house for the domestic worship of Isis, an Egyptian goddess much venerated in Pompeii in the first century AD. The other entrance, featuring two metal-studded, wooden doors, was flanked by two *cauponae* (inns) belonging to the house. The atrium floor was studded with marble hexagons and had an *impluvium* (basin) in the middle, with tall sides resembling flower boxes and a fountain with a tall vertical jet. The anterooms contain paintings in the 4th style (middle of the first century AD) surmounted by stuccoed mouldings in the 1st style (second century BC), which reveal how old the house is. Room 'b' is unusual: painted on to red panels are a number of figures suspended in mid-air, including in the middle, Venus fishing and soldiers bearing arms; small hunting scenes on a black background appear at the top.

50 centre left In the middle of the upper euripus *there was a fountain with a central jet and side jets; a tetrastyle temple on the same axis as the lower* euripus *was situated behind, and the fountain linked the two systems.*

50 centre right The lower euripus, *shown here from the north, was recently restored; the pergola was philologically reconstructed and the original trees replanted.*

50 bottom The fountain in the middle of the lower euripus *consisted of a basin with pillars built against the walls, on which marble statuettes stood. The water flowed over the steps in the middle, which led off from a square structure.*

garden, full of acanthus and fruit trees, and in the south-north direction, between pergola-covered avenues. At the intersection of two euripi stands a 3rd-style temple with a fountain at its base, fitted with a semicircle of inclined spouts and a vertical jet in the middle. Another very unusual fountain stood at the centre of the lower *euripus*; it was quadrangular and had a kind of pyramid in the middle, with four small 'staircases', down which the water ran, no doubt producing a pleasing sound. The water operating the fountains came from a *castellum plumbeum* situated in the north-west corner of the *insula*.

The atrium leads to a small peristyle situated in the place of the original *tablinum*, which is recognisable by the surviving traces of the south wall of the atrium. Two of the most interesting frescoed rooms in Pompeii – *oecus* 'f' and triclinium 'h' – give onto the *viridarium*. Oecus 'f' is decorated in elegant 4th-style with white panels divided at interludes by architectural compartments with trophies; the panels are surrounded by frames with miniature decorations. The ceiling, whose surface has been partly preserved and restored, is ornamented with circular and square partitions containing fine stucco reliefs. Triclinium 'h' features scenes from the history of Troy in two registers. The upper register depicts Hercules' battle with Laomedon, King of Troy, and the lower one portrays episodes from the Trojan war, featuring Achilles.

Another important feature of the house is the scenic arrangement of two *euripi*. The upper *euripus* is covered by a pergola supported by pillars decorated with Bacchic subjects and surrounded by numerous garden statues. The north wall is frescoed with a large hunting scene in an exotic setting, while the west wall depicts the myth of Diana and Actaeon. The pictures on the east wall portray the myths of Narcissus and Pyramus and Thisbe. The only known artist's signature in Pompeii, '*Lucius pinxit*' (painted by Lucius), appears here. The two paintings are separated by a 2nd-style Corinthian *aedicule*. The other, lower *euripus* runs through the huge

51 top The eastern end of the upper euripus *terminated with a summer triclinium, dominated in the centre by a distyle aedicule with an arched end containing the statuette of a crouching young man pouring water from an amphora. There is a painting on either side; the one on the left depicts the myth of Narcissus, and the one on the right, the myth of Pyramus and Thisbe.*

51 centre The west side of the upper euripus *was frescoed with the myth of Diana and Actaeon, divided into two scenes by the entrance door to the* oecus, *which featured 4th-style paintings. On the left Actaeon discovers Diana bathing; on the right he is attacked by the goddess's dogs.*

51 bottom This Hermaphroditus decorated the edges of the cascade fountain in the middle of the lower euripus, *that was clearly visible from the small temple in the middle of the upper* euripus. *The figure is lying on its side on a rock covered with the same drapery which leaves almost the whole body uncovered; the head is slightly reclining. The details show the skill of the artist, probably a local.*

THE HOUSE OF POLYBIUS (IX-13-3)

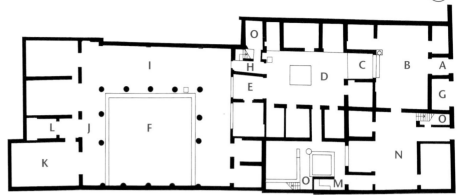

The house of Julius Polybius is one of the most impressive of those giving onto Via dell'Abbondanza, both because of its size (it occupies three-quarters of the *insula*) and because of its pictorial decorations and furnishings. It is named after the numerous election manifestos extolling the duumvirate of Julius Polybius found on its façade and those of the neighbouring houses, and on

the walls of the entrance. The house, however, may have belonged to one Julius Philippus, whose seal was found in one of the wardrobes. The monumental façade of this two-storey house was uncovered in 1910 by V. Spinazzola, while the rest of the complex was freed of volcanic debris between 1966 and 1978 by A. de Franciscis.

A graffito composition in four verses (pentameters) by an unknown poet, discovered on the façade to the left of *taberna* no.4, reads:

'*Nihil durare potest tempore perpetuo; Cum bene Sol nituit redditur Oceano, Decrescit Phoebe quae modo plena fuit. Sic Venerum feritas saepe fit aura levis.*' (Nothing can last for ever; when the sun has run its course, it sinks into the ocean. The moon wanes where once it was full. Thus the wounds of love often disappear like a puff of wind).

The structures and decorations were completely restored recently

(1997). The house as it appears today is a combination of at least two older row houses, which has produced a very unusual building. An atrium (Q) was built on the site where there used to be a *viridarium*, producing a sequence of rooms unusual in Pompeii, namely a vestibule, a covered courtyard, a *tablinum* – which became an antechamber, the atrium, the *tablinum* and finally the peristyle. The white façade, decorated in the 1st style with rectangular, rusticated ashlars, closed at the top by

a toothed cornice, together with the doors, with projecting stucco pilaster strips surmounted by a moulded cornice, gave the house an imposing, austere look, despite the fact that two shops opened onto the road during the last phase. Sadly, much has been lost. The house was being restored when Vesuvius erupted in AD 79, as revealed by a group of broken amphoras – still seen in the north-west corner of the covered courtyard (A) – which may have been intended for use in *opus signinum*, and a heap of the

A Entrance
B Covered courtyard
C Antechamber
D Atrium
E Tablinum
F Peristyle
G Shop
H Corridor
I East portico
J North portico
K Triclinium 'EE'
L Couch recess
M Kitchen
N Servants' quarters
O Staircase leading to top floor

52 The façade of the House of Polybius, which gives onto Via dell'Abbondanza, appears solemn and austere; this was evidently the image that the owner of the house wished to give of himself, as he played an active part in town politics.

52-53 The east portico is divided into quadrangles corresponding to the intercolumniations and decorated with an unusual tympanum motif with a red background and a circular relief in the middle. Cupboards and chests for household articles stand against the wall.

53 top The covered courtyard immediately inside the entrance is decorated in the 1st style. Note the imitation door on the left of the antechamber.

53 top centre The wall outside the servants' quarters' kitchen bore a fresco portraying a scene of sacrifice and an auspicious serpent. The gallery leading to the rooms on the top floor can be seen at the top right.

yellow pozzolana (volcanic ash) used to make mortar.

The main entrance is situated at no.3. The vestibule leads to a covered courtyard ornamented with magnificent 1st-style structural decorations, which were due to be replaced. When the house was first built, the large opening of the *tablinum* was in the middle of the north wall of this courtyard; on the right was the entrance to the corridor leading to the *viridarium* behind it, and on the left was a door into a

53 bottom centre The peristyle has three porticoed sides and one with engaged half-columns; the lower part of the columns was stuccoed in yellow.

53 bottom The atrium is paved with river stones; the well-head that covers the mouth of the cistern below can be seen in the foreground. Behind it are the tablinum *and the passage to the peristyle.*

cubiculum. Later, but still during the 1st-style period, the *tablinum* became an antechamber, the original corridor lost its function and was incorporated in other rooms, and the entrance to the *cubiculum* was walled up, although its presence was hinted at by a painting.

A Tuscan atrium was built in place of the *viridarium* behind the original *tablinum*; the atrium had a cobbled floor and an *impluvium* with a base of coloured marble *crustae*, *opus signinum* edging, and diamond patterns made of white tesserae. A series of living rooms decorated in the 3rd style, separated by a corridor that leads to the service area, give onto the west side of the atrium. On the north side are the *tablinum*, the adytum leading to the peristyle, and a *lararium*. The peristyle has a colonnaded Tuscan portico on three sides, and half-

columns are built onto the western side. The east ambulatory is particularly interesting from an architectural/ decorative standpoint; it has a tympanum motif which divides the space into quadrangular sectors corresponding to the intercolumniations. The tympana have a red background with a white relief disc in the middle. On the east wall is a frieze within a 3rd-style decorative structure featuring a sequence of birds, theatrical masks, fruit and landscapes.

The reception rooms give onto the north ambulatory; the splendid triclinium to the west is decorated in the 3rd style with a black background, and there is a magnificent mythological landscape on the east wall depicting the dramatic sequences from the Punishment of Dirce. Sadly the room was being restored at the time of the eruption and the other walls had not

been decorated; perhaps it was intended to keep the decoration on the east wall and renew that of the other walls.

The decorations of the other rooms on the north side of the peristyle, also in the 3rd style, are equally interesting; the ceiling decorations of these rooms have also survived. The most important findings here include a set of clothes chests under the east portico and the bronze statue of a youth (possibly Apollo or Ephebe), which was used as a lamp-holder, which were found in triclinium EE at the end of the peristyle. This triclinium is one of the most interesting in the house; the bronze remains of the triclinium couches and the banqueting service of the house were found on the floor of this room. The best items were probably being stored here temporarily, while the house was restored.

54 top left
This magnificent oecus frescoed with elegant 4th-style decorations, which were probably completed shortly before the eruption of AD 79, is situated in the centre of the north portico.

54 centre left
This painting in the middle of the west wall of the cubiculum at the end of the south portico, shows Mars with helmet, lance and shield; the goddess Venus is portrayed on the opposite wall.

54 top right This 4th-style architectural view decorated the upper part of the end wall of the cubiculum featuring Mars and Venus.

54 bottom right
This scene is part of the huge painting of 'The Punishment of Dirce' which dominated the east wall of the large triclinium at the end of the north portico.

55 left This bronze crater is decorated in relief with eight characters recently identified as the seven

heroes who helped Polyneices regain Thebes, headed by his brother Eteocles. The object was a valuable household ornament.

55 top right With her left hand, this half-naked Venus supports a cherub who holds up a mirror to show her reflection.

55 bottom right
This delicate flying figure against a red background decorated the cubiculum at the end of the south portico.

54 bottom left
This magnificent bronze statue of Apollo was found in the large triclinium at the end of the peristyle.

Made using the 'lost wax' technique, it imitated an archaic type of Apollo which was quite fashionable in the late first century BC.

THE HOUSE OF THE CHASTE LOVERS (IX-12-6)

Systematic archaeological exploration of the southern sector of Insula 12, Regio IX began in 1987, and had not been finished at the time of writing (1998). Although the complex appeared to belong to different properties right from the outset, it was given the name of the 'House of the Chaste Lovers' after a painting with a banqueting scene in which a couple seem to be kissing affectionately (Room 'm', north wall). Four different properties give onto Via dell'Abbondanza, and there is a fifth behind them.

A *Entrance to the bakery*
B *Grindstone area*
C *Kneading room*
D *Oven*
E *Hanging garden*
F *Triclinium*
G *Peristyle*
H *Drawing room with incomplete decoration*
I *Stable*
J *Passagewaj*

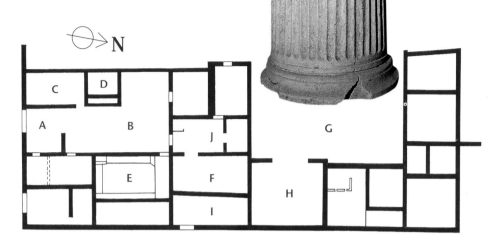

The building at no.6 was a bakery (*pistrinum*). The entrance room has two doorways; the eastern doorway leads to a small room which probably enabled the owner to check on everything that went in and out of what must have been a very busy bakery. The northern doorway led into workroom 'f', where four grindstones stood at an angle on the paved floor, while the large oven stood against the west wall at the centre. The oven has an exposed face with a round brick arch surmounted by a wall of *opus incertum* betraying evident signs of repair of earthquake damage. Immediately beyond the arch is the entrance to the large oven, formed by square blocks of Vesuvius lava stone. To the left of the oven there was a large rectangular room used for grinding the corn and making bread, which was introduced directly into the oven through a square opening in the north wall. The grindstones were operated by mules, which had a stall at the bottom left of the north wall, where the remains of a manger containing hay were found.

The other rooms on the ground floor and much of the upper floor were used for residential purposes. The upper floor was reached via a staircase from room 'I', which acted as the anteroom to the owner's quarters, and led to the most elegant part of the house, triclinium 'm'. The triclinium contains magnificent 3rd-style decorations with the walls divided into alternating red and black panels by slender stylised

56 top This marble well-head concealed the mouth of the cistern situated near the hanging garden.

56 centre left A bakery situated in Via dell'Abbondanza was being restored at the time of the eruption; the front of the large oven is shown here.

56 centre right The peristyle of the house provided a great deal of information, not only about the plants grown in it, but also about the organisation and distribution of the various areas.

56 bottom In the large drawing room, the compartments were exquisitely decorated with garlands and architectural views.

columns; delicate winged figures stand out at the centre of the red panels, while banqueting scenes are portrayed in the centre of the black panels. The east wall of this triclinium was clearly redecorated at a later stage, but with the same stylistic characteristics as before.

Another room of some interest is room 'h', a small hanging garden (about two metres above Via dell'Abbondanza) which supplied light and air to the whole of the owner's quarters. An interesting fresco on the west wall depicted Hercules being presented to 12 gods in the top part, and two auspicious serpents approaching an altar in the bottom part. On the west wall, an artist's preparatory sketch of a sacrificial

scene, made before he reproduced the same scene in a niche on the same wall, has been miraculously preserved.

Finally, room 'p' has great emotional impact: this was a stable which housed some of the mules that operated the mills. At the time of the eruption, five of them were tied to the mangers where they remained trapped, despite attempts made by

57 top The triclinium, frescoed in the 3rd style, featured banqueting scenes in the centre of the walls; a complete glass table service resting on a three-legged wooden table is portrayed here, as if to flaunt the owner's standard of living.

57 bottom This magnificent frieze, portraying a race between chariots pulled by deer and driven by cherubs, is part of the decoration of the large drawing room – still incomplete at the time of the eruption.

some of them to escape. The entire bakery complex was in the throes of being restructured, as demonstrated by the dismantled grindstones and heaps of lime scattered around here and there, even in the triclinium.

The sector around the peristyle in the middle of the *insula* is curious: it is not in keeping with that of other houses which give onto Via dell'Abbondanza, and the oldest part of the house probably gave onto the lane to the west of the *insula*. The excavations have enabled all the architectural features of the complex to be reconstructed, down to the smallest detail; even the original roof tiles and palmette *antefixae* have been recovered. The garden is particularly interesting; thorough palaeobotanical excavations have led to the recovery of all the elements required to reconstitute the trees planted, which stood in slightly raised beds protected by a trellis, as in the gardens portrayed in many Pompeiian paintings. Flower beds full of roses and ferns lined a longitudinal path with semicircles at intervals, while a pergola concealed the south wall. A fountain statue depicting a child with a dolphin was found on the low wall between the columns of the north portico, probably placed there temporarily before being installed in the garden.

The rooms on the north side of the peristyle are mainly frescoed in the 4th style, and were probably still being finished, as the central paintings had not yet been inserted on some walls. By far the most interesting is the large drawing room no.12 in the south-eastern corner of the peristyle, entered from the east portico or the garden path through a monumental prothyron with two columns surmounted by a tympanum. The trelliswork false ceiling of the room was decorated with sunken panels, with a half-cupola in the middle. The ceiling had been completed, but the walls were still being decorated with frescoes. Where the work was unfinished, either the rough plaster undercoat or the final layer of plaster with the fresco design already traced in sinopia can be seen, thus providing a detailed picture of the timing, procedures and tools used for wall frescoes. The floor was covered with bowls containing paints and tools, which further demonstrate that work was in full swing on August 24, AD 79. The excavation demonstrates, at least in this case, that the painters worked on a number of walls simultaneously, that the walls were painted very quickly, and that there was a set hierarchy among the tradesmen and a clear division of roles.

58 left A table with a precious silver service is shown in the foreground of this banqueting scene.

Two couples are reclining on the couches; the house is named after the fact that one couple is kissing tenderly.

58 right This statue of a crouching child was found at the edge of the peristyle, but must have constituted the end of a garden fountain. Note the unusual gold colour of the hair.

THE FULLERY OF STEPHANUS (I-6-7)

Fulleries were special laundries where clothes were washed and bleached and also where fabric was treated after weaving, to prepare it for cutting and sewing. Fullers (*fullones*) were organised into guilds according to their specialisation, including felters (*quactiliarii*), dyers (*offectores*), et cetera.

The fullery was excavated by V. Spinazzola between 1912 and 1914, and is named after two electoral slogans painted on the façade. The first reads 'fullones universi rogant...' (all fullers recommend...), and the second 'Stephanus rog(at)...' (Stephanus recommends...). Various items of equipment were distributed throughout the building, which was designed to operate as efficiently as possible. For example, the large entrance enabled customers to come and go without getting in each other's way, and the administrative office, where clothes were handed in or returned and payments made, was situated to the right of the entrance. The washing area, located at the end of the peristyle, consisted of three interconnecting tanks installed at different levels and five smaller basins, three on the eastern side

and two on the west. In the smaller basins, clothes were trodden with the feet in a mixture of water and soda or other alkaline substances such as human or animal urine, then transferred to the large tanks, where they were repeatedly washed and rinsed. The more delicate fabrics such as linen were washed separately; in this fullery, they were probably treated in the tank created by building up the walls of the original *impluvium* in the atrium. The clothes were then dried on large terraces on the upper floor of the house, reached by wooden staircases. To save space, the fullery had a flat roof instead of the usual pitched roof, the only one of its kind to survive in Pompeii. If there was not enough room on the terraces, the fullers also had permission from the magistrates to dry clothes along the road. When the clothes were dry, they were folded and placed under a press, positioned between the atrium and the entrance hall, before delivery to their owners.

The water needed for the laundry business was partly supplied by the public aqueduct (as can be deduced from the discovery of a lead water pipe covered with a few centimetres of earth that conveyed water beneath the pavement); the rest of the water used was rainwater collected from the flat roof and the pitched roofing of the peristyle. The workers may well have prepared and eaten their meals in the workplace; there is a kitchen to the right of the tanks which was found full of pans, with a gridiron and a tripod on the hob, at the time of excavation. Customers probably waited for their clothes in a large room that gave onto the atrium.

The entrance door, which consists of vertical wooden elements, was barred at the time of the eruption, and is now preserved in the form of a plaster cast leaning against the wall. A number of bodies were found behind the door during the excavations, probably those of the workers and owners of the fullery. One of them was carrying gold and silver coins amounting to 1,090 sesterces – perhaps the day's takings.

The house only became a fullery in the years immediately prior to the eruption; in fact it has all the features of a private dwelling. The wall decorations, appropriate to a residential property, are in the 4th style, dating from after the earthquake of AD 62. The frescoes in the

59 top right A painting on the wall opposite the fullery entrance in Via dell'Abbondanza portrayed Venus in a boat drawn by two elephants (the Indian Venus). Under the picture, which attracted the attention of passers-by, was an advertising slogan that praised the work of the fullery.

59 bottom right The large drawing room of the previous house was converted into a waiting room for customers who came to collect their clean clothes.

drawing room, which gives onto the atrium, are particularly interesting. They feature large red panels separated by architectural compartments, with a flying figure painted on the central panel; the upper part portrays fantastical buildings, with still lifes and pastoral sanctuaries, set against a white background. The owners probably restored the house after the earthquake, but were persuaded by the seismic swarm some years later to sell it to a buyer, who turned it into a fullery. The original house, which dates from the second century BC, included a shop with an apartment on the upper floor situated to the left of the entrance, and a number of rooms on the west of the peristyle, originally belonging to house no.8. Before AD 62 the house was decorated in the 2nd style, as is evident in room 'h', which gives onto the peristyle. During that period, one of the loveliest rooms in the house was the terrace which overlooked the peristyle from the upper floor and had a portico made of grey Nuceria-tuff half-columns.

59 top left The *impluvium* of the previous house was converted into a vat used to wash the most delicate items. The staircase leading to the top floor can be seen in the background.

59 bottom left The vats used to treat fabrics were of different heights, and each one overflowed into the next, so that the tallest vat, in which the last rinse took place, always contained clean water.

N

A Entrance
B Ostiary
C Atrium
D Drawing room
E Triclinium
F Tablinum
G Peristyle
H Vats
I Kitchen

60-61 This drawing shows the various rooms constituting the Fullery of Stephanus. From left to right: the entrance where the press was situated, the atrium with the impluvium, converted into a tank for washing the more delicate items, and the flat roof above used for hanging out clothes and sulphur treatment, the peristyle with a small garden, and three large tanks built at decreasing levels, at the side of which the oval treading basins (lacunae fullonicae) can be seen.

THE HOUSE OF MENANDER (I-10-4)

This house, excavated by A. Maiuri in 1930–31, is one of the most important in Pompeii because of its elegant floor and wall decorations and the exquisite furnishings found in it. The house probably belonged to one Quintus Poppeus; his family boasted kinship with Poppea, the second wife of Nero, whose bronze seal was found in the servants' quarters. The luxurious mansion, which irregularly occupied much of the *insula* in AD 79, had been extended from the first century BC onwards at the expense of the neighbouring houses. Various clues tell us that it was being restored at the time of the eruption. The columns of the small atrium of the baths, which were under restoration, were lying on the ground in the corridor, which separated the peristyle from the servants' quarters; a temporary kitchen had been set up in room no.3 north-east of the atrium, and some amphoras full of good-quality plaster ready for use were stored in the kitchen serving the baths area. It is therefore likely that the house was only partly habitable.

The main nucleus of the house has a classical layout, with the vestibule, atrium, *tablinum* and peristyle on the same axis. Passers-by could see the whole house at a glance, as the vanishing point of an admirable architectural perspective was located

A Vestibule	**G** Staircase to top floor	**L** Kitchen quarters
B Atrium		**M** Small atrium of baths
C Tablinum	**H** Ala	
D Peristyle	**I** Green oecus	**N** Laconicum
E Exedra	**J** Large drawing room	**O** Tepidarium
F Lararia	**K** Servants' quarters	**P** Calidarium

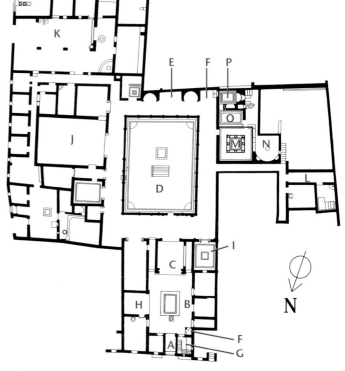

frescoed with 4th-style paintings; paintings of maritime scenes are featured in the upper part. The domestic lararium stood in the north-west corner.

62 top This view of the house from the entrance clearly shows the perfect axial alignment of the successive architectural volumes.

62 bottom The atrium, containing a compluvium, was

63 top left This pair of cluster earrings consists of beads strung on gold threads.

63 top right This hollow gold ring is ornamented by an oval cornelian setting with an engraved image.

63 centre left In the middle of the south side of the atrium was an ala *(waiting room)* frescoed in the 4th style with paintings of the Trojan war. The large tablinum *on the right almost seems to be open so that people passing by on the street could see right through the house, as far as the end of the peristyle.*

63 centre right On the back wall of the peristyle, next to the niche of Menander, there is an apse with a 4th-style landscape

dominated by a shrine with Venus and a cherub. The 2nd-style hemispherical calotte, decorated in relief with acanthus volutes, is very interesting.

63 bottom The end wall of the peristyle featured a series of niches and apses. The comic poet Menander is portrayed on the wall painted yellow in the central niche, which is situated on the same axis as the peristyle, the tablinum, *the atrium and the entrance; the portrait opposite may be that of Euripides.*

in the rectangular *exedra* (no.23) in the middle of the south side of the peristyle. The architect seems to have designed the structural elements of the house around this perspective view, installing two Corinthian columns as the door jambs of the *tablinum*, and regulating the space between the columns of the north and south portico of the peristyle to lengthen the perspective and direct it towards the rectangular *exedra*.

The house is named after the decorative plan of this room, as two seated Greek poets (Menander on the right and possibly Euripides on the left) are depicted on the side walls. On the south wall (seen from the street), tragedy masks stand out against a yellow background. The imposing

entrance, with pillared door jambs surmounted by Corinthian capitals made of tuff, leads to a large atrium which has a marble *impluvium* with moulded edges in the middle and a *compluvium* at the top with box-shaped *cymae* decorated with palmettes and spouts in the shape of dolphins' heads. The walls were decorated in the 4th style, with a Nile frieze depicting pygmies and crocodiles in the top part.

In the north-west corner there was a domestic *lararium* whose base was decorated with imitation marble, and a small temple with two pediments, Tuscan columns and stuccoed cornices. The south side of this temple, originally a wooden grid, is preserved in the form of a plaster cast. The room between the *lararium* and the vestibule housed a

winding masonry staircase that led to the rooms on the upper floor, above those on the west side. The *ala* (waiting room) on the east side of the atrium was decorated in the 4th style. The pictures in the central panels portray the end of the Trojan war, with the death of Laocoon to the south, the Trojan horse to the east, and the capture of Helen and Cassandra in the presence of Priam to the north.

Beyond the large *tablinum*, which is sumptuously decorated in the 4th style, stands the peristyle, a four-sided

stripe with a vine shoot issuing from a *cantharos* and flying cupids, figured pictures in the middle of the panels, and a splendid frieze portraying Centaurs and Lapithae against a red background above the panels.

The multi-coloured mosaic floor of *opus vermiculatum* is also very beautiful, the threshold is decorated with intertwining curved lines, alternating with squares with rosettes, and the background with squares edged by black bands; in the middle, scenes of life on the Nile are portrayed within a

portico with Doric columns closed at the bottom by a magnificently decorated *pluteus* depicting herons among plants, hunting scenes and fantastic gardens, almost denying the existence of the wall, to suggest a continuation of the real garden. All the rooms adjacent to the peristyle are luxuriously decorated; in the north-west corner there is a magnificent 4th-style room with a green background divided into panels by a vertical black

64 top These cluster earrings are formed by gold globes and semi-precious stones strung on a structure of gold threads. The hooks from which the earrings hung closed like a brooch.

64 centre This magnificent multi-coloured opus vermiculatum mosaic picture, portraying a Nile scene, is situated in the middle of the floor of the green oecus in the north-west corner of the peristyle. The picture is framed by a mosaic decoration with a triple braid motif.

64 bottom This silver cup, which is part of the luxurious furnishings of the house, is made in two layers: a smooth, thicker lining and an embossed outer layer on which idyllic scenes are portrayed. Here, a boat rowed by a young man can be seen. The craftsman who made the cup might have been one Apelles, whose name appears on the base.

braided frame (*emblema*). In the middle of the eastern ambulatory there is a huge drawing room built over older dwellings which, as demonstrated by specimens still visible, have 1st-style wall and floor decorations.

In the south-western corner of the portico there is a second *lararium* with a masonry altar and arched niche that contained five wooden busts, probably of ancestors, now preserved in the form of plaster casts. The bathing area is organised around a small octastyle atrium, with walls decorated in the 2nd style. The mosaic floors are particularly interesting; the floor between the *tepidarium* and the *calidarium* portrays an ithyphallic servant bearing ointments and perfumes, while the floor of the *calidarium* is decorated with a coloured mosaic portraying a tuft of acanthus with a bird, surrounded by fish, dolphins and marine figures.

The service area for the baths was built at a lower level than the baths. It was here that the precious silver service of the house, comprising 118 items stored in a wooden case, was found. The entire bath complex was being restored and rebuilt at the time of the eruption in AD 79.

Finally, in the south-east corner of the *insula* were the servants' quarters

where the remains of a handcart were found; pieces of the original metal found here were used to restore this cart. The owner of the house seems to have kept a large number of agricultural implements here, suggesting they may well have had a large country estate. The part of the house entered from the street to the east of the *insula* was probably for the procurator, who supervised the numerous servants working in it.

The wealth of the house must have been well known; a number of thieves tunnelled their way into the house in ancient times, but were trapped – perhaps by the collapse of the structure – in the room south of the east walkway of the peristyle, where they were discovered with small spades and a lantern.

The house recently underwent major philological work (1997–98), which restored the original volumes and the correct sequences of solid and hollow, light and shade to the architectural whole, and this, together with the restored paintings and renewed floors, has made the House of Menander perhaps the best existing example of a patrician house in a provincial town of the first Imperial age.

64-65 This picture, in the middle of the north wall of the ala, depicts the capture of Cassandra after the Greeks entered the city of Troy.

65 right This tall-stemmed silver goblet, which portrays scenes from the loves of Mars and Venus, was part of the household furnishings, as well.

BETWEEN VIA DELL'ABBONDANZA AND VIA DI STABIA

A The Holconius Crossroads
B The House of the Cithara Player
C The Stabian Baths
D The Brothel
E The Bakery of Popidius Priscus

67 top The House of the Cithara Player overlooked some of the major roads of Pompeii (Via Stabia, Via dell'Abbondanza and Vico del Menandro), which were lined with shops and business premises.

67 centre The distyle exedra, situated at the centre of the middle peristyle gave onto the large open area, offering a delightful view of the plants surrounding the swimming pool.

This was the heart of the town, which linked the oldest part with the more recently built districts. It was a busy commercial area, but also full of magnificent homes and important public buildings. The irregularity of the *insulae,* and consequently of the buildings in them, is due to the use of land left free of buildings outside the oldest part of the town. However, it is here, among the narrow, irregular lanes, that the spirit of a city which grew as a result of thriving business activities can best be appreciated.

66 This painting, originally on the south wall of the large drawing room in the middle peristyle of the House of the Cithara Player, portrays the myth of Antiope.

The bacchante, driven mad and condemned by the gods to run ceaselessly throughout Greece, finally found peace in Phocis, where she met Phocus, who became her companion.

THE HOUSE OF THE CITHARA PLAYER (I-4-5)

The House of the Cithara Player, excavated in three different stages between 1853 and 1861, is named after a bronze statue of Apollo playing the cithara found near the large pool of the middle peristyle on November 8 1853. The owner was one Lucius Popidius Secundus, nicknamed Augustianus because he was a member of Nero's retinue. A graffito on a column of the southern peristyle reads '*Luci, Augustiane, (h)ab(eas) prop(itium) Caes(arem) Ner(onem) tu(u)m*' (Oh, Lucius Augustianus, keep your Caesar Nero propitious!). The Popidius family was one of the most politically active in Pompeii in the years following the earthquake of AD 62; in fact, 45 of their election manifestos appear along Via dell'Abbondanza. The house, which occupies much of the *insula*, is the result of successive extensions, and by AD 79, it had an area of some 2,700 square metres. Some of the shops fronting onto Via dell'Abbondanza and Via di Stabia may also have belonged to the same person; the bakery and annexed confectioner's shop in the north-west corner of the *insula* appear to have belonged to Lucius Popidius.

The house is laid out at different heights because the whole *insula* is built on a north-south slope. The main entrance is at no. 5 Via di Stabia, and there was a second entrance to the north of the house at no. 25 Via dell'Abbondanza. A third entrance in the south-eastern part of the *insula*, on Via del Menandro, led to the servants' quarters of the house and the annexed stables. Those entering the building from no.5 had a spectacular view of the house; it was possible to look through the vestibule to the Tuscan atrium with its marble *impluvium*, the *tablinum* situated at a higher level, its door jambs decorated with two bronze busts, the south colonnade of the middle peristyle, a large drawing room, and a *cubiculum* in which the picture of Apollo playing the cithara, painted in the middle of the east wall, represents the focal point of the whole: the architect had deliberately created a perspective *trompe l'œil* effect. The most luxurious part of the house was the part surrounding the central and southern peristyles. The central peristyle was surrounded by a portico with Corinthian columns, and the end wall on the south side, shared with the south peristyle, had seven large windows which could be closed with wooden shutters, to separate the two huge rooms.

Between the columns, a series of *oscilla* portraying dancing fauns and bacchantes hung from the architrave. In the centre of the middle peristyle there is a large, rectangular swimming pool completely lined with waterproof *opus signinum*. The swimming pool was supplied with water from a smaller semi-circular tank on the west side, in turn filled by two jets of water, which probably issued from the two central columns of the west portico. The edges of the swimming pool were decorated with bronze statues of a wild boar attacked by two dogs, a lion and a deer, and a snake rising up from its coils.

The most attractive rooms of the house were built round the peristyle. They include the *distyle exedra* (no. 18), decorated in the 4th style; the large triclinium (no. 19), which had a magnificent black and white mosaic and elegant 3rd-style decorations, with a large fresco depicting the myth of Antiope in the middle of the south wall; the *oecus* (no. 20), with three frescoes depicting a life-size Apollo and Poseidon at the service of Laomedon, Nemesis and the Swan, and Venus and Mars; and the large room (no. 21), with a huge fresco of the Judgement of Paris dominating the centre of the north wall.

The south peristyle featured slender, fluted Composite columns, which rested on an *opus signinum* stylobate decorated with white tesserae. The *viridarium* was raised some 70 centimetres above the floor of the ambulatories. The large *exedra* in the south-eastern corner of the peristyle is especially interesting; the entrance was divided into three by two pillars, the

four sides. This part of the house may have been used for the many servants and the freedman who supervised the running of the household.

The house had a magnificent bathing area to the west of the middle peristyle. It was accessible from that peristyle or via the atrium of the house at entrance no. 5. The bathing area comprised the three essential rooms: the *apodyterium* (changing room, no.38) to the south, the *tepidarium* (no.40) in the middle, and the *calidarium* to the north; its walls were frescoed with an imaginary garden inside a wooden fence, and a black and white, geometric mosaic covered the floor. In the east wall was an apse containing the *labrum* for the fresh-water fountain, while the pool for hot baths was on the north side. The hypocaust, to the north, had *tegulae*

mammatae covering its walls to heat this room as well as the *calidarium*; hot air was allowed to circulate beneath the floor, which was supported on *suspensurae*. The kitchen and the latrine, unusual for Pompeii, closed by a door, were also in the hypocaust. At the time of the eruption, the house was at an advanced stage of restoration, and some parts were about to be converted for business use. Little is now left of the magnificence of the building. The paintings and ornaments have been transferred to the Archaeological Museum in Naples, but, after years of neglect, extensive restoration work has begun, drawing attention
to one of the most fascinating houses in Pompeii.

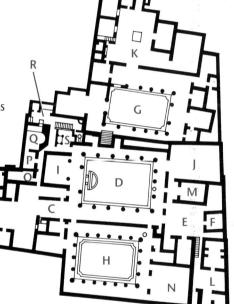

N

floor was decorated with a white mosaic framed by a large double and quadruple band of black tesserae meanders, and the walls were richly frescoed in the 4th style. The east wall was decorated with the myth of Iphigenia in Tauris, while the south wall depicts Dionysus' discovery of Ariadne on Naxos. Sadly, the picture which once decorated the north wall has been lost. A wide brick staircase led from the middle peristyle to the third, northern peristyle, which had some beautiful living rooms on the east and west sides frescoed in the 4th style. Various *cubiculi* were built around the large atrium, which had an entrance to the Via dell'Abbondanza house in its north wall. A narrow staircase in the middle of the west side led to the upper floor, which looked over the atrium on all

A Vestibule
B Atrium
C Tablinum
D Middle peristyle
   with swimming pool
E Drawing room
F Cubiculum
G Upper peristyle
H Lower peristyle
I Distyle exedra
J Large drawing room
K Atrium
L Servants' quarters
   with stables
M Cubiculum
N Distyle drawing room
O Apodyterium
P Tepidarium
Q Calidarium
R Kitchen
S Small atrium

67 bottom The middle peristyle features a colonnade that was restored on various occasions, even in ancient times. The large swimming pool, ornamented by various bronze statuettes, including the famous one of a wild boar attacked by dogs, stood in the middle of the unroofed area.

THE HOLCONIUS CROSSROADS

The crossroads between Via dell'Abbondanza and Via di Stabia, together with the Orpheus crossroads, is one of the nerve centres of the town, where both commercial traffic and urban routes converged. Before it could enter the town centre's numerous narrow streets, those coming into Pompeii from nearby towns or the villas in the fertile Sarnus Valley would have had to travel some distance along the main roads which converged at crossroads like this one. The Holconius crossroads, the junction of Via

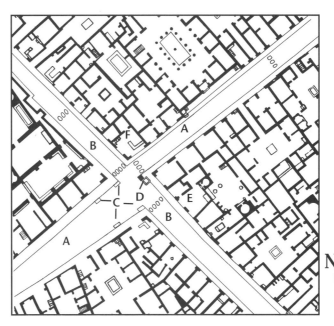

A Via dell'Abbondanza
B Via di Stabia
C The four-faced Holconius Arch
D Public fountain
E Bakery
F Thermopolium

68 top This statue portrays Holconius Rufus, one of the leading citizens of Pompeii. The armour he is wearing testifies to his title of tribunus militum a populo, *granted to him by Augustus.*

dell'Abbondanza and Via di Stabia, is also one of the most attractive spots in the old part of the town. To the north, the façades of the houses and *tabernae* can be viewed against the background of Vesuvius. To the south, Via Stabia descends slowly but surely to the Stabian Gate, one of the oldest gates in Pompeii. In ancient times, it was possible to see beyond the gate as far as the River Sarnus, which was so important to Pompeii. Looking to the east, a succession of balconies and porches, election manifestos and advertising slogans adorned the brightly coloured façades, which bordered the length of Via dell'Abbondanza, all the way to the distant Sarnus Gate. To the west, around a slight bend, the road rises to the Forum, once so impressive, with its monumental entrance of tall columns atop a flight of steps, which spanned the width of the road.

Much of Pompeii's history and trade traversed this crossroads; vehicular traffic, however, was confined to the roads leading north, east and south, but was prevented from making the ascent to the Forum by a tall barrier built of blocks of Vesuvius lava stone. This section of Via dell'Abbondanza leading to the Forum was, therefore, presumably a large pedestrian precinct.

The south-eastern corner of the crossroads was occupied by a large bakery with annexed confectioner's shop; the grindstones and bread ovens could be seen from the street. The north-west corner is occupied by the Stabian Baths, whose austere walls were made of square blocks of grey Nuceria tuff. The south-west and north-east corners were

occupied by the crowded refreshment stalls. A public fountain with a square lava-stone basin stood in the roadway; the pillar from which the water pipe projected was decorated with a relief bust of a woman wearing her hair in the fan-shaped style, fashionable at the time. The tall water tower, designed for water distribution, stands against the north side of the fountain: it is made of regular blocks of tuff and limestone with long vertical slits housing the water pipes.

What gave the whole area its monumental appearance was the four-sided arch which stood in the widest section of the roadbed at the start of Via dell'Abbondanza's ascent to the Forum. The arch, which covered an area of nearly 100 square metres, rested on four large, marble-faced *opus latericium* pillars. Honorary statues of the Holconia family stood in front of the pillars, and there was probably a statue, an equestrian group or even a *tholos* above them. During excavations, the head of a statue of a woman and a fragment of an inscription praising Holconia, public priestess, were found near the south-west pedestal. The statue of M. Holconius Rufus (now in the Naples National Museum) was found by the north-west pillar, in its original position. This statue was positively identified from an inscription on its podium, stating that Marcus Holconius Rufus, son of Marcus, was a military officer, chosen by the people, had the honour of being one of the first priests of Augustus, held the office of *duumvir* five times, and was finally honoured as patron of the town.

68 bottom The crossroads of Via dell'Abbondanza and Via di Stabia is one of the most important in Pompeii; it shows the orderly layout devised when the town's population increased. This complex crossroads is completed by pedestrian crossings, a castellum plumbeum and a basalt fountain.

69 top The west side of the baths gymnasium was occupied by a swimming pool flanked by two nymphaea, entered through large

entrances with round arches in walls magnificently decorated with coloured stucco reliefs.

69 bottom The large unroofed area in the centre of the baths complex is a gymnasium, where bathers probably performed their exercises before commencing the bathing cycle. The porticoes surrounding it feature low, squat Doric columns ornamented by necking with symmetrical volutes and a tongue cornice.

70-71 This drawing reconstructs the original appearance of the Stabian Baths. The rooms, located around a large trapezoidal courtyard, were divided into the men's section (on the left) and the women's section

(on the right), which were entirely separate. The heating systems and water and sanitary installations, together with the exquisite wall decorations in the numerous rooms are shown.

A Entrance from Via
   dell'Abbondanza
B Peristyle
C Vestibule
D The men's
   apodyterium
E The men's
   tepidarium
F The men's
   calidarium
G Frigidarium
   and balneum

H Nymphaea
I Swimming pool
J Latrine
K Entrance from
   Vico del Lupanare
L The women's
   apodyterium
M The women's
   tepidarium
N The women's
   calidarium
O Praefurnium

THE STABIAN BATHS (VII-1-8)

The Stabian Baths, the largest baths complex in Pompeii, occupy much of the southern sector of Insula VII-1. The complex, named after the Stabian Gate, was excavated between 1853 and 1858 under the supervision of M. Ruggiero. The site had already been visited by raiders in the years following the eruption of AD 79, and clear traces of their presence were found during the excavations. This explains the bareness of the complex, and especially the lack of furnishings and statues. The complex as seen today dates from the second century BC, although, prior to this time, the area was probably occupied by smaller baths serving a gymnasium, which must have stood on the same site. The main entrance is situated in the middle of the façade which fronts onto Via dell'Abbondanza. The corresponding pavement and the vestibule, furnished with benches, were paved with pale limestone slabs. Two more entrances were in use at the time of the eruption, one from Vicolo del Lupanare, and the other from Via di Stabia. The other entrances were no longer in use, because, although they were repaired after the earthquake of AD 62, the earth tremors that took

place in subsequent years rendered them unstable and they were walled up. All these entrances were made of opus quadratum consisting of grey Nuceria tuff, and had a simple elegance provided by decorative details in the 1st style.

The large entrance on Via dell' Abbondanza led into a trapezoidal space, porticoed on three sides, which served as a gymnasium. The west side, which had no portico, housed the swimming pool, which had two rooms, one to each side, containing shallow pools (possibly nymphaea), and a large changing room to the south. The façade of these rooms, which overlooked the gymnasium, was finely decorated in the 4th style with multicoloured stucco bas-reliefs, many of which still survive. The portico was formed by low Doric columns made of grey Nuceria tuff (later covered with a thick layer of plaster, fluted to imitate marble), closed at the top by unusual necking with symmetrical volutes and a tongued cornice. Among the many service rooms on the north side was a large latrine (O) and a large rectangular room (R), identified by the excavators as a sphaeristerium (a room for playing ball), because a marble sphere was found there.

The baths proper were situated on the eastern side; the women's sector

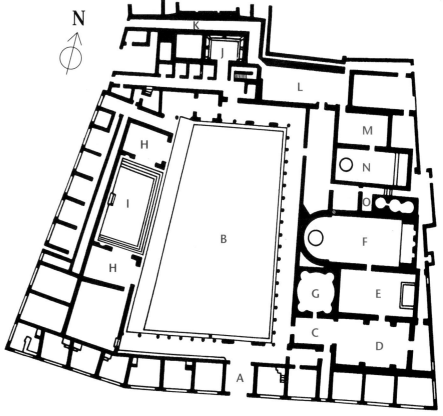

72 top *The* apodyterium *in the men's sector is preceded by a smaller room, the vestibule, which had a barrel vault decorated with a complex stucco relief. The back wall gave onto the palaestra, and there was a small glazed circular window at the top.*

72 centre *The* tepidarium *was heated with the aid of the* tegulae mammatae *that lined the walls and the* suspensurae *that supported the floor. The pool, built against the east wall, was covered with marble slabs.*

to the north and the men's sector to the south were separated by the large hypocaust, which supplied the steam and hot water required by both sectors. The entrance to the men's sector was situated in the south-east corner of the portico. Bathers crossed an antechamber which led to the changing room, identified by the presence of a bench and a series of niches – used for placing clothes inside – along the sides of the room. The antechamber and the changing room are magnificently decorated with stucco relief *clipei* (shields) with cupids, nymphs, weapons and floral patterns in the centre; these shields are supported by a web of curved patterns that sometimes form sunburst backgrounds against which exquisite reliefs of flying deities stand out. The luxury of these two rooms is accentuated by the 4th-style frescoes on the walls, and by the floor of large

marble slabs. After undressing, bathers entered the *tepidarium*, where they left a cloth for drying themselves and glass ointment jars, and accustomed themselves to the higher temperature; lukewarm baths could also be taken here. They next went into the *calidarium*, which was filled with damp steam, and where the temperature reached around 40°C. On the short side, to the east, there was a rectangular marble pool for hot baths. To increase perspiration, bathers drank cool water from a *labrum* (a marble basin) in the apse of the opposite wall. The room was illuminated by a skylight in the centre of the vault of the apse, which would also have acted as a temperature regulation valve when the room became too hot. After the sauna, bathers returned to the *tepidarium* to dry themselves, apply ointment and, probably, have a massage. The two rooms were heated with the aid of

cavity walls containing *tegulae mammatae*, and *suspensurae* underneath the floor, which allowed the hot air produced by the hypocaust to circulate under it.

Finally, bathers entered the *frigidarium*, accessible through the antechamber, where they took a cold bath to cleanse the body of sweat and ointment, and firm the skin. The *frigidarium* of the Stabian Baths was designed around the usual circular plan, with a large pool for cold water baths in the middle; the tambour walls contained four apsidal niches, and were decorated with garden scenes bounded by wooden screens. The truncated, cone-shaped roof, closed at the top with a glass skylight, was frescoed in a deep blue colour to imitate the starry night sky.

The women's baths, located in the north section of the east side, was not connected to the men's. Its entrance

was on Vicolo del Lupanare, and bathers followed a winding route: first they went to the changing room (11), which had a cold water pool built against the west wall, giving the room a double-purpose as the *frigidarium*. A long, low red bench and the usual series of niches where the clothes were left, ran around the walls of the room. Graffiti of large boats with unfurled sails and birds are drawn on the pillars, which separate the first three niches on the east side. The floor, formed by diamond-shaped brick tiles bordered by a lattice of white tesserae, is particularly interesting.

The *tepidarium* underwent a transformation in the last few years of its existence. During the first stage, the walls contained a number of niches, but these were later filled in and all the walls, including the barrel-vaults, were covered with *tegulae mammatae*; the socle was covered with marble slabs and the walls decorated with elegant, slender columns with stucco reliefs which supported a cornice with lotus flowers. The *calidarium* is attractive: the floor is covered with white mosaic tiles, framed by a black strip, and the walls, with their red background, are divided by yellow pilaster strips resting on a low plinth of marble slabs. The projecting stucco pilaster strips are topped with vaguely Corinthian capitals. The capitals support an architrave with a continuous relief frieze, decorated with garlanded candelabra, alternating with marsh landscapes containing water plants and geese. Higher still, there is a lotus-flower frieze, and the whole is crowned with a fluted vault. On the east side was a marble pool for hot baths, and on the west side, the *labrum* containing cool water.

After the bathing cycle, bathers generally took a walk under the porticoes, and drank hot drinks to recover some of their lost fluids. The cost of entry to these public baths was about half an *as* – the same price as a piece of bread or a glass of wine. Oddly, entry to the baths cost at least twice as much for women. There were also some years when the elected magistrates offered the use of the baths free of charge, covering the expenses themselves.

72 bottom The frigidarium consisted of a circular pool with masonry steps down to the water. The walls, frescoed with an imaginary garden and featuring four apses, supported a truncated cone-shaped roof, closed at the top by a circular glazed opening.

72-73 The apodyterium in the men's sector features three arches made of opus latericium which support the large vaulted roof, decorated with coloured stucco to form a pattern of hexagons and circles. Benches and clothes compartments stood against the walls.

73 top This detail of the decoration of the calidarium in the women's section of the baths shows the meandered pilaster strip which has a yellow background and a vaguely Corinthian capital, surmounted by a relief stucco frieze with garlands hanging from candelabra. A frame with lotus flowers divides the frieze from the fluted barrel-vaulted ceiling.

73 bottom This detail of the stucco decoration on the ceiling of the men's vestibule shows a bacchante in a field framed by a double braid creating a square, with shields with cupids in the corners.

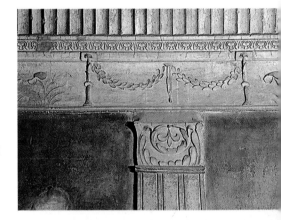

A **Vestibule**
B **Cubicles**
C **Latrine**
D **Secondary entrance**
E **Staircase to top floor**

74 top left The walls of the wide corridor separating the rooms in the brothel are stuccoed in white and present a frieze with paintings of various sexual positions.

74 bottom left In his well-known *Ars Amatoria*, Ovid described and recommended various types of intercourse, depending on the physical characteristics of the couple.

74 right The brothel was built over two floors; the top floor was reached via a staircase leading from a side street.

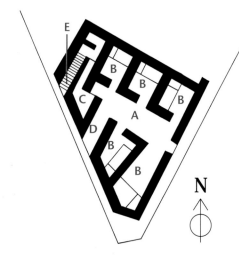

THE BROTHEL (VII-12-18)

As it was a commercial town, Pompeii had to be equipped to accommodate and entertain a large number of non-residents. As in all such towns, in addition to the numerous refreshment stalls (*thermopolia*) and lodging houses (*cauponae*), places where girls and boys sold their 'services' were required. Over 30 such venues have been identified in Pompeii. Some were modest, consisting of a single room with a masonry bed covered with a *palliasse* or a stuffed mattress, as depicted in the paintings on the walls of scenes of sexual intercourse; others were situated on the upper floors of boarding houses and reached by steep wooden staircases, while others, as in this instance, were buildings specifically intended and run as brothels.

The *lupanar* (brothel), named after the howl of the she-wolf (*lupa*) in heat, was located at the junction of two alleys, and occupied both the ground and upper floors. In the last years of the town's existence, it seems to have been run by two men called Africanus and Victor, as indicated by a number of graffiti found in the rooms. There were two separate entrances to the ground floor, the first at no.18 Vicolo del Lupanare and the second, convenient for those coming directly from the Forum, at no.19 of the alley to the south-west. Both entrances led into a kind of central salon around which five prostitutes' chambers

containing the characteristic masonry beds were built. The latrine was situated on the west side, near entrance no.19.

The walls of the chambers were entirely plastered in white, and almost completely covered with graffiti left by clients and the girls who worked there. It is practically certain that all the graffiti date from after AD 72, as the imprint of a coin of that date was left in the fresh plaster. The tone of the graffiti is predictable: some writers boast of making love to numerous girls, others make declarations of love, others advise visitors to take care, others express jealousy, and so on. The walls of the central salon were decorated with simple carpet-border patterns and stylised garlands against a white background, while the upper part, above the doors leading into the chambers was decorated with a frieze containing a series of pictures portraying individual scenes of sexual intercourse, constituting a kind of advertisement for the erotic services on offer. A picture in the middle of the north wall depicts Priapus in front of a fig tree, holding the testicles of a double phallus in each hand.

The top floor was reached by a staircase leading from no.20 in the road that ran down to the Forum. The staircase had a door with a bell, and led to a *menianum*, a kind of outer corridor, which gave access to five more small rooms. The position of the *menianum* corresponded to the balcony projecting from the outer walls, which also sheltered the pavement below. The rooms on the upper floor probably had wooden beds and contained more elegant 4th-style decorations, with no erotic allusions. Although prostitution was very common in Pompeii, as in the rest of the Roman world, it was considered disgraceful, on a par with acting or money-lending. For this reason, prostitutes were generally disqualified from holding office as magistrates. Apart from visitors passing through Pompeii, the brothels were frequented by slaves and freedmen, while free citizens had girls brought to their homes or took advantage of the servants. If someone wished to defame a respectable person they might accuse them of patronising brothels. However, no ethical distinction was made between heterosexual and homosexual practices.

THE BAKERY OF POPIDIUS PRISCUS (VII-2-22)

The bakery was probably owned by N. Popidius Priscus, whose house was located in the same *insula*, behind the bakery. The house and the bakery were connected by a small door in the rear of the bakery. The workroom had a large entrance on Vicolo Storto, and does not seem to have had a sales counter. This suggests that the products were sold wholesale, and a procession of delivery men, carrying baskets full of loaves on their backs, probably set off from here in the mornings to the shops and *tabernae* of the town.

The bakery used four large grindstones and one small one, which stood in a row at a suitable distance apart to enable the mules to turn them without getting in each other's way. The grindstone consisted of an hourglass-shaped moving part (*catillus*), the bottom section of which was inserted into a fixed, conical part (*meta*), while the top section contained the cereal to be ground. The *catillus*, which was the part most subject to wear, could be inverted, extending the life of the grindstone considerably. The *catillus* was turned on the *meta* with the aid of two square parts fitted alongside the narrowest section, with a seating, into which wooden arms were inserted and secured by pegs; the mules were tied to these wooden arms. Mules were the best animals for this job because, when blinkered and urged on by a servant, they worked constantly for long periods of time.

The two characteristic elements of the grindstone were made of basalt lava quarried from the slopes of Vesuvius, which was highly suitable and much sought-after because it was porous and very hard, so that no fragments broke off during grinding. After grinding, the flour was sieved, and the residues used to make low-quality bread which was mainly bought and eaten by servants. The bread dough was prepared either by hand or in mixing machines consisting of a cylindrical container, in which horizontal blades on a wooden shaft were turned to mix and knead the dough. The remains of one of these machines were found behind the oven in the workroom. The dough was divided into round loaves, each marked with a double cross to form eight segments, as demonstrated by the 81 loaves, already baked and

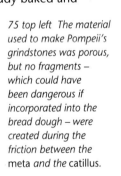

75 top left The material used to make Pompeii's grindstones was porous, but no fragments – which could have been dangerous if incorporated into the bread dough – were created during the friction between the meta and the catillus.

75 bottom left All baking operations took place in the same building; the heat of the oven kept the flour dry, helping the yeast to rise.

75 top right The loaves were usually circular and marked with a double cross so that they were easier to cut.

75 bottom right This painting, found in the tablinum of house VII-3-30, shows a bread stall.

ready for sale, found in the Modestus bakery. (VII-1-36).

Kneading troughs stood on masonry podia on the south side of the bakery, and containers for the first cooling of the bread were ranged on the north side. The oven, which had a large, polygonal combustion chamber and a baking chamber with a conical roof, was made of brick *opus caementicium*, and had a long flue at the front. The housing for the water containers was also situated at the front; one container was used to cool the working implements, and the other to wet the surface of the loaves halfway through cooking time, to produce a fragrant, shiny crust. The tank, in which the corn was washed before grinding, was located to the rear of the workroom.

By the late Republican period, bread-baking by families was replaced in Pompeii by almost industrial-scale production. The town was served by some 30 bakeries with an average of

76-77 The bakery
shown in this
reconstruction is
popularly known as
that of Vicolo Storto.

three or four grindstones each; they only made bread for use in the town, and only about 20 of them had shops, while the others supplied bread mainly to *tabernae* and *cauponae*. No corn depots were found in the town; corn was probably stored in farms outside town and brought in to the bakeries daily by the *saccarii*, who had their own guild.

A Grindstone area
B Bread larder
C Bread-making area
D Oven
E Atrium

THE THEATRE DISTRICT

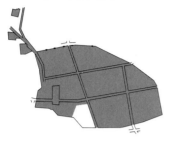

■ The Triangular Forum

■ The Samnite Palaestra

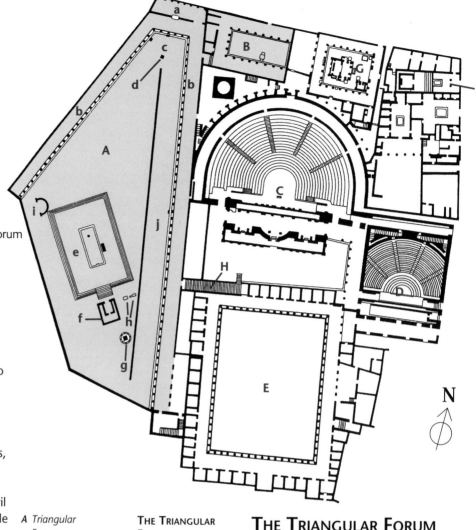

A Triangular Forum
B Samnite Palaestra
C Large Theatre
D Odeon
E Theatre Quadriporticus
F Temple of Jupiter Meilichios
G Temple of Isis
H Monumental staircase

THE TRIANGULAR FORUM
a Propylaea
b Portico
c Fountain
d Pedestal of Marcellus
e Doric temple
f Tomb
g Tholos
h Altars
i Schola
j Stadium

*T*owards the end of the Samnite era (second century BC), there seems to have been a definite will in Pompeii to participate in Greek culture and the Greek lifestyle. This can be seen in private urban homes, where an attempt was made to create the illusion of the scenery of Hellenic villas, and in public monuments, as whole districts were laid out in the Greek style. In fact, the rebuilding of the Civil Forum, the restructuring of the Temple of Apollo, the construction of the Theatre District and the monumentalisation of the main roads connecting the major cultural and financial centres of the town were all part of a single plan intended to connect the town with the cultural movements of Greece and the Hellenistic east that were sweeping through the Western world. This was the period when Cato the Censor vainly called upon Roman citizens in the Senate to preserve sacred traditions and ancestral worship.

THE TRIANGULAR FORUM AND THE SAMNITE PALAESTRA

The Triangular Forum is one of the most attractive places in Pompeii. It stands on a tall ridge of lava overlooking the Sarnus Valley and the open country of Stabianus, together with the Gulf of Naples. It was occupied from the sixth century BC, when a Doric temple of Greek or Etruscan origin was built. The sacred land took the form of a sanctuary, separated from the town that was growing up around the Temple of Apollo. Little is known of what happened in later centuries; it is certain, however, that the area received much attention in the second century BC, when local magistrates decided to monumentalise part of the town in accordance with Hellenistic models. The plan was to rebuild the façades of the streets leading to the Civil Forum and the Triangular Forum, using large, square, dressed blocks of grey Nuceria tuff to make monumental façades with pilaster strips, columns and cornices. This operation created a stylistic link between the three most important

78 The façade of the Doric temple, the stylobate of which was reached via a short staircase, presents an unusual south-east orientation, perhaps so that it could be seen by those sailing down the River Sarnus. In the foreground is one of the capitals with a flattened echinus, enabling the temple to be dated at the sixth century BC.

orientation. Little remains of it apart from the stereobate; despite many studies, no conclusive theories have been drawn. The sixth-century BC temple was a peripteral Doric building, which was very unusual in that it had seven columns on the short sides and 11 on the long sides. Some scholars explain this anomaly by suggesting that the original temple, probably made of wood, had four columns on the façade and six on the long sides (the usual configuration) and that other columns were added in the intercolumniations at a later stage for reasons of stability. The number of columns then remained the same when the structure was changed from wood to Sarnus stone, to ensure its preservation. The two surviving capitals each have an unusually flat echinus, and

centres in the town: the Civil Forum, the Temple of Apollo and the Triangular Forum. The Triangular Forum is entered via an imposing entrance, (*propylaeum*), formed by six tall, elegant Ionic columns between two excellently crafted corner half-columns. Those approaching the entrance by walking down Via dei Teatri from Via dell'Abbondanza were met with the spectacular sight of the *opus quadratum* façades of the houses, ornamented by pilaster strips, with the impressive entrance at the end, only partly disturbed at the end of the first century BC, by the construction of the public fountain by the column on the far right. Two doors led into the sacred area, which is roughly triangular; three sections are porticoed with 95 Doric columns, while the south-western section consisted of a balustrade with a magnificent view over the Gulf and the River Sarnus estuary. The colonnade, and especially the foundations of the stylobate, were probably inspected after the earthquake of 62 BC and then restored, as suggested by recent stratigraphic investigations. A low wall runs parallel to the eastern colonnade, bordering on a wide corridor that runs along the area from north to south. It has been given various interpretations: it was probably a stadium (although it is only 90 metres, half a stadium, in length) used for athletics and horse races, held in conjunction with religious festivals. The temple is situated towards the western edge of the sacred area, and has an unusual north-west/south-east

the structure greatly resembles that of the Paestum Basilica and that of the Palatine Tables at Metapontum (sixth century BC). The long *cella* (shrine bearing the deity's image) must have been fronted by a pronaos with two Corinthian columns, probably dating from a later restoration. The altar contains an off-centre rectangular base on the east side, suggesting the existence of a similar base on the west side, in which case the temple may have been dedicated to two deities, probably Minerva and Hercules, as suggested by the *antefixae* (roof ornaments) of their images on the temple, and an incomplete inscription in Oscan painted on a tuff pillar near the Theatre Crossroads. The temple must have been badly damaged in AD 62, but no restoration work had been started prior to the eruption in AD 79. The Samnite Palaestra, an integral part of the Triangular Forum design, is in the north-eastern corner. It has three porticoed sides of the Doric order; the altar and pedestal used for prize-giving and other ceremonies stood on the south side.

THE THEATRE COMPLEX

The Large Theatre, the Odeon and the Theatre Quadriporticus constitute a unified architectural complex forming part of the second-century BC monumentalisation plan for the town, which was definitely inspired by Greek Hellenistic models.

THE LARGE THEATRE

The site for the construction of the theatre was chosen because of the slope behind the rib of lava on which an ancient temple already stood; this emphasises the religious connotations of the theatre, especially in Ancient Greece. Two-thirds of the *cavea*

(terraces) rested on the natural crag, while the rest was supported by impressive constructions made of *opus incertum*. Inscriptions tell us that the theatre as it looks today is the result of restoration sponsored by the Holconius family (the same family that built the four-sided arch at the Holconius Crossroads) and carried out by freedman Marcus Artorius Primus. The first, which appears three times, reads: '*M.M. Holconii Rufus et Celer cryptam, tribunalia, theatrum, s(ua) p(ecunia)*' (Marcus Holconius Rufus and Marcus Holconius Celer rebuilt the *crypta* [the ring-shaped covered passageway between the *media cavea* and the *summa cavea*], the boxes and the marble terraces at their own expense). The second reads: '*M. Artorius M. (libertus) Primus, architectus*', indicating that the architect responsible for the reconstruction work on the theatre,

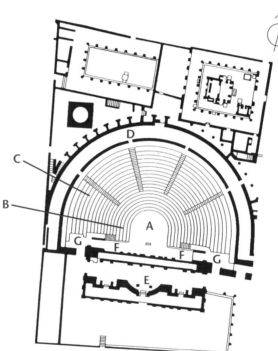

80 top An aerial view of the Theatre District.

80 centre The Large Theatre, the Odeon and the Quadriporticus were connected by a portico; this roofed area probably acted as a passageway between the theatres and the Quadriporticus, where spectators strolled during the interval between shows.

A Orchestra
B Ima cavea
C Media cavea
D Crypta
E Stage
F Parodoi
G Tribunes

N

Marcus Artorius Primus, was a freedman, as was usual in Roman times. In addition to the inscriptions, the Holconius family's generosity was commemorated by a statue on the stage dedicated to Marcus Holconius Rufus and by a *bisellium* (a two-person bronze seat) at the centre of the bottom row of the *media cavea*, inscribed in bronze.

The theatre *cavea* was divided into the usual three sections: the *ima cavea* (front or lower terraces), where the town magistrates sat; the *media cavea* (middle terraces), designed for the wealthier

classes; and the *summa cavea* (back or upper terraces), to which the lower classes flocked. The *ima cavea* was entered from covered passageways (*parodoi*) at the sides of the stage, while the *media cavea* and *summa cavea* were accessed from the *crypta* (circular passageway). The *media cavea* was divided into seven wedges by five staircases leading up to the doorways in the *crypta*, and there were two staircases from the crypta up to the *summa cavea*. The *crypta* could be reached from different directions: from the east

portico of the Triangular Forum, from Via del Tempio di Iside (north), and from Via di Stabia (south) via a narrow tunnel and a steep staircase.

The elected magistrates who financed public performances at the theatre sat on the raised platforms above the *parodoi*, that were reached by separate staircases. The stage was connected to the walls of the *parodoi* to form a single building; the front part of the stage (*proscenium*) had an apsidal space in the middle and a staircase at either side, flanked by two niches,

which gave access to the stage. The large, two-storey stage had three openings: the main door in an apse in the centre and the two side doors in rectangular niches. The openings were framed by columns with entablatures, which probably supported niches with pediments on the top storey. Between the openings there were pillars with smaller niches housing honorary statues, and colonnaded wings with marble and coloured stucco. Behind the stage there was a long ramp allowing actors to enter the stage through the three

80 bottom The cavea of the theatre rested on the natural slope of the plateau on which the Triangular Forum was built. The stage, made entirely of opus latericium, was restored on several occasions in ancient times.

80-81 Theatre masks often appear in still lifes; in this mosaic, a tragedy mask and a comedy mask stand

on a shelf, and a double flute rests on a pillar behind them.

82-83 This drawing illustrates the Large Theatre's two-storey proscenium, which contained three doors. The coloured sculptural decorations are based on those of similar buildings in a better state of preservation and a fresco found in Herculaneum.

84 top left In this fresco fragment, an actor with wreathed head is about to put on the tragedy mask.

84 top right This large fragment of painting shows the various planes of a theatre set design; the curtain above dropped vertically onto the stage.

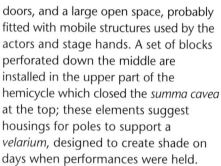

84 centre This detail shows a fairly young actor with a mask pushed up onto his hair; the masks were tied with leather laces.

84 bottom The popularity of the theatre and all types of performance held there is demonstrated by this marble slab with tragedy, comedy and satire masks carved on both sides, found in the House of the Golden Cherubs (VI-16-7).

doors, and a large open space, probably fitted with mobile structures used by the actors and stage hands. A set of blocks perforated down the middle are installed in the upper part of the hemicycle which closed the *summa cavea* at the top; these elements suggest housings for poles to support a *velarium*, designed to create shade on days when performances were held.

At the peak of its splendour, the building could hold over 5,000 spectators. It is not known what kind of performance was normally given at this theatre; *atellanae* (comic performances named after Atella, the town where they originated) were no doubt very successful. These shows always featured the same comic characterisations: *maccus* (the buffoon), *bucco* (the fat fool), *pappus* (the deceived old man) and *dossenus* (the rogue). Comedies by Plautus and Terence in Latin, tragedies, and other minor forms, like pantomime, may also have been staged. The Pompeiians' love for the theatre is well documented in the large number of frescoes alluding to the theatrical world, with masks, actors and sets. The names of the great actors are unknown, although they had a great following in the Roman world. In Pompeii a chief actor called Paris is mentioned in a theatre announcement.

THE ODEON

The circumstances under which the Odeon was built are known from an inscription, a copy of which is preserved on the architrave of the Via di Stabia entrance: '*C. Quinctius C.f. Valg(us), M. Porcius M.f. duovir(i) dec(urionum) decr(eto) theatrum tectum fac(iundum) locar(unt) eidemq(ue) prob(arunt)*' (By decree of the *decurions*, Caius Quintus Valgus, son of Caius, and Marcus Porcius, son of Marcus, *duumvir*, put out to tender the construction of the roofed theatre and tested it themselves). The two *duumviri* in question are also the ones who sponsored the construction of the amphitheatre and donated a new altar to the Temple of Apollo. They were among the personalities who

85 left Little is known of what music was played in ancient times, but a great deal of information is available about the instruments and the way they were used. In this picture, a seated girl strums a small harp with her right hand and holds a five-stringed lyre in her left.

85 top right The whole cavea of the Odeon is artificially substructed. The ima cavea, which contained the bisellia, had wider terraces made of basalt stone, while the media cavea, like the amphitheatre, was made of grey tuff.

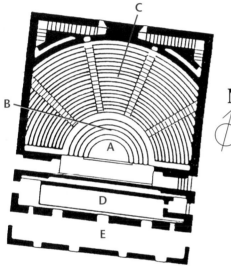

C

B

A

N

A *Orchestra*
B *Ima cavea*
C *Media cavea*
D *Stage*
E *Service area*

D

E

dominated the political and economic life of much of Campania after Sulla's victory over the Italic allies.

The Odeon is a roofed building which imitates many of the forms of the Large Theatre; it was connected to the latter by a porticoed corner area which joined the east *parodos* of the theatre to the west *parodos* of the Odeon. However, the Odeon was only built after 80 BC, and seems to have been the first building sponsored by the new ruling class imposed by Sulla. This has led some researchers to suggest that the building may have been a meeting place for Sulla's veterans, who were given a house in Pompeii and a piece of farm land outside the city walls after the war, when the colony was founded. Another hypothesis is that the

85 bottom right The semicircular stairway leading to the seats in the media cavea was very elegant; two kneeling telamones, supporting a shelf with their elbows, were carved on the lower part of the outer walls of this staircase. The parapet that separated the ima cavea from the media cavea terminated in two winged griffins.

85

newcomers completed the complex – the costly monumentalisation project, which had begun the previous century with the building of the Triangular Forum and the Large Theatre – in order to ingratiate themselves with the people.

The building is certainly described as a *theatrum tectum* (roofed theatre), and all the architectural elements suggest that it was intended to house spectators divided by social class for the purpose of watching entertainment performed on a stage. Because of the acoustics and the fact that the area was roofed, it is generally believed that musical and poetic recitals, recitations and mime shows were held there. The Odeon stands entirely inside a rectangular area with walls made of *opus quasi reticulatum*, with the auditorium in the northern half and the stage in the southern half. The *ima cavea* consisted of four basalt stone terraces deep enough to contain a *bisellium*; the fourth terrace was protected at the rear by a parapet made of grey Nuceria tuff, terminating at either end in winged griffins, whose heads have been lost.

Behind the parapet there was a corridor giving access to the seats in the *media cavea*, reached from two unusual semicircular staircases with four steps situated between the *parodoi* and the stage. Alongside the *parodoi*, the outer walls of the terraces

(*analemmata*) were decorated at the lower ends with tuff telamones, depicted kneeling on a quadrangular base and supporting a shelf which probably held an amphora or a statue; similar decorations appear in the *tepidarium* of the Forum Baths. The *media cavea* could also be entered from above, via the staircase situated between the semicircle of the *cavea* and the corner of the building. The *media cavea* was divided into five wedges by staircases made of lava stone, while the seats were made of grey Nuceria tuff with moulded edges. The lower part of the seats on these terraces were indented so that

the feet of the spectators in the row behind did not disturb those in front, as in the amphitheatre. There was no *summa cavea*.

The *tribunalia* (raised boxes for honoured guests or those who had financed the entertainment) were situated in the upper part of the *parodoi*. The *orchestra* is perfectly semicircular, and has a floor made of multicoloured marble *crustae*, added in the age of Augustus by *duumvir* Marcus Oculatius Vero, as demonstrated by an inscription in bronze lettering found there.

The front of the stage is very simple, consisting of a low wall with

86 left These magnificent bronze pan-pipes were undoubtedly used in buildings like the Odeon, as suggested by the proscenium represented in the lower register.

86-87 This famous mosaic by Dioscurides of Samos portrays a very unusual concert: on the right and in the middle, two musicians dance to the sound of a drum and a pair of cymbals, accompanied by a double-flute player and a boy who seems to be blowing a small horn.

87 top Cymbals were commonly used at religious festivals and dance performances, where they set the rhythm of the dance.

87 right Music accompanied festivals; in this painting, which seems to be a homage to Bacchus, a double-flute player and a cymbal player perform on a gallery covered with vines.

no decoration. The stage itself is equally basic; apart from the usual three openings used for performances, it was simply decorated with architectural frescoes in the 2nd style. Behind the stage was a building-width ambulatory, which could be entered from the Quadriporticus area or Via di Stabia; four other doorways opened onto an irregularly shaped back area. All these entrances were closed by wooden doors. As previously mentioned, the Odeon had a saddle roof supported by wooden trusses, already in use in Pompeii at the beginning of the first century BC. The building could hold 1,000 spectators, and resembles a theatre found at Sarno and the Naples Odeon, where Nero himself liked to perform.

THE THEATRE QUADRIPORTICUS

The Quadriporticus was on a scenic site, below the sacred area of the Doric Temple and behind the Large Theatre. The building was erected in the late second century BC, immediately after the Large Theatre. The Quadriporticus was usually entered from Via Stabia, along a wide passage behind the Odeon.

The entrance to the area was monumental to a certain extent; it consisted of three Ionic columns at the top of a flight of three steps which led down to the same level as

the porticoes in the large square.

The attractive scenic stairway in the western section of the north side of the building forms a stylistic link between the Quadriporticus and the sacred area of the Doric Temple, and it is therefore possible that some sporting contests took place in the stadium, as previously suggested (see The Triangular Forum).

The quadrangular Quadriporticus has 74 Doric columns, 15 on the north and south sides and 22 on the east and west sides. Under the ambulatories there is a continuous series of small, almost square rooms with an upper floor, which are not interconnected.

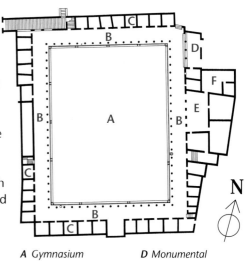

A Gymnasium
B Porticoes
C Chambers
D Monumental entrance
E Dining room
F Service rooms

THE TEMPLE OF JUPITER MEILICHIOS

An Oscan inscription found near the Stabian Gate enables a small temple in the north-east corner of the Theatre District to be identified fairly reliably: 'The aediles Maius Siuttius, son of Maius, and Numerius Pontius, son of Maius, set the boundaries of this road as far as the Stabian Bridge; the boundaries were set for a length of ten perches. These aediles also set the boundaries of Via Pompeiiana for three perches as far as the Temple of Jupiter Meilichios.'

The front part is porticoed, and the roof rests on two columns, of which the bases and one of the Vesuvius lava Doric capitals have been traced. Beyond the portico is an unroofed area dominated by a beautiful tuff altar with a *dosseret* with volutes and a frieze with triglyphs and plain metopes: a clear example of Doric and Ionic styles being combined. Beyond the altar, a staircase leads to the tall podium on which the temple proper is built. It is an Italic temple, with a four-column pronaos on the façade and two columns on the sides. The simple shrine had a pedestal on the end wall to hold the religious statues.

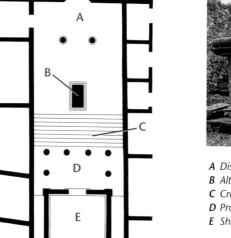

88 left The Quadriporticus originally had two different functions: it housed spectators during intervals between performances, and acted as a gymnasium in which the youth of Pompeii engaged in sporting activities. After the earthquake of AD 62, it was used as a

barracks for the gladiators who fought in the Amphitheatre. The Quadriporticus was one of the first architectural structures to be excavated, and was partly restored and reconstructed to enable the first visitors to understand its use and functions.

88 top right The rather imposing altar and the wide staircase leading to the Temple of Jupiter Meilichios gave the

small temple a solemn, severe appearance. The area was surrounded by walls to isolate it from the rest of the district.

A Distyle portico
B Altar
C Crepidoma
D Pronaos
E Shrine

88 bottom right This sculpture, found in the Temple of Jupiter Meilichios, has been interpreted by some scholars as Aesculapius, god of medicine. On the basis of reliable pictorial comparisons they also attribute the small temple to Aesculapius, although the presence of this statue does not invalidate strong evidence connecting the temple with Jupiter.

THE TEMPLE OF ISIS

The cult of Isis reached Pompeii quite early on, probably around 100 BC, from Puteoli, and it seems odd that in a town like Pompeii, which was still mainly of the Samnite culture, it immediately gained many converts. It seems even more unusual that the temple of a cult, which promised salvation after death to all the faithful (unlike the Greek and Roman religions) was situated in the theatre and gymnasium district, where the youth of Pompeii trained and the ancient warrior nobility met. Sadly, little remains of the original temple, which was destroyed by the earthquake in AD 62, and completely rebuilt in unusual circumstances, as described by the inscription found on the entrance door: 'N(umerius) Popidius N(umeri) f(ilius) Celsinus aedem Isidis terrae motu conlapsam a fundamento p(equnia) s(ua) restituit; hunc decuriones ob liberalitatem, cum esset annorum sexs, ordine suo gratis adlegeretur' (Numerius Popidius Celsinus, son of Numerius, paid for the Temple of Isis to be rebuilt from its foundations, which had collapsed as a result of the earthquake. To repay his generosity, the *decurions* accepted him into their order free of charge, although he was only six years old). This inscription provides a great deal of information. It indicates the concern of a father to pave the way for his six-year-old son to enter politics and hold the most important offices in the town because he, as a freedman, could never hold public office. It is also

89 left The Temple of Isis is not one of the best proportioned, as shown in this reconstruction drawing: the clear distinction between the pronaos and shrine makes it look wider than it is deep, partly because of the two side niches. The sacred nature of the building was accentuated by the numerous altars and statues surrounding it.

A Entrance
B Portico
C Temple pronaos
D Temple shrine
E Sacred well
F Purgatorium
G Assembly room
H Teaching hall

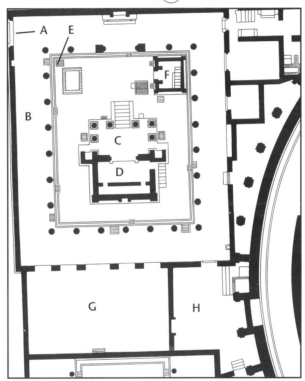

89 top right This magnificent head of Isis probably belonged to an acrolith, *a sculpture in which the naked parts are made of marble, and those covered by clothing consist of wood.*

89 bottom right This sculpture, made of Pentelikon marble, portrays Isis with somewhat archaic features. The goddess, leaning slightly forward, is wearing a chiton that clings to her body like a delicate veil, enhancing her figure. In her right hand she once held a sistrum, now sadly lost, and in her left, lying along her body, is the hankt, the symbol of life.

symptomatic of the importance of the cult of Isis in Pompeii, that a wealthy Pompeiian freedman chose to restore the Temple of Isis rather than a temple devoted to the traditional deities, in order to achieve his ends. It also tells us that the leading assembly of the town, that of the decurions, appreciated Numerius' gesture so much, that it was willing to accept his son, a future free man, into the *curia*, in spite of his young age. The inscription also demonstrates that the earthquake was so violent that the temple had to be rebuilt from the foundations. As the liturgy of the cult required specific rooms and spaces, the temple built by Numerius was probably identical to the previous one.

The temple is entered from the north side, from the road named after the temple (Via del Tempio di Iside). From outside, the temple appears to be totally isolated by a high wall which was decorated with a red plinth and a white upper part, framed to imitate an isodomic work; sadly, hardly any of these remains are left. The simple entrance was closed by a door with

90 top left
The temple, the altars, the purgatorium, *the sacred well and the finely frescoed porticoes provided a very attractive setting for performance of the liturgy of the cult, whose followers multiplied in the last years of Pompeii's existence.*

90 bottom left
The discovery of the temple, practically intact, aroused great excitement throughout the cultural world of the day, and artists visiting Pompeii in those years never failed to immortalise it in drawings or paintings.

Sadly, many of the furnishings and decorations were removed, and are now housed in the Naples National Museum.

90 right
This painting, from the assembly room, depicts an Egyptian landscape with an island, in the middle of which stands an aedicule containing the sarcophagus of Osiris; a priest performs sacrifices on a small altar opposite. A fisherman with rod and line, wearing a wide-brimmed hat, can be seen in the background.

three panels, of which only the middle one could be opened, as demonstrated by the hinges found. The portico is very unusual; the north and south colonnades consist of eight columns, while the west colonnade has seven and the east colonnade six. There was no central column in the east colonnade, and the wider intercolumniation was framed by two pillars with engaged half-columns, which were almost certainly taller than the other columns, as this entrance was designed to appear as the main access to the pronaos, and the procession of worshippers entered here. The brick columns had no base, but rested directly on the original stylobate; the column shafts were covered with a thick layer of red plaster in the lower third and white plaster in the fluted upper part. The capitals, of the composite Tuscan type, supported a wooden architrave and a pitched roof with eight rows of tiles ending in *antefixae* of gorgon masks with wings on their foreheads. Between the columns were six smaller altars, possibly for votive offerings. The end walls of

the porticoes were elegantly decorated in the 4th style; characters from the court of Isis alternated with Egyptian landscapes in the centre of panels with a red background, and the panels were separated by architectural compartments with pictures of naval battles and still lifes. The panels were bordered at the top by a magnificent continuous frieze of plant volutes on a black background, with characters and animals associated with Isis. The sacred building stood in the middle of the open space, paved with tuff slabs. The walls of the temple, which was of the Italic type, were almost entirely made of brick covered with plaster, while the podium was made of *opus incertum*. The pronaos was reached from a staircase situated at the central intercolumnation, which was wider than the side ones. The columns, of the Corinthian order, supported an entablature with a projecting cornice. Little is known of the roof, which must have been a saddle roof with clay decorations. The shrine was not very deep, and had a large entrance. Against the back wall there was a long bench with two bases for statues, probably those of Isis and Osiris. Six moulded grey tuff shelves supported religious statuettes on the side walls, which were decorated in geometrical patterned reliefs. The shrine could also be reached through a small door in the south wall of the temple, at the end of an outside staircase. On the front of the shrine, to the sides, were two niches framed by Corinthian pilaster strips with pediments, where statues of Harpocrates and Anubis probably stood; in fact, two altars at the sides of the pronaos were dedicated to those deities. At the sides of the staircase leading to the pronaos were two small dedicatory pillars; a magnificent slab bearing an inscription in hieroglyphics (which probably came from Heracleopolis) was found on the left-hand pillar. A statue of Dionysus with the panther was found in a niche in the middle of the back of the shrine; at the sides of the niche, two large relief stucco ears indicated that the deities were listening to worshippers' prayers.

The altar was not on the same axis as the temple, but further to the left, so as not to hinder processions making their way to the temple. The excavation journals recount that 'the ashes and burnt bones of the victims ...' were found on top of the altar. The remains of sacrifices and offerings were tipped into a kind of sacred well in the north-east corner of the temple, which must have had a saddle roof, as shown in many documentary pictures executed at the time of the excavation. In the south-east corner was the *purgatorium*, a small, open enclosure entered through a door in the north side; from here, a small staircase led to a basement shrine, in which sacred water from the Nile, used for purification, was stored. The outer walls were finely decorated in stucco with relief depictions of pairs of lovers, including Mars and Venus, Perseus and Andromeda.

From the west portico, five arched doorways led into a large rectangular room. This large room, which was

practically intact when excavated, was richly decorated: the black mosaic floor in the north sector was inlaid, in white tesserae, with the names of Numerius Popidius Celsinus, his father Ampliatus and his mother Corelia Celsa, to commemorate their generosity. The walls, exquisitely frescoed in the 4th style, featured seven large panels, five portraying Nile landscapes and two depicting scenes from the myth of Io: Io received in Egypt by Isis, and Argo watching over Io. The remains of a female *acrolith*, probably Isis herself (the naked parts – head, feet, hands – were made of marble, while the drapery was sculpted in wood), were found in this large room, together with many other objects relating to the cult, including a sistrum. This room has been given various interpretations, but it was probably the place where worshippers of Isis gathered and ritual banquets were held.

The west portico led to another large room behind the Large Theatre buildings; this was wholly covered in white plaster, and figures and scenes of the cult of Isis were portrayed in no particular order. This room probably served for religious instruction and as a store for sacred ornaments and vestments; in fact, a large number of religious objects were discovered there. Nearly all the ornaments, including the statue of Isis donated by Lucius Caecilius Phoebus, the herms of Norbanus Sorex, Dionysus and the Panther, Venus wringing out her hair, and almost all the detachable paintings, have been removed, and are now on display in the National Museum in Naples, in a wing dedicated to the worship of Isis in Pompeii. The discovery of the Temple of Isis between

1764 and 1765 aroused great interest; many famous artists and illustrators flocked to the site, and a myriad of watercolours, frescoes, drawings and prints have immortalised the charm and mystery of the temple.

91 bottom left The sistrum, a kind of metal rattle with movable metal parts that ran through holes, was used by the cult of Isis.

91 top right This painting, found in the assembly room behind the temple, depicts the myth of Io, who was persecuted by Hera for her love affair with Zeus, took refuge in Egypt, and was welcomed by the goddess Isis at the sanctuary of Canopus in the Delta. Only one other version of this subject, unusual in Pompeiian art, is known.

91 bottom right This painting, also from the assembly room, depicts a small distyle *temple* standing on an island connected to the mainland by a bridge; an altar and a votive column can be seen in the foreground. The colours and the rocky background contrast with the stretch of water to form a very attractive landscape.

THE CIVIL FORUM

*A*s in all Ancient Roman cities, Pompeii's Forum was the heart of the community who lived in the town and crowded the fertile countryside surrounding it. This was where the townspeople came to conduct their administrative and legal business; to take part in solemn religious ceremonies in honour of the gods who watched over the town; to elect magistrates every year to represent the community; to find out about municipal edicts and those issued by the central government in Rome; to watch gymnastic and gladiatorial games, and to hire specialist personnel like lawyers and doctors. All kinds of goods were traded and all sorts of market traders and idlers gathered here; this was also where strict masters gave their lessons and handed out their pupils' punishments.

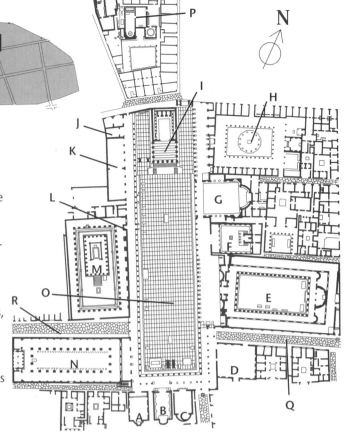

A The Hall of
    the Duumviri
B The Curia
C The Hall of
    the Aediles
D The Comitium
E The Building
    of Eumachia
F The Temple
    of Vespasian
G The Temple of
    the Public Lares
H The Macellum
I The Temple
    of Jupiter
J The Latrine
K The Forum
    Holitorium
L The Mensa
    Ponderaria
M The Temple
    of Apollo
N The Basilica
O The Forum Square
P The Forum Baths
Q Via dell'Abbondanza
R Via Marina

92 This view of the Civil Forum from above shows the perfectly rectangular shape of the huge unroofed area.

The civil section with the public buildings to the south emblematically faces the religious section with the Temple of Jupiter to the north.

All this is demonstrated by an exceptional find in the Praedia of Julia Felix: a painted frieze 70 centimetres high and 31 metres long, of which less than ten metres survives, representing everyday life in the Pompeii Forum.

An astonishing crowd of shopkeepers, tradesmen, baggage wagons, hauliers, fabric merchants, shoemakers, iron- and bronzeworkers, vegetable sellers and cattle merchants throng under and in front of the porticoes, but three scenes are of particular interest. In the first, a number of male figures are reading the latest news from a panel, on which the text is divided into columns; in the second, a lady accompanied by a servant girl is giving alms to an old man leaning on a stick with one hand outstretched; in the third, a teacher is having a pupil whipped in front of his classmates.

The Forum as it appears today dates from the second half of the second century BC. In its oldest period (sixth–fifth century BC), two roads met in the southern part of the Forum, namely the road leading from the north (the current Via del Foro and its continuation, Via delle Scuole) and the road leading from the west (the present Via Marina with its continuation of Via dell'Abbondanza), which then ran slightly further north, under the present Building of Eumachia. An elongated but irregular open area used as a marketplace was created round this crossroads, partly because the Temple of Apollo was situated nearby. Some *tabernae* were later built round this space.

When peace came to the Mediterranean after the end of the Second Punic War, new markets opened up, both in the west (Spain) and in the east (Asia Minor), bringing new wealth to the entire Italic world. The population of Pompeii increased considerably when many people moved there from towns destroyed by Hannibal. These newcomers immediately took their place in urban life, and the town was greatly enriched by trade and agriculture. Part of this wealth was invested in the monumentalisation of the town, in accordance with examples imported by the newcomers from the Hellenistic cities of Asia Minor.

The old marketplace was transformed into one of the most rational and elegant forums in any Italic town. A rectangular section was surrounded on three sides (east, west and south) by porticoes consisting of severe Doric columns, and entirely paved with slabs of grey tuff – a new material introduced into the local building techniques from quarries in the Nuceria area; it was tough and strong but easy to carve.

The great temple dedicated to the Capitoline triad – Jupiter, Juno and Minerva – stood out on the north side against the slopes of Vesuvius. Local government buildings were erected on the south side, and the monumental Basilica to the west. The Temple of Apollo was completely redesigned, and standard weights and measures were introduced. The *macellum* (meat and fish market) was built on the east side, and the *comitium* (for town elections) in the south-eastern corner. Numerous shops survived among these buildings, too. Later, from the age of Augustus on, the shops were replaced by the Temple of the Public Lares, the structure called the Temple of Vespasian, and the Building of Eumachia. These later constructions blocked off the two streets that had led to the Forum from the east. The large rectangular area was filled with bases supporting honorary and equestrian statues, and the *suggestum* (the

platform from which candidates called on citizens to vote for them) was built in the centre of the western side.

The Forum was entered from Via Marina or Via dell'Abbondanza from two monumental staircases surmounted by columns with tympana which presented a vision of order and grandeur to visitors. The earthquake of AD 62 seriously damaged the Forum, and hardly any of the buildings that gave onto it had been completely restored at the time of the eruption in AD 79; the Pompeiians, however, had started extensive restoration work.

Two places of worship dating from the Julio-Claudian era (first half of the first century AD) were largely rebuilt: the Temple of the Public Lares, to appease the Penates after the earthquake, and the Temple of Vespasian, in the hope of obtaining economic aid from Rome to deal with the state of emergency. The Forum represents a unified, functional architectural whole, in which all the

93 left Even after the eruption of AD 79, the Forum was easily identifiable; the columns of the Temple of Jupiter and those of the porticoes emerged from the volcanic debris, acting as markers enabling unscrupulous excavators to strip the square of nearly all its decorations, statues and architectural elements in the years following the disaster.

93 right This fresco, from the Praedia of Julia Felix, shows how the Forum looked to the inhabitants of Pompeii. A series of equestrian statues stood against the west wall, and the columns of the porticoes were decorated by garlands.

94-95 This is what the Civil Forum looked like shortly before the eruption. This bird's-eye view shows it from the south, with the apses of the three municipal buildings in the foreground and the Temple of Jupiter on the opposite side, flanked by two honorary arches.

elements combine to display the cultural strength, economic capacity and optimism of the town, in an area accessible to all citizens.

The Forum was surrounded by porticoes on three sides. The grey tuff colonnade built during the second century BC survives on the south side and in the eastern section as far as Via dell'Abbondanza; it features two rows of Doric columns with triglyphs and plain metopes. The tuff columns in the west portico and the rest of the east portico had been replaced with white travertine. In some parts of the west side the portico still has two storeys; the columns of the upper row are of the Ionic order. The upper storey was reached by staircases at the edges of the porticoes; one still survives in the south-west

corner, between the municipal buildings and the Basilica. The portico alongside the *macellum* is different: the columns are of the Corinthian order, and they stand on an Attic base with a double torus. The lower third is decorated with bean motifs and the upper two-thirds fluted, while the acanthus leaves on the capital are unfinished. The architrave has a sharply projecting decorated cornice surmounted by plinths, which must have supported an upper row of columns. According to very recent hypotheses, a single row of unroofed columns or a series of statues were positioned alongside the Temple of the Public Lares, on the line of the stylobate. The floor of the ambulatories was made mainly of *opus signinum* or lava cement decorated with travertine *crustae* (south side). The large square, originally paved with tuff slabs in the second century BC, was repaved with travertine slabs after the earthquake, but the work was not complete at the time of the eruption. Along the west and south porticoes was a row of equestrian statues, of which only the pedestals survive. Three larger bases were placed along the south side after the earthquake. A fourth, smaller base occupies the centre of the space in front of the arched base, which may have supported a statue of Augustus, while the others supported statues of court personalities or local aristocracy.

MUNICIPAL BUILDINGS

The south side of the Forum is occupied by three buildings intended for the administration of the town; they were badly damaged by the earthquake of AD 62, but because of their special importance, restoration work had started almost immediately afterwards, mainly using *opus latericium*. The stratigraphic surveys conducted by A. Maiuri in the 1950s demonstrate that the original buildings dated from the second century BC and that, when the earthquake damage was repaired, they

were extended by moving the façades towards the Forum. The three buildings are almost equal in size, only differing in their internal layout, but their specific function is unclear. The central building is the most impressive and might be the *curia* (the place where the town Senate formed by the decurions met); it has also been suggested that it might be the *tabularium* (the archive of all the official deeds and documents of the local authorities). A double staircase led to a landing at the same height as the floor of the great hall; a large rectangular niche was situated in the back wall, while a tall podium bearing pillars ran along the side walls. If this building was the *tabularium*, cupboards containing documents were probably placed on the podium, whereas if it was the *curia*, the podium may have had honorary statues alongside the pillars, and seats for members of the assembly would have been arranged in the centre. The west building has a solemn, elegant appearance, and the marble slab floor, laid prior to the earthquake of AD 62, still survives. A large apse was situated in the end wall and there are three rectangular niches in the side walls; the apse and niches contained honorary statues. This building may have been the headquarters of the *duumviri* or, if the central building was

the *tabularium*, this may have been the *curia*. The third building, to the east, must have been completely faced with marble; the slabs which formed the socle still survive on the outside wall. The hall is bounded to the south by a large *exedra*, which contained a statuary group. This building was probably used as a meeting room for the two aediles, the second most important town magistrates, or the *duumviri*.

THE COMITIUM

The *comitium*, situated in the south-eastern corner of the Forum, was the building where the town magistrates (the *duumviri* and aediles) were elected. The unroofed, almost square building was bounded by fairly high walls. During its first incarnation, towards the end of the second century BC, it had five entrances on the west and north sides, allowing voters to enter from the Forum and exit onto Via dell'Abbondanza. Later, following the earthquake of AD 62, three of the entrances on the west side and four on the north side were closed with *opus incertum*, possibly to make the structure more stable. The east and south walls were wholly decorated with marble and coloured stucco; each wall contained five niches, which would have held honorary statues. The floor was

originally paved with marble slabs, some pieces of which were found by the walls. The one physical element that distinguishes this building is a rostrum, built against the south wall and reached by a staircase. The highest-ranking senior magistrate, who supervised the voting operations, which took place in front of the rostrum, sat here. Voters entered from the Forum; after identifying themselves by handing in their *tesserula* (a kind of electoral certificate), they received a *tabella* (a waxed wooden tablet which could be folded in half). They wrote the names of the candidates they wished to vote for on the tablets, which were then placed in the ballot box (*arca* or *cista*), before leaving by the doors onto Via dell'Abbondanza. It was here that the magistrate announced the four winners of the election, that is, two *duumviri* and two aediles.

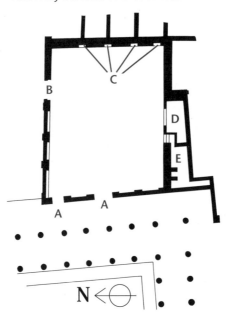

A Entrances from the Forum
B Entrance from Via dell' Abbondanza
C Niches for honorary statues
D Rostrum
E Service Rooms

96 left The municipal buildings that occupied the south side of the Forum were entirely covered with pedestals for statues and a small archway. Honorary statues near the seat of political power were an undoubtedly much sought-after reward.

96 top right The Hall of the Duumviri is the best-preserved hall; its

marble floor, white plastered walls and niches with rear apse gave it an austere, solemn appearance.

96 bottom right The Comitium occupied the south-eastern corner of the Forum; it could be entered from Via dell'Abbondanza and also from the Forum, through large entrances used during elections.

THE BUILDING OF EUMACHIA

A very unusual building in the south part of the east side of the Forum has been identified as the headquarters of the fullers' guild (namely for fabric manufacturers, dyers and washers), although not all the experts agree with this theory. Two inscriptions, an incomplete one on the architrave of the east portico of the Forum, and another at the secondary entrance in Via dell'Abbondanza, cast some light on the nature of this building. The latter reads 'Eumachia L(uci) f(ilia) sacerd(os) publ(ica) nomine suo et M(arci) Numistri Frontonis fili chalcidicum, cryptam, porticum Concordiae Augustae Pietati sua pecunia fecit eademque dedicavit' (Eumachia, public priestess, had the *chalcidicum*, *crypta* and portico built in her name and that of her son Marcus Numistrius Fronto, and dedicated its construction to the *Pietas Concordia Augusta*).

The building was erected towards the end of the first century BC by creating an artificial terrace between the Forum, Via dell'Abbondanza and the lane behind the building. It was built onto the two-storey, east colonnade of the Forum, where the first inscription was located. The *chalcidicum* referred to in the inscription is the area between the colonnade and the front of the main building; it was a kind of vestibule which could be closed at the sides with a metal gate. The founder seems to have wished to oblige visitors to enter the *chalcidicum* from the square rather than from the sides. The whole area was covered with a saddle roof on wooden trusses. The west slope of the roof conveyed rainwater directly into the Forum, and the east slope, connected to the pitched roof of the porticoes, conveyed it into the building. The front of the building, faced with high-quality marble, was perfectly symmetrical with a magnificently decorated central entrance, which had a marble portal decorated in relief with an acanthus branch inhabited by a variety of fauna.

The quality and style of the relief work suggest that it was not carried out by local artists; the craftsmanship is directly comparable with that of the *Ara Pacis* in Rome. At the sides of the entrance there are two large apsidal *exedrae* flanked by rectangular niches with inscriptions at the base in praise of Romulus and Aeneas, imitating those in the Forum of Augustus in Rome; the niches may well have contained statues of the Emperor's legendary ancestors. At the far ends were two rectangular *exedrae* which could be reached by a staircase. If, as believed by some experts, the building was the wool market, these would have been the rostra used for wool auctions; however, others believe they were used for making speeches at Imperial festivals. The fact that the building was used for official purposes is demonstrated by the set of bases for honorary statues situated

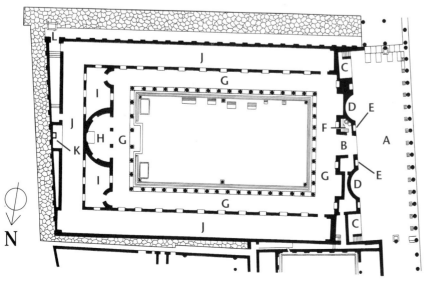

A Chalcidicum
B Entrance
C Auction galleries
D Apses with honorary statues
E Niches with eulogies
F Urine collection
G Porticoes
H Apse with statue of Livia
I Gardens
J Crypta
K Niche with statue of the Priestess Eumachia
L Exit onto Via dell'Abbondanza

N

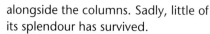

98 top left This inscription, carved on the architrave of the Forum portico in front of the building, states that Eumachia, daughter of Lucius and public priestess of Venus, built the entrance, the crypta *and the porticoes on her own behalf and that of her son Marcus Numistrius Fronto at her own expense, and dedicated it to the harmony and devotion of Augustus.*

98 bottom left The statue of the Priestess Eumachia stands in an intentionally secluded position, in a niche next to the large apse that housed the far more important statue of Livia,

as if to demonstrate the civic activities of the priestess without any calculated expectation of honours.

98 top right The flower gardens behind the rear façade of the building and at the sides of the apse created a pleasant sight for those using the Forum entrance.

98 bottom right The frieze surrounding the entrance was lying on the ground to the left of it at the time of the eruption, because restoration work was being carried out. It featured a succession of acanthus volutes ornamented by insects, birds and snakes.

alongside the columns. Sadly, little of its splendour has survived.

As the axis of the building diverges slightly from that of the Forum and the monumental portico, a space was created between the inner and outer fronts of the building, which was filled with a number of service rooms. The rooms to the north were used as stores, while the room to the south consisted of a platform with a large terracotta vessel built into it, designed to collect urine, used by the fullers as a bleach.

The huge inner courtyard was surrounded by a four-sided portico with marble Corinthian columns, which some experts believe had two storeys. On the east side, on the same axis as the entrance and preceded by two columns supporting a tympanum, there is a large apse with a marble statue in the middle representing Augustus' wife, the Empress Livia, venerated as an example of harmony and devotion and portrayed as a richly ornamented deity with a cornucopia in her arms. The large apse had two small gardens at the sides which could be seen from the windows flanking it and from the two semi-circular niches at the ends. A large covered gallery (*crypta*) whose numerous windows borrowed light from the portico, runs behind the portico on three sides. In the middle of the east ambulatory of the *crypta*, alongside the large apse of Livia, is a niche where a life-sized marble statue of Eumachia was found. The statue was dedicated by the fullers, as demonstrated by the inscription: '*Eumachiae L(uci) f(iliae) sacerd(oti) publ(icae) fullones*' (Dedicated by the fullers to Eumachia, daughter of Lucius). The niche, and indeed the entire complex, could also be entered from Via dell'Abbondanza; a secondary entrance was situated in the south-east corner. Near this entrance is a travertine fountain decorated with the image of abundance which, perhaps intentionally, recalls the statue of Livia in the large apse in the peristyle.

On this side too, the building had a monumental exterior; the whole outer façade overlooking Via dell'Abbondanza was framed with projecting pilaster strips surmounted by pediments alternated with lunettes.

The whole building echoes the noble ideals of artistic form and decoration which held sway in Rome, and a strong message of support for Augustus' policies is in evidence, which no doubt served as electoral propaganda.

Eumachia's tomb near the Nuceria Gate also expressed an unusual, Classical-style, formal language that ennobled the figure of the public priestess, associating her with the Imperial family and therefore bringing her to the attention of the citizens of Pompeii. Sadly, little survives of this large, important building, as it was damaged by the earthquake of AD 62 and stripped of much of its marble and statues before it was restored; even the precious portal was detached and laid on the ground.

THE TEMPLE OF VESPASIAN

A *The Forum portico*
B *Entrance*
C *The Temple portico*
D *Altar*
E *Shrine*
F *Stairs leading
  to shrine*

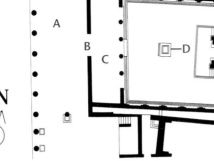

N

99 top The Temple of Vespasian was wholly covered with marble slabs, hardly any trace of which remains. The walls of the unroofed area, with their sequence of panels alternately containing tympana and lunettes, are particularly interesting.

99 bottom The altar standing in the middle of the unroofed area between the entrance and the temple, was decorated with a sacrificial scene on the side facing the Forum. The arrangement of the characters, the naturalism and the delicacy of the surface show it dates it from the Julio-Claudian period.

Roughly in the middle of the east side of the Forum, between the Building of Eumachia and the Temple of the Public Lares, but set back a little, stands a small temple built on the site of the shops that once faced onto the square. The space in front of the temple had strong paving made of lava cement and marble *crustae*, and there was probably a lean-to roof, which sloped down to the square, although no trace of columns along the façade remains, and the stylobate now seen is the result of an eighteenth-century restoration, as revealed by recent archaeological surveys. The *opus latericium* façade must have been completely faced with marble slabs, and many of the holes found in it would have been used to insert fixing cramps. The entrance leads into a porticoed area, supported by four columns, which acts as a vestibule. Rainwater from the pitched roof was collected by a tuff channel which conveyed it into a tank below. The temple was wholly enclosed by a very high *peribolos* wall, decorated with projecting pilaster strips which supported alternate tympana and lunettes, in the same style as the south outer wall of the Building of Eumachia. A small door in the back wall, on the right-hand side, led to three rooms behind the temple, which were used by religious members. The temple proper was built onto the east wall, and the magnificent altar, covered in marble slabs with relief decoration, stood in the middle. The temple, which was faced entirely with marble, consisted of a tall podium, probably surmounted by a tetrastyle pronaos, with the central intercolumnation wider than the others so that the inner shrine could be seen. The façade of the inner shrine had two *antae*, and a pedestal for a single statue standing against the back wall. The podium was reached by two lateral

staircases concealed from the view of those entering the temple.

The magnificent altar in the centre of the unroofed area was surmounted by a slab ornamented with a *dosseret*, and the sides were faced with four white marble slabs with relief decorations. The west face, the one seen immediately on entering the temple, represents a sacrifice: a veiled priest performs libations on a tripod covered with spring vegetables, assisted by ministers of the cult, a double-flute player and two lictors, while the *popa*, the priest's assistant who carried the hammer and killed the victim, and another assistant led the bull to be sacrificed. In the background of the sacrificial scene, can be seen garlands between the columns of a tetrastyle temple, with a round shield holding back a drape. Some articles used during religious ceremonies are portrayed on the north and south sides of the altar: the north slab shows the *stola* (long outer garment) which the priest wore over his shoulders, the *lituus* (sacrificial rod) and the *acerra* (a box containing incense), surmounted by a festoon of flowers and fruit suspended between two *bucranes*), while the south slab portrays the *patera* (dish), the *simpulum* (a kind of ladle) and a three-lobed *oinochoe*, again under a hanging augural garland. The east side, facing the temple, is decorated with a crown of oak leaves between two laurel branches.

To whom was the small temple dedicated, and when was it built? An inscription found in Pompeii, whose origin has been lost, but which must have come from the Forum, reads '*Mamia P(ubli) f(ilia) sacerdos public(a) Genio Aug(usti) solo et pecunia sua*' (Mamia, daughter of Publius, public priestess, on her own land and

at her own expense, [dedicated a temple] to the Genius of Augustus). The inscription fits the cornice of the shrine of this temple, and all the portrayals on the altar relate to the cult of the Genius of Augustus, instituted in Rome in 7 BC. The oak-leaf crown was awarded to Augustus by the Senate for bringing peace to the Roman world, and it was used to represent the Emperor from that time on. The two laurel branches are also associated with Augustus. Finally, the sacrifice of a bull, as depicted on the Forum side of the altar, was the prerogative of living Emperors, and as examination of the slabs reveals that they have undergone restoration, it is assumed that the temple and the altar were dedicated to Augustus during his lifetime, and later adapted to the cult of Vespasian, who was in a position to do a great deal for the town when it was seriously damaged by the earthquake of AD 62.

THE SANCTUARY OF THE PUBLIC LARES

This is definitely the most unusual of all the public buildings in Pompeii, especially because of its perimeter, in which architectural recesses and projections alternate in a pattern more usual in the Hellenistic east. Of all the buildings on the east side, this is the one closest in alignment to the colonnade, which borders the open space of the Forum. Only eight basalt bases survive around the edge, to which marble slabs were probably fixed with iron pins, traces of which have been found. It is not certain whether columns were mounted on these bases; the enclosed area was definitely not roofed, so probably there was a row of columns surmounted by an architrave which did not support a pitched roof.

The building developed around an almost square, open area, as suggested by the exquisite floor of marble slabs (*opus sectile*) of different types and colours, which form a regular geometrical pattern of framed squares

and circles. An altar stood in the middle of the floor, as indicated by the remains found here. On the back wall is a large semicircular apse, flanked by two small niches with two pilaster strips surmounted by a small pediment. The apse has a low podium round the semicircular side, with a rectangular projection in the middle, corresponding to a niche in the wall. Above the podium there was a row of columns which supported a projecting cornice and which formed an *aedicule* with architrave and tympanum in a position corresponding to the niche. The apse was closed at the top by a hemispherical dome, probably coffered. Along the sides, in perfect symmetry, were two large rectangular *exedrae* flanked by two niches practically identical to those on either side of the apse. The two *exedrae* had two columns on the façade between the *anta* pillars which supported an entablature with tympanum and cornice; the end wall contained a single statue pedestal. At the sides, between the apse and the two *exedrae*, there were two niches of similar style to the others, but situated inside a round arch supported by pilaster strips on a tall podium.

Many theories have been postulated about the function of this strange building; it seems fairly clear that it was intended to house statues of some importance, and it was long believed that the town lares were worshipped here. However, it is more likely that this building housed statues of the Imperial family, as suggested by comparisons with other towns in Roman Italy and the provinces. The building was certainly erected after the age of Augustus, but before the earthquake of AD 62, which caused such serious damage that some of the decorations were removed altogether. It is not unlikely that some of the precious decorations were stripped by clandestine raiders (*fossores*) who knew the wealth of the town and its monuments, and looted what they could in the years after the eruption.

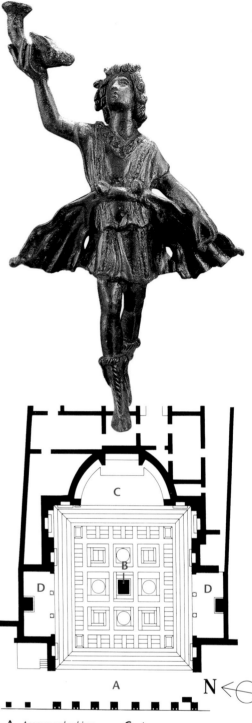

A Area overlooking the Forum
B Altar
C Apse
D Distyle niche

100 top left Very little remains of the marble decoration that must have ornamented the building of the Public Lares; much of the magnificent floor, which featured an unusual geometrical pattern made of coloured marble, has also been lost.

100 bottom left This painted lararium shows the positions of the participants in a propitiatory rite. At the sides, two servants pour wine from their horns; in the middle, a priest holding the horn of plenty performs libations to the sound of a double flute, while two young servants bring a pig for sacrifice and a tray of offerings.

Below, auspicious serpents approach an altar with eggs.

100 right This statuette, found in the House of the Golden Cherubs, is one of a pair; the figure holds a horn with a goat's head, from which wine flowed to an altar in the centre, where a priest performed libations.

THE MACELLUM

The *macellum* was the building used as a public market, especially for meat and fish. In Pompeii, it occupied the northern part of the east side of the Forum. Construction of this large west-facing building started in the late second century BC. Later, with the reorganisation of the eastern side of the Forum, it acquired the layout that survives today. The serious damage it suffered in the earthquake of AD 62 was not immediately repaired, and at the time of the eruption in AD 79 the area was still a huge building site, and the market was being held elsewhere. The area in front of the building, roofed by a two-storey portico in the same way as Eumachia's *chalcidicum*, was designed to demonstrate explicit support for the Imperial cult. Between the columns of the Forum portico and the façade of the Macellum there was a veritable gallery of honorary statues, as demonstrated by the facing rows of pedestals which must have supported

rested on the side walls. In the middle of the back wall, there was a niche flanked by two magnificent marble columns of the Corinthian order, and there were two smallish entrance doors at the sides of the *aedicule*. Two other entrances led into the building, one of which stood in the middle of the north side with a niche and painted propitiatory serpents; the other, which stood in the eastern section of the south side, was used by those arriving from the lane to the south (Via del Balcone Pensile), which was closed to the west by the Temple of the Public Lares.

The huge internal area had a portico on four sides, while the *tholos* stood in the middle. The south side was occupied by 11 *tabernae*, while on the west and north sides, the shops opened to the outside, and were closed off to the internal area. In the middle of the open area stood a polygonal building resting on 12 bases, with a conical roof that covered a huge counter designed for the sale and cleaning of fish, which were kept constantly cool by a fountain in the

101 left The area in front of the entrance to the Macellum was a veritable gallery of statues, demonstrating support for the Imperial cult. Magnificent Corinthian columns characterised this section of the portico, which must have been built on two levels.

101 top right The sacred area in the centre of the east portico was well suited to the monumentality of the building. A staircase flanked by two podia led to a large room dominated by the statue of an emperor, with a pair of honorary statues on either side.

101 bottom right A 12-sided tholos containing stalls for the sale of fish stood in the middle of the unroofed area.

them. A number of shops, which some experts interpret as *tabernae argentariae* (moneychangers), gave onto this *chalcidicum*; their depth increased from south to north because the Forum was on a different axis from the Macellum.

The monumental entrance to the Macellum consisted of a room with two marble-covered pedestals on the façade, which may have housed either two statues or two columns supporting an entablature that also

A *Chalcidicum*
B *Monumental entrance*
C *Money-changers*
D *Entrance from Via degli Augustali*
E *Access from Via del Balcone Pensile*
F *Porticoes*
G *Tholos used for the sale of fish*
H *Tabernae*
I *Shrine*
J *Religious college*
K *Room used for the sale of fish*

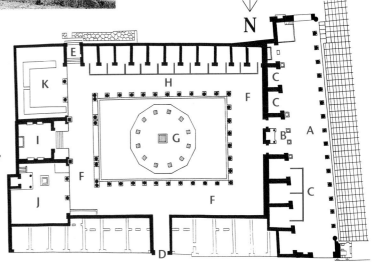

102 top left All
that remains of
this exquisite 4th-style
wall decoration,
documented in
numerous early
nineteenth-century
drawings, is a large
section in the north-
west corner of the
portico.

102 bottom left This
statue, once believed
to represent
Augustus' sister
Octavia, actually
portrayed a local
personality.

middle. The cobbled floor was surrounded by a marble gutter so that the water and waste liquids did not spread through the open area, but flowed into a drain underneath. This was discovered by stratigraphic techniques, which detected the water pipe and the drain full of fish bones and scales.

The eastern side is of particular interest. A small shrine stands in the middle, on the same axis as the Forum entrance. On the uncolonnaded front, a staircase flanked by two podia leads to a room with an *aedicule* at the end, only the base of which survives; it must have housed the statue of an Emperor, part of which (an arm with a hand holding a sphere) was found during excavation. Two niches on each of the two side walls also contained honorary statues, two of which have been found; the man and woman portrayed were originally believed to be Augustus' nephew and sister Marcellus and Octavia, but are more likely to have been local personalities who sponsored the rebuilding of the Macellum, portrayed in accordance with Imperial iconography. The originals are housed in the National Museum in Naples, and have been replaced by two copies.

On the north side of the shrine is another large room of unknown function; its façade is divided into three by two columns standing on a quadrangular plinth. In the south-east corner there is an *aedicule* made of *opus latericium*, which must have contained a religious statue, since a low altar covered with marble slabs stands in front of it. The room was entirely covered with frescoes of colonnades with garlands and cupids in the middle; sadly, all that survives of these decorations is the nineteenth-century descriptions. The most likely hypothesis, in view of the table covered with marble slabs which stands against the south wall, is that sacrificial banquets were held here by a religious organisation.

On the opposite side, to the south of the small shrine, was another room where fish was sold on a long counter with a channel running along it which conveyed running water. This room presented a strident contrast with the preceding ones, although it was ornamented by two columns on the façade like the room to the north, and an elegant 4th-style painting with a central picture depicting the personification of the River Sarnus (which was teeming with fish), surrounded by nymphs and the goddess of abundance. A large section of the rich decoration that adorned the back wall of the portico has survived in the north-west corner. The 4th-style fresco has survived up to almost its entire original height; panels depicting winged sprites with girls behind them and one portraying Penelope recognising Ulysses stand out in the middle section, while the large panels in the upper part contain still lifes. The Macellum recently underwent a thorough restoration, and as much as possible of its original character has been regained.

102 right This male
figure, portrayed in
heroic nakedness,
was long interpreted
as Augustus' nephew
Marcellus. In fact it
was another local
personality, perhaps
the one who
sponsored the
restoration of the
building.

THE TEMPLE OF JUPITER

The Temple of Jupiter, flanked by two triumphal arches, dominates the north side of the Forum. For those arriving from Via dell'Abbondanza, the view from the south was breathtaking: not only was the symmetry of the great sacred building clearly apparent, but it was also possible to see beyond the triumphal arch on the right-hand side to a third arch at the beginning of Via di Mercurio, through which the monumental façades of the houses could be glimpsed, with the impressive Tower of Mercury in the background. This sight gave the impression of a large town containing

A *Altar*
B *Access staircase*
C *Pedestals for equestrian statues*
D *Pronaos*
E *Shrine*
F *Shrines for the Capitoline Triad*
G *Stairs to mezzanine floor*
H *Triumphal arch (Augustus?)*
I *Triumphal arch (Germanicus?)*

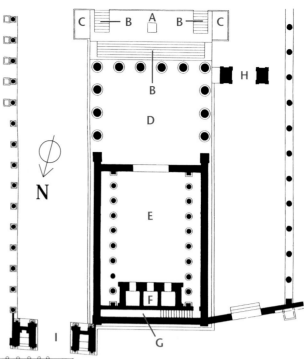

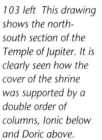

N

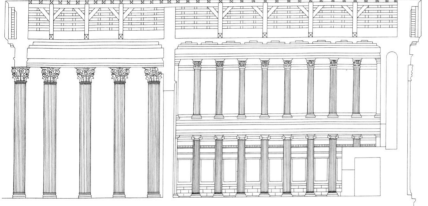

103 left This drawing shows the north-south section of the Temple of Jupiter. It is clearly seen how the cover of the shrine was supported by a double order of columns, Ionic below and Doric above.

103 right The sides of the temple reveal the progressive extension and reconstruction work undergone by the sacred building, which dominated the Forum; the successive brick additions are clearly visible.

monuments and scenery of incomparable beauty.

The temple was included in the general Forum layout dating from the second century BC; in fact, the axis of the temple corresponds to that of the great square. The original religious building, which was slightly smaller, had a staircase as wide as its entire front, leading up to a tall podium, columns on the façade and a shrine in the lower half. The podium contained three barrel-vaulted basement rooms used to store religious ornaments, vestments and votive offerings. These rooms were reached by a staircase in the middle of the slope leading up to the temple, which was later replaced by an opening on the east side of the podium. A large altar (4.30m x 6.60m) belonging to this phase of the temple has been identified by test excavations some three metres from the present front of the podium. The temple may have been dedicated to Jupiter even at this early stage. Extensive changes were made immediately after 80 BC,

when Sulla's colonists made their presence felt in the religious life of the town, and the temple was transformed into a *Capitolium* dedicated to the sacred triad of Jupiter, Juno and Minerva, venerated on the Capitol in Rome. The podium (17m x 37m) was slightly lengthened towards the centre of the square and the great sacrificial altar was eliminated; a new altar was built in front of the temple much later, but so far away that some experts believe it was not a sacrificial element but the base for a statue of Augustus.

The temple was entered by two lateral staircases, built into the podium to form a large platform in the middle and a smaller one on either side. A new altar was erected on the central platform, and two equestrian statues were placed on the side platforms. This information was supplied by an unusual source: a well-known Pompeiian banker, Lucius Caecilius Jucundus, had two friezes sculpted for a domestic altar, one of

which represents the north side of the Forum. The two narrow staircases at the entrance to the temple led to a landing from which a flight of stairs almost as wide as the building leads up to the pronaos floor. The temple walls were completely rebuilt at this second stage. Six slender Corinthian columns were built on the front and four on the sides, using grey Nuceria tuff covered with very fine plaster; the elaborate capitals were made in two parts. The large roofed area, characteristic of Etrusco-Italic temples, was created between the three colonnaded sides and the front of the shrine. The floor of the large pronaos was paved with travertine slabs, but this paving probably dates from a restoration in the early first century AD.

The shrine occupies the northern half of the high podium; at the outer corners of the façade and the rear wall, it has two pillars with tuff Composite capitals, with Ionic elements (volutes) and Corinthian elements (acanthus leaves). The entrance door leads into a large room divided into a nave and two aisles by two two-storey colonnades; the lower storey is Ionic and the upper storey is Corinthian. The aisles are narrow, and the two storeys of columns seem to act as a scenic backdrop to the statues on the back wall. The floor in the centre of the shrine was made of *opus sectile*, and decorated with diamond-shaped tiles laid in a pattern to create the effect of many cubes seen from an angle, while the outer bands and the intercolumniations of the aisles were made of black and white mosaic.

Similar floors can be observed in the shrine of the Temple of Apollo and in the *tablinum* of the House of the Faun. The walls were originally decorated with 1st-style incrustation paintings, but later, after 80 BC, these were replaced by 2nd-style decoration with red *orthostates* divided by imitation marble pilaster strips, framed above and below by multicoloured rustication; a mock corbel closed the decoration at the top. The wainscot seems to have been restored and replaced by a decoration in the 3rd style. At the end of the shrine was the podium which supported the three religious statues; it was decorated by half-columns on the front and at the corners. Inside the podium there were three narrow rooms entered through three small doors.

All that has been found of the religious statues is the face mask of Juno and the colossal head of Jupiter, now replaced by a copy, while the original is housed in the National Museum in Naples. The earthquake of AD 62 seriously damaged the temple, and the damage had not yet been repaired at the time of the eruption in AD 79. A huge bust in the process of being recarved and numerous pieces of decorative marble deposited in the rooms beneath the podium suggest that the temple was used temporarily as a workshop. The fact that the temple was dedicated to the Capitoline Triad is demonstrated by an inscription found there during the excavations conducted between 1816 and 1817.

Two triumphal arches of unknown attribution were built at the sides of the *Capitolium* at the beginning of the first century AD. It has been suggested that the right-hand arch alongside the façade was dedicated to Augustus, and the left-hand arch alongside the end wall, which coincides with the northern boundary of the Forum, to Germanicus. Both are made of *opus latericium* covered with marble slabs and surmounted by equestrian groups. Some researchers also believe that both arches may originally have been aligned with the front of the temple, and that the left-hand arch was later moved back to give more prominence to the portico in front of the Macellum. The latter arch is very

interesting; the arch itself rests on a base of travertine slabs, and there is a pair of *aedicules* on the two faces which must have been flanked by columns, the bases of which rested on a projecting cornice that edged the socle. Sadly, all that remains of this magnificence is a few small slabs of marble.

104 top left A triumphal arch made of opus latericium, which has been tentatively attributed to Augustus, stood on the left of the temple façade.

104 bottom left The Corinthian columns that occupy the front of the temple were found lying on the ground during the excavations; the one in the east corner was only raised in the early twentieth century.

104 top right A second triumphal arch, attributed to Germanicus, stands on the right of the sacred building, acting as a boundary between the Forum and the wide street behind it. The monument was faced with marble, and the niches contained honorary statues.

104 bottom right The temple shrine which housed the Capitoline Triad had a nave and two aisles separated by Ionic columns. The large head of Jupiter found here was, at the time of the eruption, being recarved into what would have been an entirely different statue.

THE PUBLIC LATRINE

A large public latrine, with the load-bearing structures made of *opus latericium*, stands in the north-west corner of the Forum, under the outermost edge of the portico. The latrine was entered through a small door which led first into an antechamber, to prevent the interior from being seen from the Forum, and then into the room containing the seats. A deep drainage channel flushed continuously with running water, ran round three sides of the room; blocks of lava stone supported planking containing holes which straddled the channel. At the time of the eruption the latrine was probably not in use, as the damage suffered in the earthquake of AD 62 was still being repaired.

THE FORUM HOLITORIUM

The Forum Holitorium, a large rectangular room in the northern section of the west side of the Forum, was the place where cereals and dried pulses were sold. It consisted of eight large openings flanked by stout pillars made of *opus latericium*. The floor was made of *opus signinum* decorated with multicoloured marble *crustae*. The building was damaged in the earthquake of AD 62 and had not been completely restored at the time of the eruption; the roof was still missing, and the walls had not yet been plastered. It is currently used as an archaeological store.

THE MENSA PONDERARIA

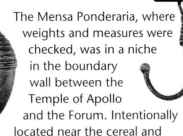

The Mensa Ponderaria, where weights and measures were checked, was in a niche in the boundary wall between the Temple of Apollo and the Forum. Intentionally located near the cereal and dried-pulse market (Forum Holitorium), it consists of a horizontal limestone bench containing nine circular cavities of different capacities with a hole in the bottom, through which the measured product ran out. A smaller table with three cavities rested on it, so that 12 different quantities could be measured. The table was installed in the Samnite era (late second century BC), so the measures were Oscan, as demonstrated by the names inscribed in the cavities.

With Romanisation, the Oscan measurements had to be adapted to the Roman ones, as proved by this epigraph carved into the face of the marble counter: '*A(ulus) Clodius A(uli) f(ilius) Flaccus N(umerius) Arcaeus N(umeri) f(ilius) Arellian(us) Caledus d(uo) v(iri) i(ure) d(icundo) mensuras exaequandas ex dec(urionum) decr(eto)*' (Judges and *duumviri* Aulus Clodius Flaccus, son of Aulus, and Numerius Arcaeus Arellianus Caledus, son of Numerius, [had the task] of equalising the measurements, as resolved by the *decurions*).

105 top left The steelyard was a typical weighing instrument, which required the arm to be in balance with the fulcrum; the product to be weighed was placed on a scale-pan hooked to the end nearest the fulcrum and the counterweight, which was mobile, determined the weight in accordance with the measurements marked on the arm.

105 top right This terracotta loom weight served to hold taut the yarn fixed horizontally and vertically to the work surface.

105 centre These marked lead weights were probably used on scales with a central fulcrum and a pan at each end; the fixed weight was placed on one, and the product to be weighed on the other.

105 bottom left There were also measuring instruments for liquids; a set of quadrangular-bodied bottles, which are fractions or multiples of one another can be seen here.

105 bottom right These two stone weights were also used for weighing on instruments with two balanced scale-pans; in this case, one weighs half as much as the other.

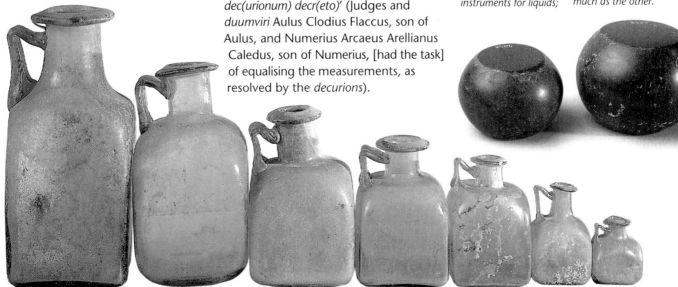

THE BASILICA

The outermost sector on the west side of the Forum is occupied by the Basilica, which was definitely the most important and monumental of all the public buildings in Pompeii in terms of architecture, and the most expensive in financial terms. The Basilica was the place where business transactions and the administration of justice were conducted, as it was the location of the court presided over by the leading town officials, the *duumviri*. It was also a natural meeting place, as it was always full of people.

The Basilica was built in the second half of the second century BC, as suggested by some graffiti in Oscan, and is therefore the oldest surviving Roman building of this kind. Another graffito found on an inner wall of the building, which reads as follows, is very helpful in dating it: '*C(aius) Pumidius Dipilus heic fuit a(nte) d(iem) V nonas octobreis M(arco) Lepid(o) Q(uinto) Catul(o) co(n)s(ulibus)*' (Caius Pumidius Dipilus

was here five days before the nones of October [October 3] when Marcus Lepidus and Quintus Catulus were consuls [78 BC]). It is not known why Caius Pumidius Dipilus went to the Pompeii Basilica, but it is certain that the building was already in use in the early decades of the first century BC.

The building appears to have been constructed in accordance with the usual criteria, although the main entrance was not on the longer side, but on the short side overlooking the Forum. This variation is understandable; that was the most important side, and it was a much easier access point for those arriving from the square and from Via dell'Abbondanza. There were two more entrances on the long sides; the northern entrance was used by those entering from Via Marina, and the southern entrance by those arriving from Vico di Chiampionnet, although the latter seems to have been added later, during the age of Augustus. The

A The Forum portico
B Entrance from Via Marina
C Entrance from Vico di Chiampionnet
D Chalcidicum
E Porticoes
F Steps to basement archive
G Tribunal
H Pedestal for honorary statue
I Ancient well

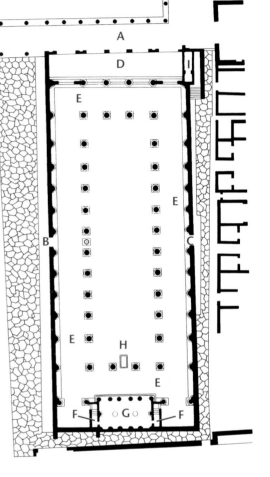

N

main entrance from the east was preceded by an unroofed *chalcidicum*, a kind of vestibule entered from the Forum portico through five openings framed by pillars made of large blocks of grey tuff, which could be closed with metal gates if required. The building's entrance is impressive: the façade consisted of four magnificent Ionic columns with four-sided capitals; the columns stood on basalt plinths which divided a flight of four basalt steps to form five entrances. The three main entrances are formed by the central intercolumnations, while the two side entrances were opened in a brick wall attached to the two outer columns and the side walls of the Basilica.

106 These magnificent, high-quality Ionic capitals carved in grey tuff surmounted the columns at the top of the entrance staircase on the Forum side.

107 The architectural area, on which the Basilica stands, appears impressive and, indeed, two activities of great importance for Pompeiian life were performed here: the administration of justice and the recording of business transactions. Its architectural and monumental design were highly advanced for the period when it was built.

Inside the large hall there is a two-storey four-sided portico with 28 fluted Ionic columns some 11 metres tall, matched on the side walls by 24 Ionic half-columns, thus creating a nave and two aisles, the nave being roughly twice as wide as the aisles. The side walls were decorated in the 1st style to imitate an *isodomic* structure with stucco reliefs.

interesting side of the building; a two-storey *avant-corps*, with a basement room of the same width, is built onto the end wall. The basement room was reached by two staircases at either side of the *avant-corps*, and may have housed the Basilica archives. The first floor, which stands on a two-metre-high podium, is the actual tribunal, which was open on the side facing the

it was reached from the *chalcidicum*, probably by a wooden ladder. In the western part of this long, narrow room is a well, whose shaft is lined with *opus incertum*, which A. Maiuri explored to a depth of some 21 metres without reaching the bottom. In the eastern part of the room was a tank which was evidently filled with water brought up from the well by a waterwheel. It has

The columns, made of *opus latericium*, are an original feature of the construction; the shaft and the outer fluting are formed by elongated pentagonal bricks arranged in a sunburst pattern. There are several theories regarding the roof; some experts believe that the nave may even have been unroofed. However, the most widely accepted theory is that the Basilica had a huge, single-truss, double-pitched roof, covered with tiles, terminating in *antefixae* of perforated palmettes. Some of the tiles are stamped with the name Ni. Pupie (Numerius Popidius), a tile manufacturer and former magistrate of Samnite Pompeii.

The west side is the most

centre of the Basilica, with four Corinthian columns between two Corinthian *anta* columns; six half-columns divided the west wall, and one divided the shorter walls. Little is known about the upper storey, although one definitely existed, but the reconstruction now in existence is of questionable accuracy. To the sides of the *tribunal* were twin rooms framed at the front by two *anta* columns; these may have been offices, where various operations concerning the activities conducted in the Basilica were handled.

A small rectangular room on a floor-level higher than the rest of the Basilica was built onto the outside of the building in the south-west corner;

been impossible to establish what it had to do with the Basilica. Being at a higher level, it may have supplied an internal fountain, which was removed after the earthquake of AD 62. In any event, the well can no longer have been in use, as much of it was obstructed when it was discovered; it may have fallen into disuse when Pompeii was supplied with drinking water by Agrippa's aqueduct, which brought water to the town from the River Serinus.

THE TEMPLE OF APOLLO

The cult of Apollo was undoubtedly one of the most important in Pompeii; in fact, the god was considered the protector of the town until Sulla's colonists imposed the cult of the Capitoline Triad (80 BC). Stratigraphic excavations conducted in the sacred area of the temple have uncovered evidence, which enables the entire history of the temple to be traced,

confirming that a temple dedicated to Apollo was built on the western spur of the lava plateau in the early sixth century BC. Practically nothing is known of this original building; it can only be assumed that it was made of wood covered with slabs of decorated terracotta, as suggested by numerous fragments found in the sacred *fossae* (trenches). When the earlier building was demolished to make room for the new one, all the sacred articles were stored in trenches consecrated in the

temple area. At this first stage the sacred area was situated in a position of incomparable beauty, much higher than the Doric temple of the Triangular Forum, and overlooked the entire gulf and the plain with the River Sarnus running through it.

In view of its position, one of the purposes of the temple was to show that the site was occupied, and to demonstrate the strength of those who built it. Whether the temple indicates the presence of the Greeks

or the Etruscans is a subject of much debate. The worship of Apollo existed in Cumae and Naples, Greek cities which greatly influenced the cultural development of the coastal towns of Campania, but there is strong evidence of this worship among the Etruscans too, as demonstrated by the Temple of Apollo at Veii. The votive offerings discovered in the temple do not help to resolve the issue, as both Etruscan products and items of Greek workmanship were found.

In its earliest period the temple occupied a larger area. The *peribolos* wall was found to the west under the House of Tryptolemus (VII-7-5), and the building must have occupied part of the Forum area to the east; in fact, other votive offerings have been identified near the west portico of the Forum. The reorganisation of the entire area in the second century BC, when the Civil Forum and all the annexed public buildings were erected, reduced the area of the

A **Entrance from Via Marina**
B **Porticoes**
C **Statue of Artemis**
D **Statue of Apollo**
E **Altar**
F **Sundial**
G **Staircase leading to temple**
H **Pronaos**
I **Shrine**
J **Omphalos**
K **Pedestal of religious statue**
L **Mensa ponderaria**
M **Forum, west portico**

108 right A replica of the statue of Apollo shooting arrows was found in fragments in the west part of the town, but was assigned to the Temple of Apollo thanks to features similar to those of the statue of Artemis.

108 right The bronze statue of Artemis shooting arrows stood against the west portico.

109 top The Temple of Apollo, with its porticoes, statues, votive offerings and trenches, helps reconstruct significant stages in the history and cultural trends affecting the urban community.

109 centre The Doric portico was being converted to the Ionic order after the earthquake of AD 62.

109 bottom The area in front of the pronaos was occupied by the altar, around which worshippers gathered for religious ceremonies.

110-111 This reconstruction drawing indicates what the Temple of Apollo must have looked like before the disastrous earthquake of AD 62.

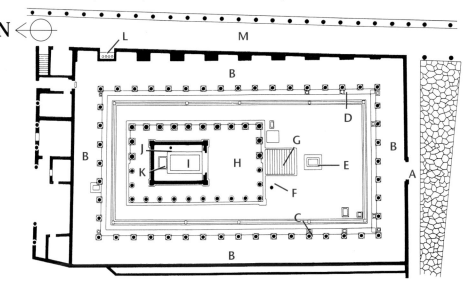

N ←

temple, but also coincided with the overall rebuilding of the sacred site.

The cult of Apollo continued to play a very important role in the life of Pompeii; the temple was connected to the Forum by 11 large entrances, which were only closed when the Capitolium became predominant as a result of pressure by Sulla's colonists (80 BC). The west side also had a number of entrances giving onto a small street that was later eliminated, but these were closed in the last years of the first century BC, as demonstrated by an inscription found here. Like many of the buildings in Pompeii, the Temple of Apollo was seriously damaged in the earthquake of AD 62, and restoration work had not been completed at the time of the eruption. The building was probably visited by clandestine raiders in subsequent years, as suggested by the lack of some of the furnishings which should have been found there. The excavation of the building, conducted in several stages, began in 1816, and it was understood by the first researchers to be the Temple of

Venus. The discovery of the temple caused an immediate sensation; many artists flocked to the site and produced documentary evidence of great importance, although there is no lack of somewhat personal, if not overimaginative interpretations.

The temple area is entered from Via Marina; the area is surrounded by a peristyle consisting of 17 columns on the long sides and nine on the short sides. At the time of its construction the grey Nuceria tuff columns were of the Composite order; the shaft was entirely fluted and the architrave featured triglyphs and metopes of a Doric flavour, while the four-sided capital suggests the Ionic order. Some experts believe that there was a second row of columns above the first, but no trace of them has ever been found, nor is that theory borne out by any historical evidence.

After the earthquake of AD 62, the lower third of the columns was covered with a thick layer of plaster, modelled into bean-shaped patterns painted yellow; the capitals were also covered with stucco and roughly

remodelled into the Corinthian order, then painted red, blue and yellow. The architrave was covered with a layer of plaster, which concealed the triglyphs, and later decorated with garlands and griffins, of which no trace remains, apart from the excavation documentation. This documentation states that the back walls were frescoed with a paratactic structure, with panels separated by architectural landscapes with a central picture. Scenes of the Trojan war were painted in the niches formed when the doors that once led to the Forum were bricked up.

A number of statues (all of which are now housed in the Archaeological Museum in Naples) stood on pedestals outside the portico. These included bronze statues of Apollo and Artemis portrayed as archers, copies of which

Corinthian order, supported an entablature with figured tympanum, lending some truth to the theory that the fragments of a pediment found in house VI-17-41, which portrayed the myth of Apollo and Marsyas, belonged to the temple, and possibly formed part of this entablature. The shrine had a floor made of *opus sectile* formed by green and white stone and slate diamonds, arranged to create a pattern of cubes, like the floors of the shrine of the Temple of Jupiter and the *tablinum* in the House of the Faun. Here, the cube pattern is surrounded by a band of slate, which, in turn is surrounded by a white mosaic. The slate band still bears an inscription in Oscan, made with metal-filled holes, which states,

112 top This earthenware slab (West Insula, VI-17-42), belonging to the temple frieze, portrays Artemis on the right, a Nike on the left and a dog at the bottom centre, in haut-relief. Artemis wears a huntress's chiton and the quiver on her back.

112 centre The theory that this earthenware slab found in the West Insula (VI-17-42) belongs to the frieze in the Temple of Apollo is reliable. The slab bears a frieze with flowers, between which the holes used to nail it to the building can be seen.

112 bottom This slab, found in the West Insula (VI-17-42), seems to belong to the Temple of Apollo; it depicts an offeror wearing a chiton and himation, about to take something from a casket with four low legs.

are now displayed in the temple. The unroofed area was paved with tuff slabs. The temple proper stands in the northern sector of the sacred area, oriented in the usual direction, with the façade facing south-east. The entrance to the temple area is directly in line with with the temple. In front of it stands an altar of Greek marble dedicated by the two *duumviri* and two aediles immediately after 80 BC. To the left of the altar, near the temple podium, stands a white marble Ionic column surmounted by a sundial. An inscription in the middle of the shaft, which forms an integral part of the monolith, states that it was donated by the *duumviri* Lucius Sepunius Sandilianus and Marcus Erennius Epidianus.

The temple is a mixture of Greek and Etrusco-Italic stylistic elements. Towards the rear of the tall podium, which has a long, wide staircase at the front, stands the shrine, surrounded by a peristyle consisting of six columns at the front and nine on the long sides – unusual for Greek architecture. The columns, of the

'*U. Kampaniìs… kvaisstur kulbennieìs tanginud Appelluneìs eitiuvad… ùps annu aaman affed*' (Quaestor Oppius Campanus… sponsored the building… by resolution of the council, which was paid for by the offerings to Apollo). Both the floor and the inscription date from the second half of the second century BC.

Near the back wall, but not attached to it, stood a pedestal which must have supported a statue of the deity, but this has never been found. On the west side, an element with a special oval shape representing the omphalos, the attribute of Apollo of Delphi, is embedded in the floor. The inner walls of the shrine have 1st-style incrustation decoration, while the outer walls, framed with cabled pilaster strips on tuff bases, are decorated with panels containing stucco reliefs, surrounded by a cornice of stylised ovoli. In conclusion, the Temple of Apollo enables the entire history of Pompeii to be reconstructed from its origins to its tragic burial, and its structures bear witness to the social and cultural changes undergone by the town during its long life.

THE TEMPLE OF FORTUNA AUGUSTA

A Via del Foro
B Via della Fontana Augusta
C Staircase leading to temple
D Altar
E Pronaos
F Shrine
G Distyle apse
H Dedicatory niches
I Service quarters

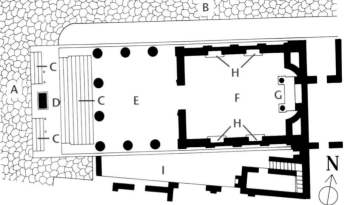

113 top The triumphal arch on the left, very dubiously attributed to Caligula, constituted the entrance to Via di Mercurio.

113 bottom The temple stood in the centre of the crossroads; sadly, the damage suffered during the earthquake of AD 62 left it bare, and there is no sign that restoration work ever began. The façade of the tetrastyle temple featured Corinthian columns, the capitals of which were left on the floor of the pronaos.

114-115 This is what the Temple of Fortuna Augusta must have looked like: a classic prostyle tetrastyle temple, preceded by a tall staircase, divided by an altar on a platform.

An inscription found on the architrave of the shrine in this temple describes the circumstances of its construction: 'M(arcus) Tullius M(arci) f(ilius) d(uo) v(ir) i(ure) d(icundo) tert(ium) quinq(uennalis) augur, tr(ibunus) mil(itum) a pop(ulo), aedem Fortunae August(ae) solo et peq(unia) sua' (Marcus Tullius, son of Marcus, *duumvir* and three times judge, quinquennial, augur and military officer elected by the people, erected the Temple of Fortuna Augusta on his land at his own expense). The Tullia family, to which Cicero also belonged, was widespread in Arpinum and central Italy. The family followed Sulla to Pompeii, and its members were frequently elected magistrates of the town. The inscription demonstrates that Marcus Tullius was the most outstanding member of the family. He was not only *duumvir* three times, but was once also quinquennial (the official who revised the electoral registers and selected possible candidates for the judiciary). However, the office of military officer is the one which demonstrates his relationship with Augustus; it was the Emperor himself who awarded this office, enabling holders to attain the rank of knight. After building the temple, Marcus Tullius must have chosen a number of slaves to form the College of Priests for the cult (*ministri Fortunae Augustae*). The College of Priests, on receiving authorisation from the *decurions*, undertook to donate a statue of Fortune, or a statue of the Emperor whenever a new one was appointed. The five inscriptions found in the temple area appear to relate to the Emperors who held office until AD 62 (the year when the temple was destroyed by the earthquake), namely Augustus, Tiberius, Caligula, Claudius and Nero.

The temple was built at the crossroads between Via del Foro and Via di Nola, on a site previously occupied by shops and probably by a house, as suggested by some floors decorated with *opus signinum*, found behind and beneath the podium on the south side. The temple was the Etrusco-Italic type, and was built in the last years of the first century BC. The front faced west, and featured a large staircase with two flights separated by a long, narrow landing; the lower flight of steps is interrupted in the centre by a podium supporting the altar. The body of the temple consisted of a pronaos with four Corinthian columns on the façade and three on the long sides; the shrine, situated towards the back of the podium, had a large apse in the back wall with an *aedicule* in the middle supported by two columns, where the statue of Fortune, with the attributes of the oar and the rudder, must have stood.

On each side wall there were two rectangular niches which must have contained honorary statues, two of which were found during the excavations conducted in 1822; the first is a man's figure wearing a toga, once incorrectly believed to be Cicero, and the second is a woman's figure, from which the face mask is missing. The temple was closed at the front by an iron gate, traces of which can still be seen on the edge of the landing at altar-level. Rooms for the priests were built on the south side of the temple, also on land owned by Marcus Tullius. As a result of the the area being pedestrianised and the construction of the porticoed pavement, the temple area was connected with the Forum. The temple certainly stood in a strategic position; anyone arriving from Naples or Herculaneum along Via Consolare suddenly found the magnificent marble-faced temple towering over them. It must have been particularly splendid, as

the Corinthian capitals still preserved on the podium of the temple feature excellent workmanship and high-quality marble. The earthquake of AD 62 damaged the entire building, and little repair work was carried out; in fact, much of the material that collapsed may well have been reused for other purposes. One interesting theory is that the marble slabs decorated with relief scenes of sacrifice in the Temple of Vespasian originally covered the altar of the Temple of Fortuna Augusta; in fact, in terms of size and stylistic similarity, they do correspond to the rest of the temple.

THE FORUM BATHS

The Forum Baths were the only ones in operation when Pompeii was buried by volcanic debris. The damage caused by the earthquake of AD 62 was probably repaired immediately so that normal business could be resumed. It is thought that the baths complex, divided into male and female sections, was built immediately after 80 BC, as suggested by an inscription probably found here, which refers to the settlers who arrived in Pompeii when Sulla's colony was founded. The inscription states that the *duumvir* Lucius Caesius and the two aediles Caius Occius and Lucius Niraemius, by decision of the town Senate, had the baths built

with public money and examined them personally.

The baths occupied the central part of the *insula* (VII-5), and are largely surrounded by shops and *thermopolia*; there were no private residences on the *insula*. The male section of the baths could be reached from three different entrances, two leading to the gymnasium and one directly into the changing room. These entrances gave onto Vico delle Terme to the west, Via delle Terme to the north and Via del Foro to the east. Some 500 lanterns were found in the latter entrance.

The gymnasium is unusual in some respects. It is a three-sided portico in which the west and north sides consist of Doric tuff columns covered with a thick layer of plaster, the lower third of which is somewhat thicker and

coloured red. The south side has no portico, while the east side has a narrower portico, supported not by columns, but by pillars with a round *opus latericium* arch. The gymnasium would originally have been longer, extending towards the south, of a regular shape, with an entirely colonnaded four-sided portico, and would also have had an entrance on the Forum side, as suggested by some sealed rooms. At a later stage, the south side was sacrificed to the construction of four shops, two of which were *thermopolia*, with a back room and an upper floor. A long masonry bench runs along the north wall of the gymnasium, interrupted in the middle by a room, which is open for its whole width. As the gymnasium was used for walks after the bathing cycle, hot drinks may have been served here to replace some of the fluids lost through perspiration.

The changing room is a large barrel-vaulted room. There are masonry benches running along the long sides, but the usual niches where clothes were left are absent; they were probably replaced by wooden shelves, as suggested by the holes left by nails. The room was illuminated from the south by a glass skylight with a metal frame. The walls were frescoed in yellow and the vault, like the lunettes on the short sides, was decorated with stucco reliefs. Alongside the skylight is a stucco head of Okeanos with a flowing beard, crowned with crab's claws. The changing room gave onto the circular *frigidarium* which had a round *balneum* in the middle, covered with marble slabs, and four apsidal niches. The rectangular mouth of the cold water pipe that filled the pool can be seen on the south wall; the drainage hole on the bottom of the pool, which allowed it to be emptied, and the overflow hole are also still visible. The truncated, cone-shaped roof, which had a glazed skylight at the top, was decorated in a shell pattern. The stucco relief frieze which depicts cherubs competing in a chariot race, against a red background is particularly interesting.

From the changing room, bathers went to the *tepidarium*, which still retains its original splendour as a result of excellent, though partial

116 The southern side of the tepidarium *still features much of the coloured stucco decoration and the shelves separated by* telamones.

116-117 The southern part of the calidarium, *with the* labrum *and the openings at the top which direct light into the apsidal area, is very attractive.*

A *Entrance from Vico delle Terme*
B *Entrance from Via delle Terme*
C *Men's changing room*
D *The men's frigidarium*
E *The men's tepidarium*
F *The men's calidarium*
G *The men's labrum*
H *The men's pool*
I *Portico*
J *Entrance from Via del Foro*
K *Praefurnium*
L *Service area*
M *Women's changing room*
N *The women's tepidarium*
O *The women's calidarium*
P *Cold water pool*
Q *The women's labrum*
R *Hot water pool*

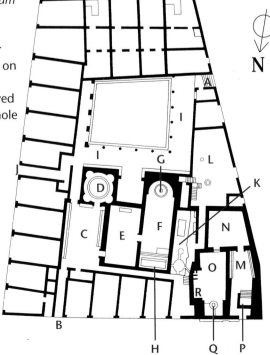

conservation. This room, which was parallel to the changing room and the *calidarium*, but shorter in length, had barrel vaults decorated with multicoloured stucco, which is well preserved in the south section. Alternate rectangular and square coffers with mythological figures in the centre decorate a lower strip in the

large, bronze brazier, donated by Marcus Nigidius Vaccula, is still preserved there, together with three low bronze benches.

The *tepidarium* led to the *calidarium*, which is of particular interest. On the short south side is a large apse surmounted by a hemispherical *calotte* with shell decorations; this side was

form of an acanthus branch; the coffers are separated by candelabras of plants, and surmounted by a strip of smaller, octagonal medallions. Higher still, in the middle of the vault, are large panels divided into diamond and rectangle shapes containing other relief pictures. This decoration dates from the restoration of AD 79.

Unlike the changing room, this room contained niches for ointments and towels. They were separated by magnificent terracotta telamones, sometimes naked, sometimes covered with animal skins, which support the cornice of ovoli, from which the vault decoration begins. The floor, of white mosaic surrounded by a black band, has been well preserved. The *tepidarium* had no internal heating system, but a

illuminated by three rectangular windows in the vault, and by an *opaion* (a circular skylight) in the centre of the *calotte*. The large monolithic marble basin (*labrum*), in the form of a *patera*, with a central spout, was situated in the apse. This basin has a long inscription in bronze lettering on the rim, which reads, '*Cn. Melissaeo Cn. f. Apro, M. Staio M. f. Rufo IIvir(is) iter(um) i(ure) d(icundo) labrum ex d(ecreto) d(ecurionum) ex p(equnia) p(ublica) f(aciundum) c(oerarunt). Constat HS DCCL'* (Cnaeus Melissaeus Aper, son of Cnaeus, and Marcus Staius Rufus, son of Marcus, as *duumviri* and judges for the second time, undertook to have the basin built with public money by resolution of the *decurions*. It cost 5,250 sesterces). The large basin was installed around AD 3-4.

The marble-covered hot-water pool was built along the opposite wall, and reached by two steps. The *calidarium* was fitted with an internal heating installation consisting of four cavity walls lined with *tegulae mammatae*, which were covered with plaster decorated with large yellow squares separated by red pilaster strips. The vault, which rested on a projecting cornice, was simply decorated with spiral fluting which prevented condensed steam from dripping onto bathers' heads. Heat was produced by the *praefurnium*, which separated the men's and women's sections. The women's section was smaller and simpler than the men's, consisting of only three rooms: the changing room, located immediately after the entrance, which contained a pool for ablutions, the *tepidarium*, heated by *tegulae mammatae*, and the *calidarium*, which contained a pool for hot baths and a *labrum* in the north-west corner of the room.

117 top The elbows of splendid terracotta telamones support the moulded cornice closing the top of the shelves used to store clothes.

117 bottom In this medallion on the vault of the tepidarium, Zeus in *the guise of an eagle, captures Ganymede.*

TOWARDS THE NOLA GATE

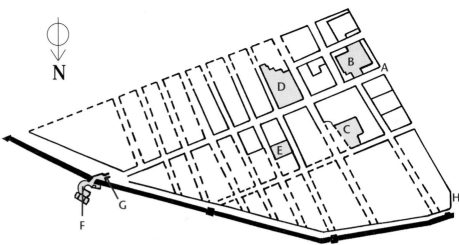

Via di Nola, which represents the north *decumanus*, runs almost parallel to the south *decumanus*, constituted by Via dell'Abbondanza. The *insulae* that developed around these roads, mainly to the east of the crossroads with Via di Stabia, seem to have formed a mainly residential area during the last decades of Pompeii's existence, since there are numerous houses of architectural significance and with special decorative features. On ground level, at the front, many did contain shops, taverns and *thermopolia*, but the bright colours and decorations found in a mainly commercial area like Via dell'Abbondanza were lacking.

Only one public complex has been found in this district to date, namely the Central Baths, which are of particular importance because their construction commenced after the earthquake of AD 62; sadly, they were never fully operational. They occupy a whole *insula*, and were designed and built with the use of such massive resources, that they would no doubt have been among the most efficient and functional, as well as the most beautiful.

THE HOUSE OF THE SILVER WEDDING (V-2-1)

In 1893, on the 25th wedding anniversary of King Umberto I of Italy, excavations began under the direction of M. Ruggero, Superintendent of Pompeii, on a large house which was named the House of the Silver Wedding in honour of the occasion. The owner, L. Albucius Celsus, known from numerous electoral inscriptions found close to the house, belonged to an ancient Pompeian family, which was very active in politics prior to the arrival of the Sulla's Roman colony. It can be assumed that this wealthy family only began to participate in the political life of Pompeii again during the last years

A The Orpheus Crossroads
B The Central Baths
C The House of the Silver Wedding
D The House of the Centenary
E The House of Lucretius Fronto
F The Nola Gate Necropolis
G The Nola Gate
H The Vesuvius Gate

118 The inner façade of the building known as the Central Baths overlooks the gymnasium; the large windows separated by massive engaged half-columns give the building a harmony of monumental proportions.

119 left This photo of the House of the Silver Wedding clearly shows the connection between the older north portico, with Doric columns, and the lower porticoes with octagonal columns, which were added later.

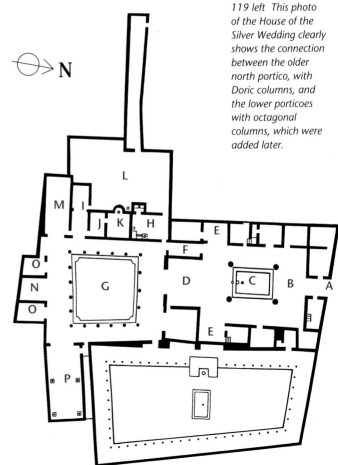

A Entrance
B Atrium
C Impluvium
D Tablinum
E Alae
F Shrine
G Peristyle
H Kitchen
I Changing room
J Tepidarium
K Calidarium
L Swimming pool
M Dining room
N Exedra
O Cubiculi
P Tetrastyle oecus

of the town's existence, although it evidently did not lose any of its ancient dignity or nobility over the preceding decades, since much of the house retains a solemn, austere appearance.

The history of the owners is told through the transformations which can still be seen in the structure of their home. The original nucleus was extremely regular, of the tetrastyle atrium type with a peristyle: the atrium was probably decorated in the 1st style and its tall doors, leading to rooms on either side, gave it a noble appearance. Behind the rooms on the south side was a single porticoed area with tuff Doric columns. During Sulla's rule, the house lost its lateral rooms, the tall entrances were closed, and the walls were entirely redecorated in the 2nd style. Later, probably after AD 62, the house regained the rooms on the sides of the atrium which, in view of its height, was divided over two floors; lower entrances were built, together with steep, narrow staircases leading to the upper floor, which had square

interior windows overlooking the lower floor of the atrium. The lower part of the atrium walls was redecorated in imitation 2nd style to match the decoration of the upper part, which was still in good condition. At the same time, three new, lower ambulatories were built onto the original single portico on the north side of the garden, giving the resulting peristyle characteristics which Vitruvius (VI-7-3) described as 'Rhodian'. The property was also extended to the west, where a baths complex was added, while a large peristyle with a pool and summer triclinium was built in another extension to the east.

The entrance is on the north side, facing onto a side street which runs parallel to Via di Nola, but along an irregular route. The tall entrance door led through the vestibule, whose floor sloped uphill, into the atrium. The atrium has a majestic appearance. The *compluvium* is supported by four tall, stout, fluted Corinthian columns made of grey tuff, covered with white plaster; the lower quarter was covered with a smooth, thicker layer coloured red at a later date. The *compluvium* was crowned by earthenware cymae with lions' heads and palmette *antefixae*. The *tablinum*, situated on the same axis as the entrance, the atrium and the peristyle and flanked by two *alae*, has 4th-style decorations; scenes of cupids with chariots and animals on a black background can be distinguished on the predella. Of the rooms leading onto the atrium, the one in the south-west corner, decorated in the 4th style, is of particular interest; the predella is unique, decorated with amusing scenes depicting pygmies.

The almost square peristyle has five Doric columns on the east side and on the other sides, six octagonal pillars, of which the lower third is circular. For the length of the intercolumniation, the architrave is frescoed with hunting scenes and surmounted by a continuous cornice of stucco ovoli.

There was also a small bath area on the west side. The changing room had a black and white mosaic floor divided into three sections: the threshold, where an aqueduct on an arched structure is depicted; the floor of the main room, which had scattered black and white tesserae surrounded by a black strip and finally, the floor of the

couch recess, which had a carpet pattern of black, white, red, green and yellow axonometric triangles inside a black and white border. The floor of the *tepidarium* was raised on *suspensurae*, allowing heat from the hypocaust to circulate beneath. Next came the *calidarium*, which had an apse on the short, west side and a hemispherical *calotte* with shell decorations; this room was adjacent to the kitchen, where the steam installation was fitted. Finally, there was a small swimming pool in the garden behind, which completed the baths complex.

Other magnificent rooms gave onto the south portico, such as a triclinium in the south-west corner, elaborately frescoed in the 4th style, and an *exedra* flanked by two *cubicula* in the middle, all decorated with magnificent 2nd-style frescoes and multicoloured mosaic floors. The *exedra* was evidently also used as a classroom by the master who taught the children of the household, as insulting graffiti about the teacher are written on the walls. The most unusual room is the tetrastyle *oecus* in the south-eastern corner. This room, which served as a dining room, had a splendid black and white mosaic floor and four octagonal columns standing on a tall plinth, which supported coffered barrel vaults decorated with stucco motifs. The walls were frescoed in the 4th style.

THE HOUSE OF THE CENTENARY (IX-8-6)

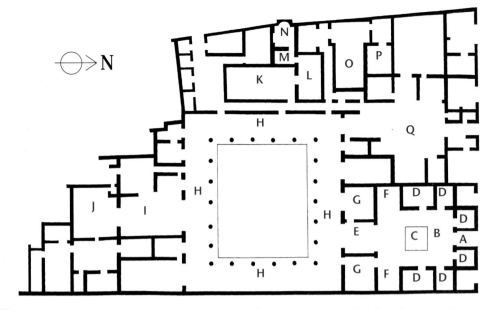

A   Vestibule
B   Atrium
C   Impluvium
D   Cubiculi
E   Tablinum
F   Alae
G   Oeci
H   Peristyle
I   Exedra
J   Nymphaeum
K   Frigidarium
L   Changing room
M   Tepidarium
N   Calidarium
O   Triclinium
P   Bed recess
Q   Atrium

120 top The large two-storey peristyle had a very attractive garden in the middle. A rectangular fountain with an apsidal niche containing the bronze statue of a young satyr pouring wine from a wineskin is situated on the same axis as the tablinum and the atrium.

The House of the Centenary, excavated in 1879 by Michele Ruggero, was named to commemorate the eighteenth centenary of the destruction of Pompeii. The owner of the house was A. Rustius Verus, as indicated by three electoral propaganda inscriptions, two at the main entrance and one at the secondary entrance, which call on citizens to elect him as aedile and *duumvir*. This residential property, one of the largest in Pompeii, is actually made of what previously were three separate houses. The *insula* has an unusual trapezoidal shape, because it lies between the double row of square *insulae* lining Via di Stabia and the rectangular *insulae* fronting onto Via di Nola. The *insula* was probably built in the first half of the second century BC, with three houses lying north-south, facing onto Via di Nola, and a number of houses lying east-west behind them. However, this theory has not been confirmed, as this part of the *insula* has not yet been excavated. During the age of Augustus (late first century BC to early first century AD), the three houses on Via di Nola and part of the first house behind it were combined to create a single residence. The extension enabled the house to be divided up into separate sections: the owner's quarters, which were the largest and occupied the whole of the eastern part, the baths area, situated in the western part alongside the apartments of the *procurator* who supervised the servants, and finally the service quarters, located in house no. 3.

The owner's quarters, which had their entrance on Via di Nola, at no.6, have the regular shape of an atrium house with a peristyle. The vestibule, which slopes gently upwards, is decorated with a black and white mosaic with a dolphin and marine griffin. The atrium, which has an upper floor, is the Tuscan type; the *impluvium* is covered with marble slabs, while the floor is decorated with white mosaic edged with black strips. Nothing is known of the *compluvium*. The various *cubiculi* that lie on either side of the atrium are decorated in the 4th style. The *tablinum*, which was on the same axis as the vestibule, the atrium and the peristyle and had two *alae*, is flanked by two *oeci* which give onto the peristyle. The left-hand *oecus* has a black background and the right-hand one has a white background, decorated with precious figured ornaments suggesting divinities.

The atrium led through a corridor to the east of the *tablinum* into the peristyle. The north colonnade of the almost square peristyle had two storeys, a portico and an upper gallery. The garden is ornamented by a rectangular pool in the centre with an apsidal niche on the north side. A magnificent fountain in the shape of a bronze sculpture, which portrays a young satyr pouring wine from a full wineskin under his arm, was found at the edge of the pool; the wine is obviously imitated by the water that fills the basin. The back wall of the west side of the peristyle is decorated with large yellow panels with a red border, in the centre of which emblems and attributes of various deities are portrayed

inside carpet-patterned frames, together with scenes depicting Perseus and Andromeda, Hercules and Hesione.

There is a spectacular architectural complex in the middle of the south side, where a large *exedra* leads through to a magnificent *nymphaeum* room. The *exedra* is largely ruined, but the emblem made of *cipolin* marble *opus sectile* still survives in the centre to demonstrate its splendour. The *nymphaeum* has a niche in the centre which once housed a glass paste mosaic and a statue of Silenus; water would have poured from the statue, before falling in small cascades into a basin in the floor. The lower part of the walls was decorated like a fantastic garden with plants, birds and myriad fish, while the upper part portrays combat between wild beasts, with an exotic landscape in the background. Visitors entering from Via di Nola could look through the atrium, the *tablinum* and the peristyle, obtaining the illusion of an imaginary space inside the house, as the design of the whole building was based around this perspective.

A long corridor led from the servants' quarters in house no.3 to the baths area behind the west portico. The baths, which were rebuilt after the earthquake of AD 62, had a *frigidarium* with a cold bathing pool on the short side of the back wall, and 4th-style wall decorations with Egyptian features. Traces of decorations dating from the previous phase have survived in the

*120 bottom
The magnificent* nymphaeum *at the end of the large drawing room has no equal in Pompeii. In the centre is an apse in which a fountain statue poured water onto the steps to form cascades and fill the basin below. There are paintings of sea creatures at the sides, and hunting scenes in exotic landscapes are frescoed on the back wall.*

121 top This famous painting was placed as a lararium *in the atrium of the servants' quarters; it portrays Bacchus, represented as a bunch of grapes, on the vineyard-covered slopes of Vesuvius. In the foreground, the usual auspicious serpent approaches an altar.*

*121 bottom
The bed recess in the procurator's quarters featured erotic paintings in a 4th-style decorative structure.*

122-123 *The House of the Centenary, so called because it was excavated in 1879, the 18th centenary of the eruption that destroyed the town, was a grandiose residence,*

magnificently decorated with sculptures, wall paintings and mosaic floors. This drawing shows a longitudinal section from the atrium to the peristyle.

changing room, which is next door, followed by the *tepidarium* and the *calidarium*. The *calidarium* had no *suspensurae* or *tegulae mammatae*, but was heated by a large oven in the cellar below (like the House of Menander), and by the walls shared with the kitchen. It had a basin in the apsidal niche and a bathtub in the rectangular niche; the walls were frescoed in the 4th style, and the floor was paved with diamond-shaped tiles. The floor of the *tepidarium* was

decorated with a black and white mosaic depicting sea creatures.

The *procurator*'s apartments consisted of a small open courtyard overlooked by a large triclinium with 3rd-style pictorial decorations portraying Theseus and the Minotaur, Hermaphroditus and Selene, Pylades, Orestes and Iphigenia, and two interconnecting rooms, one of which contains small, erotic paintings. The servants' quarters were built around the atrium, entered from no. 3 Via di Nola.

The north wall of the room to the south-west of the atrium was decorated with the famous *lararium* painting depicting Bacchus in the form of a bunch of grapes with a thyrsus and a panther, with a vineyard-covered mountain, interpreted as Vesuvius, in the background. This picture, and the statue of a young satyr at the edge of the pool in the peristyle, suggest that the Rustia family, which owned this luxurious residence, also owned vineyards on the slopes of Vesuvius from which they obtained the wealth that they flaunted in town.

123 top This painting, in the centre of the south wall of the triclinium, portrays a scene from Euripides' tragedy, Iphigenia in Tauris; it shows a discussion between Iphigenia, on the podium of a temple, Orestes sitting on a pedestal, and Pylades leaning on it a little further back.

123 bottom This painting, in the centre of the east wall of the procurator's triclinium, portrays Hermaphroditus raising a torch in his right hand and pouring wine from a tankard with his left hand. He is accompanied by a Silenus playing the lyre and a bacchante with a tambourine.

122 bottom left This flying bacchante on a yellow background (in the procurator's triclinium) is carrying a trayful of offerings in her left hand. These figures, which were very common in the Pompeiian figurative repertoire, filled the side panels and secondary parts of the walls.

122 bottom right This bacchante, holding a tray in her left hand, also comes from the triclinium. These figures were often painted in an impressionist style, with no preparatory drawing.

THE HOUSE OF MARCUS LUCRETIUS FRONTO (V-4-A)

This house was excavated in 1899–1900 under the direction of G. de Petra, who decided to roof it immediately in order to preserve the paintings and mosaics – partly because this was part of his overall plan (restoration of rooms and roofings to restore the original lighting to the house), and partly because of the beauty of the paintings that emerged from the volcanic ash. It is not known if the design of the beams put in at this time corresponds exactly to the originals, but the archaeologist was aided in this philological restoration by the studies of ancient carpentry conducted by F. Mazois. His actions, however, aroused such controversy,

that he abandoned the task and did not return until 1905.

Marcus Lucretius Fronto was the probable owner of this house, as suggested by the electoral slogans which appear along the road leading to the entrance of the house. One reads: '*Si pudor in vita quicquam prodesse putatur Lucretius hic Fronto dignus honore bono est*' (If modesty in life is believed to be of any use, then Lucretius Fronto who lives here is worthy of this great honour). The anonymous writer of this slogan evidently admired Lucretius Fronto for his modesty, while other inscriptions also state that he was *fortis et honestus* (strong and honest). These qualities led his neighbours to advise voters to elect him to the office of aedile: '*M(arcum) Lucretium Frontonem aed(ilem) vicini rogamus*' (We

floor, where the socket for the beam used to bar the door is still visible, leads into the attractive atrium, which has a strikingly intimate atmosphere. The walls are frescoed in the 3rd style, with a black background and panels framed by a white border, decorated in the centre with small hunting scenes and animals such as swans and griffins. The panels are separated by pilaster strips with a yellow background and a very delicate, vertical pattern. In the upper part, the wall is decorated with symmetrical, slender architectural patterns. The lava cement floor is decorated with scattered marble tesserae and a regular pattern of small geometrical slabs of multicoloured marble, alternating with rows of rosettes consisting of five white tesserae. In the middle of the atrium stands a marble *impluvium* with shaped

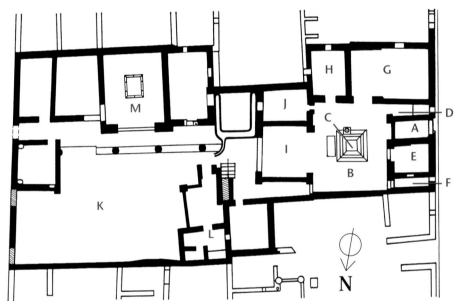

neighbours call for M. Lucretius Fronto to be elected aedile). The small but elegant and exquisitely decorated house stood in a secluded position in a small street adjacent to Via di Nola, on the north side. Its irregular shape is due to a complex history that included complete rebuilding of the house in the age of Augustus (late first century BC to early first century AD), while the restoration work performed after the earthquake of AD 62 involved only repair work and restoration of the paintings. The façade of the house, the whole of which was covered with white plaster, is protected by a canopy roof in which all the holes made for the beams are still visible. The slightly sloping vestibule, which has an *opus signinum*

A   Vestibule
B   Atrium
C   Impluvium
D   Larder
E   Cubiculum
F   Staircase
    to top floor
G   Triclinium
H   Cubiculum
I   Tablinum
J   Cubiculum
K   Peristyle
L   Kitchen
M   Triclinium

124 top Its unified decorative system makes this house very elegant. Most of the walls in the atrium and the tablinum are decorated in the 3rd style, creating continuity of form and demonstrating a well-designed decorative scheme.

sides, which received water from the matching *compluvium* above it. Two perfectly preserved holes can be seen in the corners, one of which filled the tank below, while the other conveyed overflow water out of the house through a channel laid under the floor. The *impluvium* is framed by a black and white mosaic portraying a two-ended plait. On the west side of the atrium, beyond the vestibule, there was a larder to the south and a *cubiculum* in the centre, which also had 3rd-style decorations, but with a white background. Its magnificent black and white mosaic floor consists of a threshold with five pairs of small shields and a carpet of four-pointed stars. To the north is the steep, narrow staircase

which led to the upper floor, built over the rooms along on the façade.

On the south side there were two more magnificent rooms: a large tricliniar room and a smaller *cubiculum*. The triclinium, with the couch recesses, was repainted in the 4th style after the earthquake. The yellow colour of the panels dominates, and there is a magnificent picture in the middle of the east wall portraying the episode from Euripides' tragedy, *Andromache*, in which Neoptolemus is slain at the Temple of Apollo in Delphi by Orestes, who then kidnaps his wife Hermione.

The *cubiculum* is frescoed in the 3rd style like the atrium, but the décor is far superior. The wainscot, with its purple background decorated with crosses, is

124 bottom The south wall of the tablinum features a precise linear perspective, although the structures are starting to become unreal and imaginary. In the middle area, the spaces created are filled at the sides with candelabra supporting paintings of maritime villas; a painting associated with the myth of Venus and Mars appears to hang in the centre.

125 The central panel contained the most important painting; this one, which dominated the centre of the north wall of the tablinum, portrayed Mars and Venus on the left; in the centre, Eros and groups of servant girls watch the scene.

surmounted by a predella which contains vignettes of theatrical masks and pairs of birds; the central vignette depicts a *hortus conclusus* with wooden fences. The central part is divided into panels; the side panels are separated by silver candelabra surmounted by sphinxes, and the central panel by carved ivory columns. The upper part depicts delicate imaginary buildings. The central pictures, representing Theseus and Ariadne and Venus at her Toilet are especially distinctive. Between the *impluvium* and the *tablinum* there was a rectangular marble table with lions' feet. The *tablinum* was also decorated in the 3rd style, but the quality of the frescoes is superior here. Pictures of the Triumph of Bacchus and the Loves of Mars and Venus dominate the central panels, while *pinakes* (a kind of painting portraying seaside

sanctuaries and villas) hang at the sides from elaborate candelabra. The door jambs of the *tablinum* imitate the wooden panels that usually lined the corners of rooms. To the left of the *tablinum* is the passage to the garden, and there is another attractive *cubiculum* to the right, this time frescoed in the 4th style and predominantly yellow in colour. The panels are separated by strange twisted columns; flying cherubs adorn the middle of the side panels, while the central panels bear a figure painting. The myth of Narcissus contemplating his reflection appears on the north wall, and, again, probably from Ovid, the myth of Pero breastfeeding her imprisoned father Mico, on the south wall. The latter, which represents an example of devotion, bears the following inscription on a green

background: '*Tristis inest cum pietate pudor*' (In misfortune, modesty is confronted with filial duty). Finally, the west wall with the entrance door in the middle is decorated with two portraits, one female and one male with the attributes of Mercury, which may have portrayed the children of M. Lucretius Fronto. Behind the *tablinum* lies the peristyle, whose south wall features a portico with some rooms giving onto it, and whose north wall is painted with hunting scenes in an exotic setting with life-sized animals. In the north-west corner were the kitchen, the latrine, and a staircase, which led to the upper floor of this part of the house. The rooms leading off the portico include a large triclinium decorated in the 4th style with figure paintings of Pyramus and Thisbe, and Dionysus accompanied by a Silenus playing the lyre.

126 left The painting in the middle of the north wall of the cubiculum *next to the* tablinum *portrays the myth of Narcissus, who fell in love with his own reflection. Numerous depictions of this myth appear in Pompeii.*

126 top right This painting, in the right-hand panel of the south wall, hangs from a candelabrum and portrays a series

of maritime villas, with a fishing boat and its crew in the foreground.

126 bottom right This painting, in the left-hand panel of the north wall of the tablinum, *portrays a multistorey suburban villa built on three sides, with a garden in the middle. Landscapes were very popular, as they seemed to open a window in the walls.*

THE NOLA GATE AND THE NECROPOLIS

A *The Nola Gate*
B *The ring road*
C *The tomb of Aesquillia Polla*
D *Anonymous tomb*
E *Bustum*
F *The tomb of M. Obellius Firmus*
G *Graves of praetorian guards*
H *Villa*

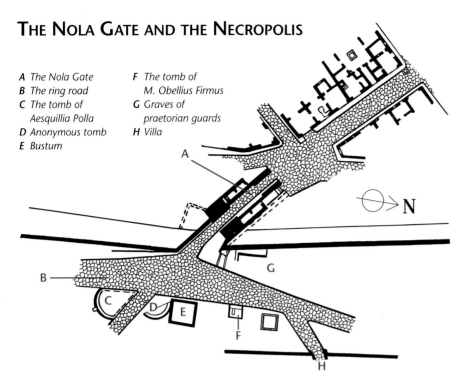

127 left The paved road that led out of the town crossed the ring road; on the east side of this crossroads there were two tombs – the tomb of Aesquillia Polla and an anonymous tomb. The latter, which stood in the north-east corner of the crossroads, had an Ionic column with a four-sided capital surmounted by an amphora which must have contained holy water in accordance with the usual funeral rites.

127 top right Via di Nola, like Via dell'Abbondanza, was a hive of activity, and was also a major route for the transport of goods into the town. Thermopolia and shops occupied almost all the façades of the insulae fronting onto the street.

127 bottom right The Orpheus crossroads, formed by Via di Stabia and Via di Nola, was just as important as the Holconius crossroads. Via di Nola, which separates Regiones V and IX, starts here and leads to the Nola Gate.

The Nola Gate stands at the eastern end of the road of the same name. It was identified in the 1813 excavations, and much of it was excavated between 1907 and 1908, when a portion of the ring road around the town and the street leading into the plain to the east were also identified, together with the structures of two *schola* tombs and an enclosure. Exploration of this area was continued in 1975 and 1978; in the last dig, the tomb of Obellius Firmus, four graves of praetorian guards and a *peribolos* wall, probably belonging to a villa, were found. The gate as it appears today was built no earlier than the third century BC, but in the absence of specific archaeological investigations, an older phase cannot be ruled out. An inscription in Oscan on the façade states that *meddix tuticus*, Vibius Popidius sponsored the construction of the gate, and tested it himself. The gate is decorated with tuff *opus quadratum* and has barrel vaults made of *opus caementicium*; the keystone of the inner façade features a tuff head of Minerva, which was quite usual in Italic towns and perhaps demonstrates the desire of the citizens to place the town gates under the protection of a deity. The gate stands well back from the line of the walls, and the road that led to it from the outside was fairly steep. This was part of the defence system; an enemy intending to attack the gate would have to climb a steep hill flanked by two ramparts which, when fully armed, would make it very difficult to approach the gate.

The road leading out of the town was paved and lined with narrow pavements edged with blocks of basalt. It ran straight to the east, crossed the whole eastern plain of the town and joined the consular road (Via Popilia), which skirted Mount Monterone where the River Sarnus begins. It also crossed the ring road (also paved), which surrounds the town and runs almost parallel to the walls. To the west side, the road overlooked the walls, in the *pomoerium* area of the town, which could not be occupied by buildings, partly for reasons of defence. The tombs were situated to the east side of the road.

The most important tomb is situated to the north: it comprises a quadrangular enclosure, whose entrance is surmounted by a pediment bearing an inscription stating that Marcus Obellius Firmus was buried there: 'To Marcus Obellius Firmus, son of Marcus, aedile, duumvir and judge. Here the *decurions* decreed the place of burial and donated 5,000 sesterces for the funeral rites. The inhabitants of the district donated 30 librae (approximately 22lb.) of incense and a *clipeus* (a shield bearing a portrait of the deceased). The ministers of the district donated 1,000 sesterces for perfumes and a *clipeus*.' This shows the great importance of Obellius Firmus during the last years of Pompeii's existence.

REGIO VI

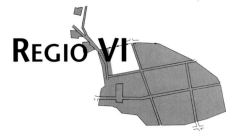

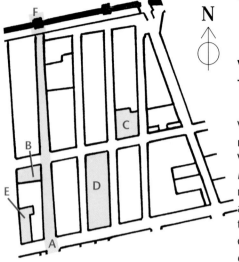

A *Via di Mercurio*
B *The House of the Small Fountain*
C *The House of the Vettii*
D *The House of the Faun*
E *The House of the Tragic Poet*
F *The Tower of Mercury*

128 bottom The road is named after the fountain near the House of the Small Fountain; the post that surmounts the basin features a relief decoration with the bust of Mercury wearing a winged hat and holding the caduceus.

128 top Via di Mercurio was closed to vehicular traffic in the first century AD, as demonstrated by the blocks and the archway known as the Arch of Caligula situated at the crossroads with Via delle Terme. The pavements and the façades of the patrician homes in the street were recently restored.

VIA DI MERCURIO AND THE TOWER OF MERCURY

Via di Mercurio is the main north-south road, along which the whole of Regio VI was built, and the two rows of *insulae* lining the road represent the main residential district. The appearance of the road is enhanced by the fact that the façades were mainly decorated with, or made of, *opus quadratum*, and it is bounded to the north by the imposing Tower of Mercury and to the south by the triumphal arch, both of which are described below. Excavated in the first half of the nineteenth century, this was long considered one of the oldest areas of urban expansion, dating from as early as the fourth century BC. Recent studies, however, date the building of luxurious private dwellings at a period no earlier than the second century BC. The road is named after a public fountain situated halfway along the road. The fountain has a square, Vesuvius lava slab basin and, on the pillar that contained the ancient water pipe, it features a relief head of Mercury with his caduceus and winged hat.

The road, which runs north-south, is situated right in the middle of Regio VI, and connects the Civil Forum area with the north walls of the town. It was closed to vehicular traffic for the last few decades of the town's existence, and is bounded to the south by an *opus latericium* triumphal arch which was originally faced with marble slabs and probably surmounted by a team of four horses drawing Victory in a chariot. To the north stands the imposing Tower of Mercury, designed to defend the northern sector, over a third of which towers above the city walls. Visitors today can see the whole town from the terrace of the tower, crenellated in ancient times, once employed for keeping watch over the huge territory to the north, which was full of villas and

covered with vines. The tower is built on three levels joined by staircases; the intermediate level gave access to the passageway along the walls that connected it to the other towers on this side of the city.

The loveliest houses in Pompeii, such as the House of the Small Fountain, the House of Apollo, the House of Meleager and the House of Castor and Pollux, front onto Via di Mercurio. There are a few shops along this road, nearly all of them at the southern end, which highlights the residential nature of this district. Some experts believe this was one of the oldest streets in Pompeii. With the aid of archaeological surveys, A. Maiuri found traces of a city gate which gave onto the cultivated land outside the walls to the north, where the tower now stands. All the villas situated to the north of the town, like the Villa of the Mosaic Columns, the Villa of Diomedes and the Villa of Cicero are aligned with Via di Mercurio, as the plots of agricultural land probably were. This road is still one of those most frequented by tourists, with the result that the street and all the façades have had to be restored, and the *opus signinum* pavements repaired.

Regio VI, which occupies the north-western part of Pompeii, slopes gently down towards the Civil Forum. It is built around Via di Mercurio which runs north-south, dividing the *regio* in half. The area is made up of two rows of *insulae* separated by a side road parallel to the Via delle Terme and Via della Fortuna Augusta stretch of the *decumanus*. It was a mainly residential area, although there were also some business premises, *tabernae* and *thermopolia*. The most important members of the nobility, both old and new, lived in this district, and it is here that the most significant buildings were found – the House of the Golden Cupids, the House of Pansa, the House of Apollo, the House of Castor and Pollux, for example – together with numerous works of art currently on display in the National Museum in Naples. Of the many houses worthy of attention, the ones selected in this chapter are best known, described on the basis of recent archaeological and historical research.

The House of the Small Fountain (VI-8-23)

This house, excavated between 1826 and 1827 by A. Bonucci, is named after the mosaic fountain situated in the small *viridarium* at the end of the house. The owner may have been one Helvius Vestalis, mentioned in an election manifesto written on the façade of the house, which reads: '*Pomari universi cum Helvio Vestale rogant…*' (All the fruiterers vote for [Holconius Priscus] together with Helvius Vestalis). The owner of this house may therefore have been the patron of the fruiterers' guild. The house consists of two distinct sections, which

129 top In order to further expand the axial perspective of the House of the Small Fountain, and to break up its narrow spaces, the decorator used the device of a large trompe l'œil *peristyle with a coloured mosaic fountain in the middle, ornamented with small bronze statues.*

129 bottom The ala *in the north-west corner of the atrium is elegantly frescoed with imaginary architectural structures against a white background; the wainscot is painted almost entirely yellow. The panels, compartments and architectural structures are decorated with priests and offerors with sacred objects.*

were originally separate houses built in the second half of the second century BC; they were combined in the age of Augustus, and connected only by two narrow passages. After they were combined, the quarters to the north of the house were probably used by servants, and those in the southern part by the owner. Much of the pictorial and mosaic decoration was renewed at this time. The house was badly damaged in the earthquake of AD 62, but the damage was soon repaired, and nearly all the walls were redecorated in the 4th style. Unfortunately, by the time it was excavated, only a few rooms were roofed; this preserved their fine frescoes, while the frescoes which would have decorated the rest of the house have practically disappeared.

The succession of rooms usual in Italic houses, alternately situated in the shade and open to the sunlight, can be seen at a glance from the road. These were the vestibule, the atrium with *compluvium*, the *tablinum* and the peristyle, which had a beautiful mosaic fountain on the back wall. The façade was stuccoed with *opus quadratum*, imitating houses with severe, noble façades made of square blocks of grey Nuceria tuff. The vestibule is on a gentle upward slope and made of *opus signinum,* decorated with a regular pattern of white tesserae. On its right-hand side is a staircase leading to the upper floor. The next room is a very high Tuscan atrium. The bottom and sides of the *impluvium* are missing; it was probably being remade at the time of the eruption, since two channels leading from the garden, which must have contained the pipes conveying water from the peristyle, can clearly be seen in the lava cement floor. The floor is decorated with rows of large marble tesserae. Rainwater from the peristyle and *compluvium* filled a large tank below, from which water was drawn through a marble opening in the side.

The atrium walls were decorated with a red wainscot and panels with a white background; sadly, the flying figures originally portrayed in the middle have been lost. The south wall is very unusual: it is decorated with three *trompe l'œil* closed doors, probably to create a symmetrical effect with the real doors on the north side. These open into an antechamber to the east, which led into the neighbouring house, a

A	Vestibule	I	Anteroom
B	Atrium	J	Ala
C	Impluvium	K	Oecus
D	Tablinum	L	Triclinium
E	Peristyle	M	Vestibule
F	Mosaic fountain	N	Atrium
G	Staircase to top	O	Tablinum
	floor	P	Kitchen
H	Cubiculum		

N

cubiculum in the centre and, to the west, an *ala* which served as a waiting room for the *tablinum*.

To the left of the vestibule is a magnificent reception room (*oecus*) with elegant 4th-style decorations, again with a red wainscot surmounted by an imaginary architectural structure on a white background, but this time featuring picturesque landscapes in the middle of the central panels, painted in an impressionistic style by a very skilled artist. The *tablinum* must also have been magnificent, but all that remains of it is the black and white mosaic floor, which has a wide border of meanders and swastikas. The slab inserted into the face of the step leading to the *tablinum* is particularly interesting; it features a relief head of the Egyptian god, Amun, among acanthus plants.

The peristyle is not particularly large. The east and north sides are porticoed with slender Doric columns, and there are two false porticoes on the south and east sides formed by Doric half-columns. The walls of the false peristyle are frescoed with large landscapes depicting a harbour, seaside villas and temples. The fountain consisted of an apsidal niche with a double-pitched roof. The niche was completely covered with a coloured mosaic decoration made of marble and glass paste tesserae and shells, while the edges of the basin were covered in marble. Water gushed through a comedy mask on the wall of the apse, and from a bronze statue of a cherub holding a goose, standing on a pedestal.

THE HOUSE OF THE VETTII (VI-15-1)

130 top left
The choice of architectural elements, and their symmetrical arrangement around the axis on which the vestibule, atrium and peristyle are situated, create an attractive expanded perspective, which highlights the areas of light and shade.

130 bottom left
The wealth of the house is demonstrated not only by the elegant wall decorations but also by the numerous garden furnishings, found practically intact. These include marble herms and magnificent bronze statues of cherubs pouring water into the fountains in the middle of the short sides of the garden.

The House of the Vettii, excavated between 1894 and 1895 by G. de Petra, caused a sensation because of its exquisite 4th-style decorations with their wealth of paintings and mythological figures, its abundance of bronze and marble statues and sculptures, and its overall architectural design.

Its magnificent state of preservation is partly due to the fact that, after the earthquake of AD 62, high-quality materials were used to restore and redecorate the house. Another important factor is that, despite being identified by raiders after the eruption, for some unknown reason, the house was not stripped and, therefore many of the works of art were found in situ. In view of the excellent condition of the house and the desire to leave everything in its place, the excavation director planned to restore and roof it immediately. This decision was a controversial one; some experts were '… concerned on the one hand by the difficulties and dangers of conservation on site, and on the other by excessive innovation and excavation …' These doubts slowed down the restoration work, which was not completed until

1905–1906, causing the colours of the atrium and part of the peristyle to fade and deteriorate.

The house was owned by the Vettii family, as demonstrated by electoral slogans on the south wall of the house and two bronze seals found in the atrium near the safes built onto the south side. The first of these seals refers to A. Vettii Convivaes; the second, with an amphora, refers to A. Vettii Restituti. A. Vettii Convivaes is also known as a witness on the waxed tablets of banker Caecilius Jucundus, and as a member of the College of Augustales.

The Vettii were a family of freedmen and members of the emerging class that ran the town from the reign of Augustus on, especially after the earthquake of AD 62. The members of this wealthy family were probably landowners and traders in wine and various agricultural products.

At the time of the eruption, the house was a combination of at least two previously separate houses, both opening to the east. They were combined in the early first century AD and, after the earthquake, were almost completely restored and frescoed in the 4th style. It is a Tuscan atrium type house, with the peristyle on the same axis as the atrium, but with the long side perpendicular to it. The house occupies the southern part of Insula 15 in Regio VI, its main entrance is to the east and its back door to the south. The view looking from the atrium to the west of the portico appears to continue into a *trompe l'œil* wall decoration, which can be seen from the road.

130 right
The triclinium in the north-eastern corner of the peristyle is a compendium of mythology, depicted in the paintings which dominate the large panels in the middle area, as well as in the host of characters portrayed in the compartments and the upper area.

The paintings in the elaborate vestibule (A-B) depict a cockfight against a black background on the left, and a sheep with a bag and a caduceus (attributes of Mercury) on the right. Opposite, on the right-hand side of the entrance door, is an apotropaic male figure placing a bag of coins (wealth) on one scale-pan and a large phallus (health) on the other. Below, a large basket of fruit represents the abundance of the house. The atrium (C), philologically reconstructed as far as the roof is magnificently frescoed, and immediately demonstrates the style

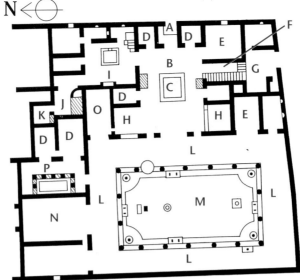

A Vestibule
B Atrium
C Impluvium
D Cubiculi
E Oecus
F Staircase to top floor
G Stable
H Alae
I Rustic quarters
J Kitchen
K Bed recess
L Portico
M Viridarium
N Room of the cherubs
O Triclinium
P Viridarium

130-131 The workshop that frescoed the oecus in the south-eastern corner of the peristyle evidently employed highly skilled decorators. This is evident, not so much in the magnificence of the whole, as the order and balance achieved between the parts. The architectural structures which fill the side panels are impressive for their geometrical rigour and the solidity of the volumes portrayed.

131 right In many patrician homes, the cult of the lares was conducted in an area situated between the servants' quarters and the owners' quarters. This magnificent frescoed lararium was located in the service atrium adjacent to the main atrium of the house.

of the house. Boys carrying objects relating to domestic cults are portrayed in windows against a black background on the wainscot; in borders above them, winged cherubs are engaged in a variety of activities relating to everyday life in the circus and the amphitheatre. Higher still, ornately decorated candelabra stand proud of the wall.

Two iron-covered safes decorated with bronze studs stood on masonry bases at the sides of the atrium. The floor of the atrium, like those of the rest of the house, is made mainly of opus signinum and lava cement, decorated with white tesserae. The vestibule is flanked by two cubiculi which also feature 4th-style decorations, but of lower quality. The left-hand cubiculum (D) is of particular interest: the wainscot has squares of fake marble, the middle section features alternate red and white panels with paintings of Ariadne abandoned by Theseus, Hero and Leander, and a frieze portraying a fish pond, and the upper zone portrays imaginary buildings.

The decorations of the *oecus* (E) in the south-east corner are of superior quality; above the wainscot, the middle and upper bands depict two different theatrical buildings on a white background, separated by a stucco cornice. There is a painting of the myth of Cyparissus in the central panel on the north wall; on the east wall there is a picture of Bacchus and Ariadne watching the battle between Pan and Cupid in the central panel, while Leda and the swan, Danae and Jupiter in the form of a shower of gold, and Jupiter

enthroned (or Alexander the Great portrayed as Helios?) are depicted in the upper part.

In the middle of the south side is a long, narrow room which contained the staircase to the upper floor and gave access to service rooms, which probably included a stable, as harnesses were found there. To the west of the atrium are two *alae* frescoed in a similar way to the atrium; here, paintings of cockfights dominate. In the north-east corner of the atrium is an opening to the rustic sector, which features a small atrium containing a *compluvium* (V), whose basin is made of tuff slabs. A staircase to the upper floor is situated on the east side, and there is a magnificent *lararium* opposite, which was probably used by both the servants and the owners of the house. This is

followed by the kitchen (W), where bronze pans still stand on metal tripods on the cinders, and a room (I) decorated with erotic paintings and an ithyphallic statue of a young man. The atrium leads into a magnificent garden with a four-sided portico, where the *viridarium* echoed to the sound of fountains playing on all four sides and in the middle of the garden. The garden was ornamented with a wide range of garden sculptures, including numerous bronze and marble statues, benches, pillars surmounted by herms and marble basins.

The Corinthian colonnade supports an architrave which had a simple border with a white background on the inside; on the outside it was decorated with a magnificent frieze of acanthus volutes stuccoed on a red background, but this

132 top This painting, on the south wall of the oecus, portrays the episode in the punishment of Dirce when Amphion and Zethus, having captured the bull, prepare to tie the unfortunate Dirce to it.

132 bottom This painting on the north wall of the triclinium depicts the moment when Daedalus shows Pasiphaë the wooden heifer he has designed as a disguise for her to mate with the bull sent by Zeus. Behind them, an old nurse points out the inventor's creation to a horrified girl. The scene takes place in the workshop.

132-133 The compartments in the triclinium feature small paintings of naumachiae surmounted by baskets containing ritual objects and theatre masks; in this case the mask is a tragedy mask and the basket contains a cantharus, a drinking horn, and a phallus covered with a purple cloth.

133 top This painting, which seems to suggest that good health is worth its weight in gold, is on the right-hand anta of the fauces at the entrance of the house.

133 bottom The atrium is richly decorated with frescoes relating to cockfighting; in this case, in the north ala, three defeated cocks are on the left, while the winner perches on a gilded goblet on the right. Sacred objects and the statuette of an athlete are laid out on the table behind them.

has been lost. Along the intercolumniations, the stylobate is decorated with various patterns traced with black and white tesserae on a background of *opus signinum*. The walls of the peristyle, also decorated in the 4th style had a paratactic design, with panels and compartments ornamented by paintings, still lifes, mythical characters, flying figures, animals and sketches of landscapes. On the far right of the north side is a landscape of a moonlit rural sanctuary set against a black background, which is exceptionally well executed.

The loveliest rooms of the house give onto the peristyle. The *oecus* (N) to the south of the east side looks magnificent, especially when it is bathed in late afternoon sunlight. Large paintings depicting the legends of Hercules

strangling the serpents, Pentheus stoned by the bacchantes, and the punishment of Dirce by Antiope's sons Amphion and Zethus, are situated in an architectural structure with unusual perspective views. On the opposite side there is a spectacular drawing room (P) with three large paintings: Pasiphaë with Daedalus giving her the wooden cow; Ixion in the underworld, bound to the wheel by Vulcan by order of Juno; and Bacchus finding Ariadne on Naxos and making her his companion. The room owes its magnificence as much to the structural characteristics of the decorations, as to the elegant, multicoloured effects and variety of themes and subjects portrayed in the paintings.

The large triclinium (Q), to which the house owes its fame, opens onto the middle of the north side of the portico. Its significance is mainly due to the exquisite frieze of cherubs against a black background, comprising nine small masterpieces, which must have enchanted banqueting guests. Starting from the left-hand door, the scenes depict: cherubs engaged in an archery competition; picking flowers and making garlands; manufacturing and purchasing perfumes; a race between chariots pulled by deer; minting coins; baking bread; harvesting and treading grapes; a festival in honour of Bacchus and Ariadne; buying and selling wine.

Beneath the candelabra, on a black

134 top This two-headed marble herm depicting Dionysus, stands on a post decorated with flowers and leaves, and was a garden ornament.

134-135 One of the most interesting human activities portrayed on the predella in the drawing room is perfume making. Here, a pair of cherubs crush the essences, others steep them, and yet others try them out on a seated psyche.

background, decorating the compartments between the panels, are some small paintings which are particularly outstanding. They represent Iphigenia in Tauris between Thoas, Orestes and Pylades, Apollo and Diana after the killing of the python, and Agamemnon on the point of sacrificing Iphigenia in Aulis. The large panels with a red background feature pairs of flying figures, which, though very effective, cannot compare with the quality and beauty of those on the black background.

To the east of the triclinium is a small secluded *viridarium* (S) with two living rooms adjacent to it. The larger one (T) is decorated in the 4th style,

and contains two well-executed paintings: Achilles recognised by Ulysses among the daughters of Lycomedes, and Augeas surprised by the drunken Hercules.

The House of the Vettii is the most frequently visited building in Pompeii, but, while this shows its great fascination for visitors of all generations, the number of people who walk through its rooms every year has caused serious deterioration.

134 bottom The atrium walls present a series of lovely sketches of cherubs. This delightful fresco is part of the decoration of the

room. It portrays a wine vendor offering a taste to a purchaser; in the meantime, two others are pouring more wine from an amphora.

135 top On another wall of the atrium, a cherub seems to be riding a harnessed crab and urging it on with a whip.

135 bottom This bacchante's face, part of another two-headed herm, had the face of a satyr on the other side. It stood on a marble column in the garden.

135

THE HOUSE OF THE FAUN (VI-12-2)

The House of the Faun, excavated by A. Bonucci between 1830 and 1832, is so called because of the bronze statuette of a dancing faun, found on a marble pedestal on the northern side of the *impluvium*. The statuette is now housed in the National Museum in Naples, and has been replaced in Pompeii with a copy, erroneously placed on a pedestal in the middle of the *impluvium*. With a floor area of approximately 3,000 square metres, this is the largest private house in Pompeii, together with the House of Pansa (VI-6-1), and like the latter it occupies a whole *insula*. The house as it appears today was largely built in the first half of the second century BC (180–170 BC), after the demolition of a small dwelling which dated from the third century BC and had occupied the centre of the *insula*.

The house was extensively

Augusta, but the original passage was retained. The house was redecorated, but still in a late form of the 1st style, as if to emphasise the austerity of this large home.

The most significant alteration was the laying of finely worked coloured mosaics (the tesserae are often no more than half a square centimetre) inspired by Alexander the Great. The most outstanding is the mosaic portraying Alexander between the first and second peristyles in the large *exedra*.

Throughout the life of the house, its owners, instead of renewing the decorations in accordance with the current style, carefully preserved the original decoration, restored it when required, and completed it when new areas were built.

The façade featured a row of shops separated by large pillars made of grey tuff with pilaster strips (or half-columns, as has recently been suggested) decorated with reliefs in the centre. At the entrance, the greeting 'HAVE' is traced in coloured tesserae on

136 left The transverse peristyle with Ionic columns and the garden with geometrically designed flower beds made this part of the house very elegant. A marble fountain with a circular basin stood in the middle of the unroofed area.

136 right The large entrance featured two Corinthian antae supporting a massive moulded architrave. The greeting 'HAVE' (welcome) was picked out in large marble crustae on the floor.

restructured towards the end of the second century BC. The *hortus* was turned into a second large peristyle of the Doric order, with a series of small rooms on the north side, while the transverse peristyle was made Ionic; the baths complex was moved to the kitchen area no.24, and in the next room, a triclinium opening onto the second peristyle was made. An additional entrance leading into the area of the second atrium was built at shop no.5 on Via della Fortuna

the lava cement pavement studded with white *crustae*. The entrance to the house is flanked by two pilasters with tuff capitals. The vestibule is decorated in the 1st style; two tetrastyle shrines with Corinthian columns on a pedestal, all made of stucco and coloured, are built against the walls on a projecting cornice decorated with coffers. The *opus sectile* floor is made of triangles of coloured marble and on the edge adjacent to the atrium, has a threshold of *opus vermiculatum* mosaic depicting

136-137 The large atrium, on the same axis as the tablinum and the 1st-style wall decoration, gave the house a noble appearance. The impluvium in the centre had marble sides, and the bottom was decorated with coloured diamonds.

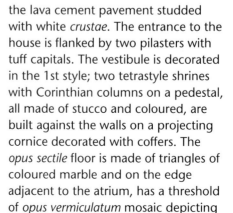

a garland with masks. The atrium walls were finished with 1st-style structural decoration, creating the illusion of an upper floor. In the centre, the sides of the exquisite *impluvium* were made of *palombino* marble and its base was made of *opus sectile* formed by diamonds of slate, *palombino* and coloured limestone.

At the sides of the atrium are various *cubiculi*, also decorated in the structural

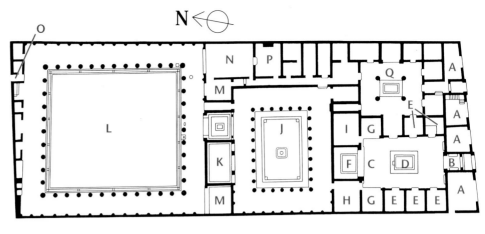

N

O

N P

M

L

Q

A

E

K

J

I G

F C D

B

A

A

A

H G E E E

A

A Shops
B Vestibule
C Atrium
D Impluvium
E Cubiculi
F Tablinum
G Alae
H Anteroom
I Oecus
J Transverse peristyle
K Exedra of the Alexander mosaic
L Peristyle
M Oeci
N Triclinium
O Posticum
P Bathing area
Q Servants' quarters

137 bottom The large, coloured mosaic decorating the floor of the distyle *exedra* between the two peristyles is of outstanding pictorial and compositional quality. It represents Alexander the Great confronting Darius at the Battle of Issus.

138-139 This illustration shows how the Tuscan atrium in the House of the Faun must have looked: brightly coloured walls decorated in the 1st style, a crushed lava floor ornamented with marble tesserae, and the impluvium, *made of* opus sectile *with a pattern of coloured diamond shapes, in the centre. The famous bronze statue, now on display in the National Museum in Naples, once stood at the edge of the* impluvium.

137

1st style. The one in the south-eastern corner has an unusual mosaic floor with an *opus vermiculatum emblema* portraying an erotic encounter between a satyr and a nymph. The *alae* serving the *tablinum* had floors beautifully decorated with an *emblema* set in coloured marble *crustae*. The *emblema* on the right depicts a cat sinking its teeth into a chicken and Nile ducks with a haul of river fish, while the one on the left portrays three white doves removing a pearl necklace from a drawer.

The rooms on either side of the *tablinum* contain two outstanding examples of *emblema* made from coloured *opus vermiculatum* mosaic; the one in the room to the east is in a square frame with a garland and theatrical masks, and portrays Dionysus as a winged boy riding a tiger with a lion's head, and the one in the room to the west shows an octopus ensnaring a lobster and a number of sea creatures.

The *tablinum*, which had door jambs in the form of fluted pillars of imitation marble, repeated on either side of the large window onto the transverse peristyle, had a particularly solemn and austere appearance. The floor was decorated with coloured diamonds of *opus sectile*, arranged in an illusional cube pattern, as in the shrines of the Temple of Apollo and the Temple of Jupiter; the central section was preceded by a coloured mosaic threshold with an axonometric meander pattern. On the north side, slightly off-centre in relation to the width of the *insula*, but on the same axis as the *tablinum*, atrium and vestibule, is a magnificent *exedra* containing the famous mosaic of the Battle of Alexander. On the south wall, the *exedra* has two slender Corinthian columns of grey tuff standing on a

pedestal between two Corinthian *anta* pillars with beautiful, red-plastered capitals. On the north side, the *exedra* overlooks the second peristyle through a large window with a low parapet almost as wide as the whole wall. The large mosaic of Alexander was preceded by a long threshold divided into three, with creatures of the Nile in the centre and Egyptian-style ducks of coloured *opus vermiculatum* mosaic on either side. Inside is the large mosaic, estimated to consist of about a million and a half, very fine coloured tesserae. The mosaic, made in situ, represents the Battle of Issus between Alexander and Darius, with the defeat and flight of Darius.

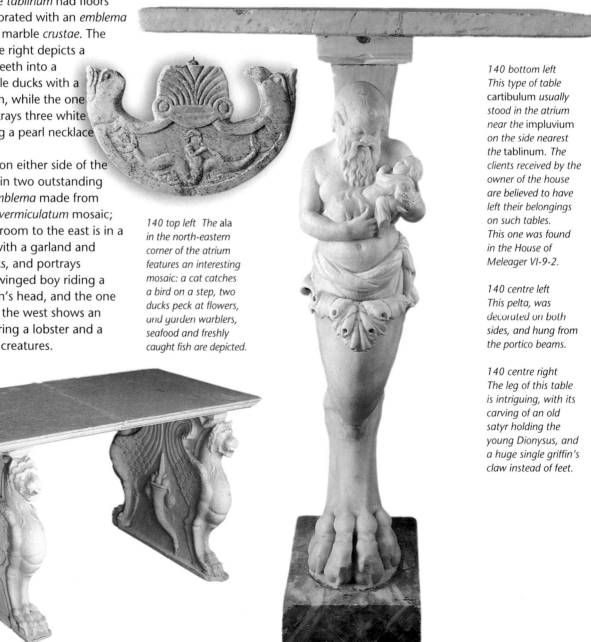

140 top left The ala in the north-eastern corner of the atrium features an interesting mosaic: a cat catches a bird on a step, two ducks peck at flowers, und gurden warblers, seafood and freshly caught fish are depicted.

140 bottom left This type of table cartibulum usually stood in the atrium near the impluvium on the side nearest the tablinum. The clients received by the owner of the house are believed to have left their belongings on such tables. This one was found in the House of Meleager VI-9-2.

140 centre left This pelta, was decoruted on both sides, and hung from the portico beams.

140 centre right The leg of this table is intriguing, with its carving of an old satyr holding the young Dionysus, and a huge single griffin's claw instead of feet.

FURNITURE

Pompeiian homes contained only the bare minimum of furniture. While the furniture in the humbler homes was spartan, in the wealthier residences it rivalled the wall decorations for beauty and artistic value.

The furniture was made of wood, marble and, more usually, bronze. One of the most common items was the couch, used as a bed in the *cubiculi* and as a sofa for conversations, reading, music and dining in the triclinia and drawing rooms.

Tables were also very common, and specimens of various materials and designs survive. Those in the atrium were generally made of marble, and were particularly elaborate. Cupboards and chests were mainly made of wood, and stood against the atrium walls.

The wealthiest homes were illuminated by bronze lamps placed on long-stemmed candelabra, or lanterns hanging from the ceiling. Fewer than 20 bronze lamps have been found in the whole of Pompeii. Homes were heated in winter by braziers and stoves, often designed to a high artistic standard.

141 top This bronze lamp, decorated with tragedy masks and a garland, would have been hung from a hook on the ceiling or from a candelabrum with a curved end.

141 centre top left The tripod of this hemispherical bronze basin is collapsible and decorated with griffins' heads and claws.

141 centre top right This table comprises a rectangular top on collapsible legs, which are held in place by crossbars and decorated with horses' heads and hooves.

141 centre bottom left Bronze chairs like this one often feature in wall paintings; the seat is flat and supported by four legs decorated with discs.

141 bottom Braziers were used to heat the various rooms of houses in winter, and this example is one of many excellent specimens found. The outer surfaces of the container are decorated with human faces, and the legs represent sphinxes.

141 centre bottom right This emblema, which portrays a lobster being caught by an octopus, under the astonished gaze of a variety of sea creatures, was featured in the room on the left of the tablinum. The picture is framed by an acanthus-leaf frieze.

The House of the Tragic Poet (VI-8-3)

This house is named after an *emblema* in the middle of the *tablinum*, which represents a theatrical scene with actors, musicians and stage sets. The owner was probably P. Aninius, who belonged to a family which appears to have established itself after 80 BC; in fact, a member of the family contributed to the rebuilding of the Stabian Baths. The house, which is not

of particularly large proportions, stands in the south-western corner of the *insula* and seems to have always covered the same site, with the only additions being the large drawing room and the kitchen, constructed on the east side of the peristyle during the later period. While the original construction appears to date from the second century BC, there is no doubt that the walls were entirely redecorated after the earthquake of AD 62, by the most skilled of all the artists working throughout the town to repair the earthquake damage.

The house was excavated under the direction of A. Bonucci in 1824–25. This was the period when all paintings and mosaics of any importance were removed to the National Archaeological Museum in Naples, thus stripping the houses of their most precious decorations, and the House of the Tragic Poet was no exception. This home, which was the Italic type, with a Tuscan atrium and its main rooms built on the same axis, stands opposite the Forum Baths

complex, on the *decumanus* leading from the Herculaneum Gate to the Nola Gate, which was a very busy road. In front of the entrance, the ornate *opus signinum* floor is decorated with large travertine tesserae. The grooves in the threshold indicate that there must have been two doors. The long vestibule walls were decorated with a red wainscot, surmounted by panels with a yellow background, divided up into compartments with a white background depicting a *trompe l'œil* wooden fence and a candelabrum. The floor was decorated with a regular pattern of black and white mosaic tesserae, with a double border of black. The section of floor nearest the entrance portrayed an almost life-sized brown dog with details such as the eyes, collar and chain picked out in coloured tesserae, and with the words 'CAVE CANEM' (beware of the dog) picked out in black tesserae on a white background underneath the picture.

The vestibule led through two small doors to the two large shops facing onto the road. The atrium was unusually luxurious; its walls largely repeat the pictorial scheme of the vestibule, with the addition of a frieze

of acanthus volutes above the middle zone, surmounted by battle scenes. The walls were decorated with excellent-quality paintings, nearly all of which relate to the Trojan cycle: the wedding of Jupiter and Juno, the departure of Chryseis, the handover of Briseis by Achilles, Venus with the dove, Poseidon and a cupid on a dolphin and, finally, a battle scene. Because the first three were in such excellent condition, they were removed and taken to the Naples Museum; the others, already in poor condition at the time of the excavation, have sadly been lost, although nineteenth-century documentary evidence survives. The atrium floor is similar to that of the vestibule: white mosaic with a pattern of large black tesserae, edged with a double strip of black. The attractive *impluvium* in the middle of the atrium has marble sides and base, edged with a black and white mosaic plait. On the north side of the *impluvium* is a marble well-head with fluted shaft and moulded edges. This was used to draw water from the tank below, which could be inspected through a cover in the side.

Various rooms give onto the atrium, including a *cubiculum* in the middle of

the west side, which contained a painting of the myth of Phrixus and Helle and a simple, 4th-style frieze of battle scenes between the Greeks and the Amazons. The *ala* in the north-east corner, which serves the *tablinum*, has a magnificent black and white mosaic floor with a threshold and a carpet section featuring geometrical patterns of squares. A steep, narrow staircase in the south-western corner of the atrium led to the upper floor, which was built across

over the front part of the house. The magnificent *tablinum* is completely open to the atrium and the peristyle, and is built on the same axis as the entrance and the atrium. The two remaining walls are decorated in the 4th style; on the east wall there was a painting of Admetus and Alcestis, and on the west wall is a door leading into a *cubiculum*. Here again, the floor is

magnificent: a mosaic picture of a musicians' rehearsal was framed with a double black meander against a white background.

The peristyle consisted of a three-sided portico with fluted Doric columns, the lower third of which were enlarged and painted red; iron cramps found here suggest that there would have been a wooden fence in the intercolumniations. On the unroofed end wall was a *trompe l'œil* wooden fence, but, sadly, the *paradeisos* (imaginary garden) within is no longer visible. A *lararium*, built in the form of a small temple with architectural components in stucco relief, is built on a tall podium onto the back wall of the *viridarium* to the west. Two *cubiculi* with 4th-style frescoes and *opus signinum* floors decorated with white tesserae, and a corridor leading to the back door of the house, give onto the west portico.

The famous painting of the Sacrifice of Iphigenia, on a red background with a carpet-pattern border, was situated under the east portico, on the back wall to the north. The kitchen with the latrine was to the right, and the large drawing

142 left This house, though not large, contains all the rooms of a typical Italic home. The focal point for people looking in from the street was the lararium *against the end wall of the* viridarium.

142 right The painting on the north wall of the east portico portrays the tragedy of Iphigenia in Aulis. Ulysses and Achilles take the girl as a sacrifice; the soothsayer Calchas, armed with a dagger, can be seen on the right; on the left, Agamemnon covers his head as he weeps, but in the heavens, Artemis is ready to replace Iphigenia with a deer.

143 top left The front of the vestibule is decorated with this mosaic realistically

portraying a chained dog. The warning 'CAVE CANEM' (beware of the dog) can be seen in the foreground.

143 bottom left This painting, on the south wall of the atrium, depicts the solemn wedding of Zeus and Hera on Mount Ida.

143 right The house is named after this mosaic picture, used as an emblema *in the* tablinum*; it shows actors preparing to perform a satyr drama – shown by the goatskin costumes worn by the two actors on the far left. A coreuta tries out a double flute in the middle; the choirmaster, wearing a himation, sits on a stool on the right and, in the background, a servant helps an actor to dress.*

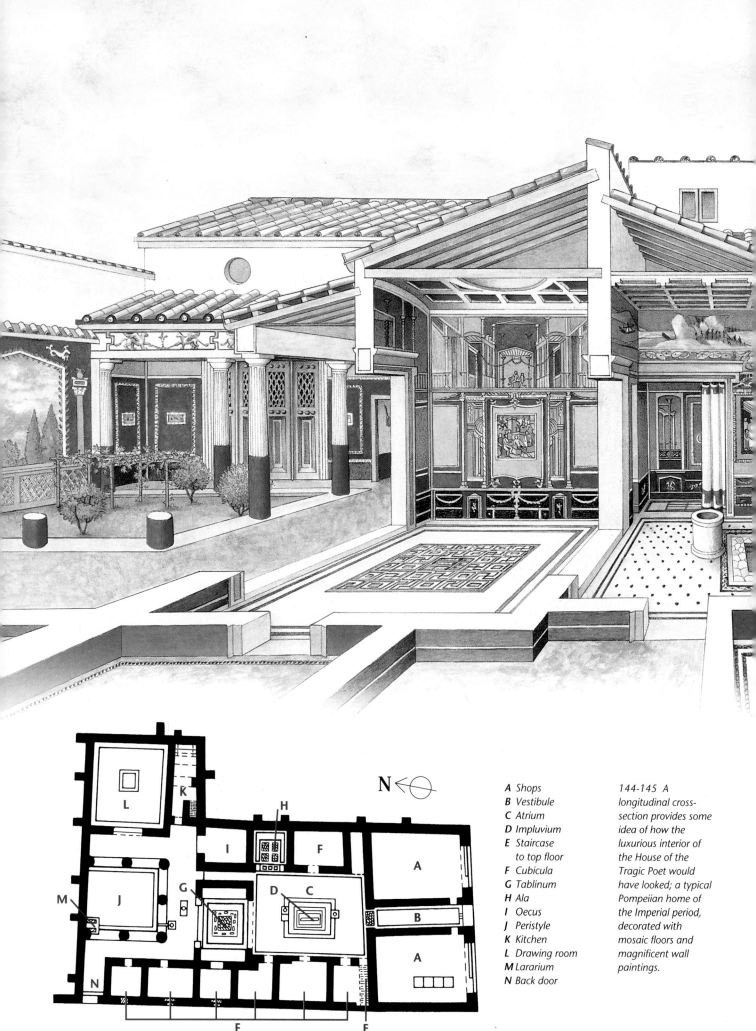

A Shops
B Vestibule
C Atrium
D Impluvium
E Staircase
  to top floor
F Cubicula
G Tablinum
H Ala
I Oecus
J Peristyle
K Kitchen
L Drawing room
M Lararium
N Back door

144-145 A longitudinal cross-section provides some idea of how the luxurious interior of the House of the Tragic Poet would have looked; a typical Pompeiian home of the Imperial period, decorated with mosaic floors and magnificent wall paintings.

room used as a triclinium, to the middle of this porticoed side. The floor of the drawing room is made of black and white mosaic surrounded by a double border of black with an *emblema* in the middle consisting of a complex geometrical pattern of fish and ducks in a frame of overlapping triangles.

The walls of the drawing room still retain their magnificent 4th-style decoration; a predella, divided into three by two pairs of pedestals, rests on the black wainscot, which is also divided into three by two stylised

pavilions. The central section is painted with a scene of centaurs hunting a lion. Slender columns, supporting a coffered *aedicule*, rise from the pedestals; the central picture on a yellow and red background hangs from the *aedicule* as if it were fixed to a tapestry drawn taut at the corners. At the sides there are other panels with flying figures. The upper section portrays imaginary buildings with seated deities and still lifes.

The paintings in the middle of the panels depict the sale of cherubs on the

north wall, Theseus abandoning Ariadne on the east wall, and Artemis and Callisto on the south wall. The House of the Tragic Poet provides a very good example of how the noble class, which emerged after the earthquake, decorated their homes, and the image they wished to convey to their fellow citizens. In fact, although it does not have an especially great floor area, this house, together with the House of the Vettii, contained more large paintings of mythological subjects than any other in Pompeii.

TOWARDS THE HERCULANEUM GATE

This part of Pompeii, situated along Via Consolare and Via delle Tombe, separated by the Herculaneum Gate, is one of the most fascinating; monuments line this ancient route, used by visitors to the town, especially the eighteenth- and nineteenth-century travellers, who, with their journals, drawings and watercolours, made Pompeii one of the most famous places in the world. The area's position gives it a wonderful panorama of the long, straight streets to the east, and the landscapes seen to the west.

This was also the first part of Pompeii to be excavated and, as such, has been badly damaged by exposure to the elements and, sadly, also by man. Nevertheless, it is an area steeped in dramatic, spectacular atmosphere, offering visitors a sense of history and the subtle pleasure of wandering among the ruins.

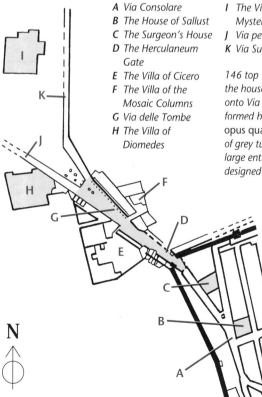

A Via Consolare
B The House of Sallust
C The Surgeon's House
D The Herculaneum Gate
E The Villa of Cicero
F The Villa of the Mosaic Columns
G Via delle Tombe
H The Villa of Diomedes
I The Villa of the Mysteries
J Via per Oplontis
K Via Superior

146 top The façade of the house that fronts onto Via Consolare was formed by impressive opus quadratum pillars of grey tuff. Shops with large entrances, designed to fit in with the architecture of the house, gave onto the road.

146 bottom The atrium and tablinum of the house still retain much of the structural 1st-style decoration which gave the area its solemn, severe appearance.

147 top After the mid-first century BC, a delightful three-sided portico, with two small rooms (diaetae) at the ends of the east and west sides, was built to replace a previously unroofed area. Most of the fresco portraying the myth of Diana and Actaeon on the back wall was lost as a result of bomb damage in the Second World War.

THE HOUSE OF SALLUST (VI-2-4)

The House of Sallust (VI-2-4), excavated between 1805 and 1809, is named after one C. Sallustius, who is nominated for election in an inscription found on the house's façade. However, the owner of the house is more likely to have been A. Cossius Libanus, a man probably of oriental descent, whose bronze seal was found in the house. When the house was excavated, its noble 1st-style decorations and the size of the living areas caused a sensation. It was originally built in the first half of the second century BC, in an area connecting the regular layout of the insulae in Regio VI with the road which ran diagonally north.

In its earliest incarnation, the structure was extremely austere and rational, and already very large; the façade was occupied by six square *tabernae* giving onto the street, with the vestibule between them. The domestic part of the house was regular in shape, with an atrium in the centre, the *tablinum* on the same axis as the entrance, flanked by twin *oeci*, *alae* at right angles to the *tablinum* and *cubiculi* at the sides; finally, a kitchen with a well for domestic needs was located in the south-west corner of the atrium. The area between the house and the boundary walls was used as a simple domestic garden, with a side exit in the east boundary wall.

Extensive modifications were made to this original layout some time after the foundation of Sulla's colony (80 BC), including the addition of a three-sided portico with magnificent fluted Ionic columns of Sarnus stone. The final transformation took place after the earthquake of AD 62, when the noble residence was turned into an inn. The two shops to the sides of the entrance were connected to the atrium and transformed into *thermopolia*; the north side of the portico was closed off to create more rooms and an upper storey, and a summer *thermopolium* was constructed in the north-eastern corner of the garden. The rooms surrounding the peristyle in the southern part of the garden made up the private part of the house. Finally, the south-west corner which became a *thermopolium*, and the north-west corner which became a bakery, were detached from the house.

This is how the house looks today. The façade, made of *opus quadratum* consisting of tuff blocks, is severely impressive. The large vestibule leads into one of the largest and tallest Tuscan atria in Pompeii. The *impluvium*, made of slabs of grey tuff, has moulded edges, and the east side had a marble table with griffins' feet, flanked by a pedestal surmounted by a bronze Herculean group with a fountain behind it, which filled a shell-shaped basin below.

Various *cubiculi*, entered through tall doors with *opus africanum* jambs consisting of large blocks of Sarnus stone, give onto the atrium, which is decorated with 1st-style reliefs. Two large *alae* at the sides of the *tablinum* served as waiting rooms for the *clientes* who flocked to this noble residence every day. At the end of the *tablinum*, which was on the same axis as the vestibule and the atrium, a large opening looked over the *viridarium*, with its Ionic portico. The *viridarium* was very attractive; the back wall was frescoed with an imaginary garden with fountains, flowers, exotic plants and birds, bordered by an imitation wooden fence. Anyone looking in from the street might have been deceived into believing that there was a garden of unusual beauty beyond the *tablinum*.

147 centre The diaeta in the west ambulatory of the peristyle is decorated on the upper part of the south wall with a magnificent fresco portraying Mars and Venus, who seem to be arguing over a small garland; at the sides, two cherubs are playing with the Mars' weapons.

147 bottom During the last years of its existence, the house was converted into a caupona, and the room to the north of the entrance became a thermopolium.

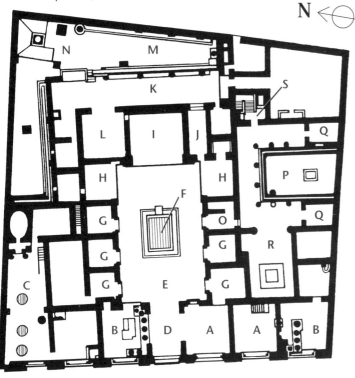

N ⟵⊙

A *Shops*
B *Thermopolia*
C *Bakery*
D *Vestibule*
E *Atrium*
F *Impluvium*
G *Cubiculi*
H *Alae*
I *Tablinum*
J *Corridor*
K *Portico*
L *Oecus*
M *Viridarium*
N *Summer triclinium*
O *Anteroom*
P *Peristyle*
Q *Diaetae*
R *Triclinium*
S *Kitchen*

THE SURGEON'S HOUSE (VI-1-10)

This house, excavated 1770–71, is so called because of the 40 surgical instruments in metal cases found here; these are now displayed in the National Archaeological Museum in Naples. The date of the house has been the subject of fierce debate between archaeologists for many years; A. Maiuri dated it at the fourth century BC, believing it to be an example of a Samnite house, but the results of recent archaeological research suggest that it dates from the middle of the third century BC.

According to stratigraphic surveys conducted by Maiuri in 1926, the house has always been the same size, and always situated in the central part of the *insula*, where it occupies an irregular site, previously flattened for an earlier building.

A *Shop*
B *Entrance*
C *Atrium*
D *Impluvium*
E *Alae*
F *Tablinum*
G *Cubiculi*
H *Triclinium*
I *Oecus*
J *Viridarium*

148 top The Surgeon's House gives onto Via Consolare, one of the oldest and busiest roads in Pompeii.

148 bottom The opus quadratum façade of the house, made of Sarnus stone, leads experts to believe this is one of the oldest residential properties in Pompeii.

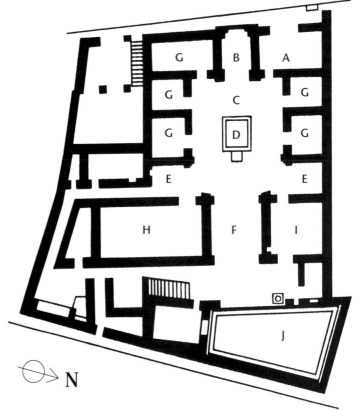

148-149 The tablinum of the house, modified on several occasions, gives onto the atrium and the peristyle behind it; this design is typical of the Italic house.

149 top left These forceps demonstrate the high degree of specialisation achieved by technicians in developing surgical instruments.

During its earliest incarnation, however, the entrance to the Surgeon's House was at a lower level and it had no *impluvium*; these facts lead some researchers to believe that the atrium was entirely roofed (a testudinate atrium), while others believe that it was unroofed, which gave the building the appearance '…of the courtyard of a country house, where the slope of the site and perhaps a cavity left intentionally in the centre, served to collect water and convey it into a tank'.

The house is laid out to an Italic plan, with the usual rooms, namely the vestibule, the atrium, the *tablinum* with its perpendicular *alae*, and finally the *hortus*, built on the same axis.

At a later stage, probably when Via Consolare was reorganised and paved, the whole house was given a floor at a higher level, mainly made of *opus signinum*. At this second stage the atrium was given a roofing system and

149 top right This *speculum uteris,* used by gynaecologists, shows the advanced level reached by the medicine of the period.

149 centre The activity of doctors is well documented in Pompeii due to the discovery of numerous cases containing surgical instruments such as scalpels, speculi and forceps.

149 bottom This painting, in the middle of the east wall of the cubiculum *on the right of the garden, shows a female artist at work.*

a Tuscan atrium-type *impluvium* and *compluvium*. The *impluvium*, made of grey Nuceria tuff slabs, collected water from the *compluvium* and passed it into the tank below, as demonstrated by the tuff mouth, which must have been surmounted by a well-head.

The atrium walls were decorated with 1st-style frescoes in the first phase, as demonstrated by some fragments, and were redecorated in the 4th style after the earthquake of AD 62. The black and white mosaic floors of the two *alae*, dating from the age of Augustus, feature a geometrically patterned threshold and a central mosaic carpet comprising a white background studded with coloured marble *crustae*, all surrounded by a black border.

A large tricliniar room stands on the right of the *tablinum*; it was redecorated in the first century AD and the walls feature 4th-style paintings, while the *opus signinum* floor has an *opus sectile emblema* in the middle. Outside the triclinium, a staircase leads to the upper storey, built over the southern part of the house and used as servants' quarters.

The Surgeon's House is one of the most remarkable in Pompeii: the condition of its well preserved structures means that it can be compared with other Pompeiian houses, which, to some extent, present the same architectural forms and expert use of materials.

THE HERCULANEUM GATE AND VIA DELLE TOMBE

The north *decumanus* of the town did not terminate in the west at a gate, because the plateau on which the town was built ended in a precipice there, preventing the road from continuing west. For this reason, the road curved north to the city gate in the north-west corner, where the Herculaneum Gate was built. From this gate, the road continued to Oplontis (now Torre Annunziata), Herculaneum and Naples, and to the numerous farms scattered over the slopes of Vesuvius.

The gate looks very impressive to those entering and leaving the town: both faces are symmetrical in appearance, with three round archways. The large archway in the middle was designed for vehicular traffic, and the smaller ones on each side for pedestrians. The paved road that runs under the gate narrows at the central archway. The stout pillars are covered with decorations of a type resembling the 1st style, with stucco-relief rustication.

Although the road leaving the town was not paved until the age of Augustus, it was certainly rebuilt from scratch after Sulla's conquest. A straight route was designed, leading from the Herculaneum Gate to Oplontis, where a military harbour had been built. The old route, now called Via Superior, curved gently east after leaving the gate, and led to the villas north of the town; the Villa of the Mysteries was reached from this road. The road slopes gradually downhill and is lined with tombs and villas. The charming aspect of this area meant that the excavators of the period decided not to bury the excavated buildings, so that the public could see not only the 'works of art', but also something of what life was like in ancient times.

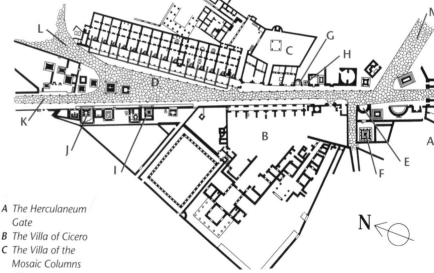

A The Herculaneum Gate
B The Villa of Cicero
C The Villa of the Mosaic Columns
D Shops
E The tomb of Mamia
F The Tomb of the Istacidi
G The Tomb of the Villa of the Mosaic Columns
H The Tomb of the Blue Vase
I The Tomb of Umbricius Sciaurus
J The Tomb of Naevoleia Tyche
K Via per Oplontis
L Via Superior
M Ring road

150 top left The Herculaneum Gate, one of the most attractive of Pompeii's city gates, must have appeared impressive to travellers; its large central archway and two small side arches give it the appearance of a triumphal arch, partly because of the stucco decoration which imitates marble opus quadratum.

150 bottom left. The tomb of the Istacidi, consisting of a tall podium surmounted by an Ionic tholos and ending in a truncated cone-shaped roof (now lost) stood immediately outside the gate.

150 top right The row of altar tombs on tall podia running along the west side of the necropolis is an impressive sight. These pictures by eighteenth-century artists circulated all over Europe, and Pompeii became an instant success in cultural circles.

150 bottom right The top part of this tomb dado contains marble doors giving access to the burial chamber in which the cinerary urns were housed.

THE VILLA OF DIOMEDES

The Villa of Diomedes is one of the largest and most luxurious in Pompeii. When excavated between 1771 and 1773 under the direction of B. Tanucci and F. La Vega it caused a sensation, not only for the wealth of its furnishings and the beautiful decorations, but also because found in the *cryptoporticus* were 18 bodies of women and children who had taken refuge there and were tragically buried by the shower of ash. The body of a richly bejewelled young woman left an imprint of breasts in the hardened mud, and this made such an impression on visitors that Théophile Gautier wrote a tragic short story about the imprint, identified as belonging to Arria Marcella. Because of the interest it aroused and its monumental architecture, the villa was the first residence outside the town to be excavated and not reburied.

The sector at road level was reached by a staircase with a two-column *prothyron* that led to a peristyle, around

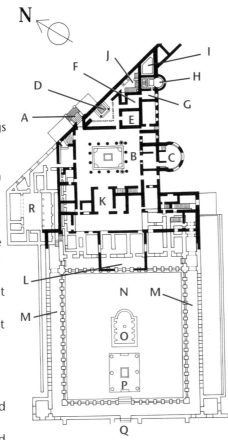

N

Upper floor	I Water basin
Lower floor	J Cistern
	K Kitchen
A Access staircase	L Tablinum
B Peristyle	M Exedra
C Couch recess	N Portico
D Balneum Frigidarium	O Garden
E Apodyterium	P Nymphaeum pool
F Frigidarium	Q Pergola
G Tepidarium	R Posticum
H Calidarium	S Servants' quarters

151 bottom right The peristyle, situated immediately inside the entrance, was built at a much higher level than the road. The bottom third of the Doric columns was coloured red, while the fluted top part was white.

which various living rooms were built, including a magnificent frescoed recess and a large apse with three large windows opening towards the south-west, offering a view of incomparable beauty.

The baths complex was built in the odd corner formed by the curve of the road; an attractive *balneum* stood in a triangular area with two porticoed sides, while the third side was frescoed with sea creatures and an imaginary garden. At the sides were the *apodyterium*, *frigidarium*, *tepidarium* and *calidarium* with the bathing pool, and an apse with beautiful 4th-style decorations and a hemispherical, shell-shaped *calotte* decorated with the signs of the zodiac.

Beyond the *tablinum*, in the middle of the western side, there was a magnificent terrace that led into a large windowed *exedra* on one side and, on the other, to a raised walkway above the peristyle. Two ramps led to the lower floor, where there was a large porticoed garden with 17 pillars on each side, a magnificent *nymphaeum* pool in the middle, and a pergola supported by six columns at one end. Along the eastern side of the garden were some magnificent living rooms richly frescoed with 4th-style paintings,

of which part of the ceiling decoration still survives. The peristyle was built in such a way that it was completely in harmony with its natural surroundings; large windows in the walls of the portico opposite the intercolumniations opened towards the outside.

The *cryptoporticus*, which matched exactly the size and shape of the peristyle above, mainly served as a cellar; the long route was illuminated by slits in the stylobate of the peristyle pillars. The servants' quarters were housed in an independent structure to the north of the house. Many of the house's paintings and all of the furnishings are now housed in the National Archaeological Museum in Naples .

151 left The back wall to the south of the magnificent calidarium *of the small baths complex was occupied by a small apse with a shell-shaped* calotte, *decorated with the signs of the zodiac.*

151 top right The large porticoed garden on the lower level of the villa featured a large fountain and a pergola supported by six columns resting on a tall base.

THE VILLA OF THE MYSTERIES

In view of its attractive architecture and Dionysian paintings, the Villa of the Mysteries is regarded as one of the most significant and best preserved of the monumental complexes outside the city walls to have been excavated. It was excavated, in part, between 1909 and 1910 by a private citizen, Aurelio Item, and was largely cleaned of volcanic pumice stone in 1929–1930 under the direction of A. Maiuri. The villa lies on an east-west axis, as did many of the dwellings in this sector; the front of the building rests on a quadrangular *basis villae*, constructed to make the sloping site level. The villa was reached from Via Superior, which ran to the east of it; the major road from the Herculaneum Gate to Oplontis was situated to the west of the villa, but it is not known if the building could be entered from this road.

The oldest incarnation of the villa dates from the early second century BC, when it would have been a regularly shaped, not so luxurious townhouse, although it did occupy an attractive position. That building was totally modernised shortly after the foundation of Sulla's colony in Pompeii (80 BC). It was extended and an extra storey was constructed, giving it the appearance of an opulent, suburban villa. It was also frescoed throughout with excellent 2nd-style paintings, including the cycle of the Dionysian Mysteries.

After the earthquake of AD 62, the villa seems to have lost the elegant, solemn appearance of a patrician villa. The owner may have sold it to someone who felt less obliged to keep up a certain image. The villa was gradually turned into a large winery, and the uses of the various rooms changed accordingly. The final stages of its transformation, which would probably have led to the eventual destruction of its exquisite decorations, was prevented by the eruption of AD 79. It is not certain who the owner was during the second half of the first century BC, when the house reached its greatest splendour; it may have been M. Livius Marcellus, since a statue of Livia with the attributes of Ceres was

A Vestibule
B Peristyle
C Atrium
D Impluvium
E Tablinum
F Windowed exedra
G Gardens
H Portico with nave and two aisles
I Kitchen area
J Bath district
K Torcularium
L Bathing area
M Torcularium
N Biclinium
O Diaetae
P Hall of the Mysteries
Q Tetrastyle atrium

found in the house. In the last years of the town's existence it was probably owned by the Istacidi, one of the most important families in Pompeii, as suggested by the fact that the seal of one of their procurators, L. Istacidus Zosimus, was found there.

The main entrance to the house was on the east side, from a side road off Via Superior. The layout was roughly symmetrical, and seems to reflect the observations of Vitruvius (VI-5-3) that, in suburban villas, the vestibule is immediately followed by the peristyle, not by the atrium as in townhouses. The vestibule, peristyle, atrium and *tablinum*, and an *exedra* with an apsidal wall that gives onto the hill sloping down to the sea, were all built on the same axis.

The entire perimeter of the villa was surrounded by a series of porticoes featuring various types of workmanship; in the front part, alongside the *basis villae*, was a hanging garden above a windowed *cryptoporticus*, which was later closed and used as a wine cellar.

The villa was entered through a long, wide vestibule divided into two sections: the first was paved and led to a small apartment (52-56) to the north, perhaps used by the villa's caretaker, and to the stables and servants' quarters to the south (35-41, 58-60); the second had an *opus signinum* floor, and masonry benches standing against the side walls and it constituted a waiting room. Here again, a small room (*cella ostiaria*) for a caretaker was situated to the north. The vestibule is followed by the peristyle, formed by a very elegant Doric colonnade of grey tuff, with six columns on the long sides and four on the short sides, which, regrettably, was closed off after AD 62 by a *pluteus,* which makes the area dark and robs air and light from all the rooms giving onto it. The pitched roof, which conveyed rainwater into the *viridarium*, terminates in elegant palmette *antefixae*. The back walls of the porticoes and the rooms around them are all decorated in the 2nd style.

The bathing area and the kitchen are situated on the south side. The bathing area (42-46) was built around an attractive small tetrastyle atrium, and comprised the *apodyterium, tepidarium, laconicum* and *calidarium*. The large kitchen, which had an open central courtyard and a brick *opus spicatum* floor, was fitted with a large bench used for cooking food and producing steam, and two ovens. A domestic *lararium* was also installed here.

A corridor on the north side of the peristyle leads to the *torcularium* (48-49), the room used for pressing grape must and making wine, where two presses were found, one of which has been restored. After harvesting, the grapes were laid in a basin (*palmentum*) and trodden. The wine produced thus was of the highest quality and particularly sweet, as the seeds and stalks were not crushed. The grape must was then collected under a press (*prelum*) and crushed repeatedly and heavily. Outside, to the north, was a huge wine cellar with numerous terracotta containers embedded in the

153 top right The biclinium, which gave onto the corridor leading from the atrium to the north portico, is magnificently decorated in the 2nd style to resemble a Corinthian oecus.

153 bottom left The tablinum is elegantly frescoed in the 3rd style with Egyptian motifs; in this case, the god Anubis is shown on the predella.

153 bottom right The biclinium between the tablinum and the Hall of the Mysteries features an unusual 2nd-style decorative scheme, in which small figured paintings are added to the architectural elements. This one, on the south wall of the biclinium, portrays a dancing satyr.

153 top left The wall separating the peristyle from the atrium was frescoed in the 2nd style and contains three openings: the central one is very wide, while the plaster cast of the door is displayed in the side sections.

153 centre left This impressive statue of Livia was found in the north-east corner of the peristyle, waiting to be installed in the large apse that was being specially prepared in a room in the northern part of the villa.

I	II	III	IV	V	V

floor, each of which had a capacity of some 200 litres of wine.

The peristyle led into the atrium through three large openings closed by double doors, two of which have been preserved in the form of plaster casts. The 2nd-style walls featured vermilion diamond shapes in the middle section and landscapes of the Nile, military trophies and paintings on wooden supports in the upper part. These have sadly been lost.

There is a sleeping area in the north part, containing bedrooms and a latrine. The *cubiculum* (no. 16), contains two bed recesses and an antechamber; the magnificent 2nd-style pictorial decoration with rows of buildings converging on a single point, and the black and white mosaic floor decoration reflect the physical division of the room. The *tablinum* (2) must originally have had a large opening onto the atrium and another onto the

exedra, but when it was restructured after the earthquake, both of these rooms were modified in size, since the role of the *tablinum* probably changed. Fortunately, the magnificent 3rd-style decoration, with Egyptian motifs against a black background, was left untouched. One of the most attractive rooms in the villa was the large apsidal *exedra* (1), which faced west and must have afforded a wonderful view through the three large windows in the

VII   VIII   IX

154-155 top
This line drawing shows the sequence of scenes which make up the painting, to be read from left to right, starting on the west wall.

154-155 bottom This photo shows scenes II, III, IV and V of the sequence, whose interpretation is controversial because the Dionysian rites were kept a close secret. It is certain, however, that the cycle is a copy of a Hellenistic original by a Campanian artist .

semicircular wall. At the sides of the *tablinum* and the *exedra* were two more small living areas, each with a large drawing room, *biclinium* and *diaeta*. They faced west onto a windowed portico. The drawing room with the paintings, after which the villa is named, is in the south sector. Oriented east-west, the drawing room has a large entrance in the west wall, a smaller one in the north-west corner, and a large window in the south wall; the last two were built after the earthquake, at the expense of the wall paintings. The floor features a carpet of palombino marble tiles. The walls are finely frescoed in the 2nd style with the famous series of large paintings, interpreted as a sequence of scenes from a Dionysian ritual. Not all experts agree on the sequence and the significance of each scene; the following is the most widely accepted theory, starting from the left-hand side of the west wall.

I. The girl to be initiated waits pensively. II. The ritual is read by a boy under the supervision of a woman, while the initiate listens attentively. III. The girl, seated, makes a propitiatory sacrifice before the initiation rite, helped by two attendants. IV. Old Silenus, delighted at the sight of Dionysus and Ariadne, sings and plays the lyre. A young satyr plays a wind instrument, and a bacchante suckles a fawn. V. The girl is frightened at the sight of Dionysus and his retinue. VI. In the centre, a drunken Dionysus leans on the seated Ariadne. In front of him is Silenus, who gives a drink to a pair of young satyrs. VII. The girl uncovers the mystic cist containing the phallus. VIII. When the pleasure is over, the girl is whipped by a winged demon to the clash of cymbals played by two bacchantes. IX. The girl, now initiated into the Dionysian mysteries, looks into a mirror held by a cherub.

156-157 This photo shows scenes VI and VII from the series of paintings decorating the Hall of the Mysteries. From left to right: an old Silenus gives a drink to a pair of young satyrs, a drunken Dionysus leans on the seated Ariadne, and a kneeling girl uncovers the cist containing the mystic phallus.

157 bottom left In scene VIII, when the pleasure is over, the girl is whipped by a winged demon to the clash of cymbals played by two bacchantes.

157 bottom right. In scene IX, the girl, now initiated into the Dionysian mysteries and radiantly beautiful, is at her toilet and looks with new eyes into a mirror held by a cherub.

THE PANORAMIC BUILDINGS OF POMPEII

A The Marine Gate
B The Suburban Baths
C The Temple of Venus
D The Imperial Villa

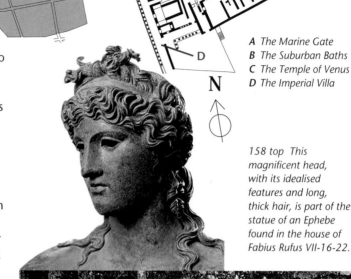

*I*n the first century BC, the whole western slope of Pompeii, from the Herculaneum Gate to the Marine Gate, and the southern section from the west to the spur on which the Triangular Forum stands, was occupied by magnificent public buildings such as the Temple of Venus, and splendid houses designed to make the most of their exceptional view over the Gulf of Naples. The Pompeiians undoubtedly spent more of their wealth on these buildings than any others, producing a unique district. Sadly, after the eruption of Vesuvius, looting, a lack of expertise among some of the early excavators, and neglect suffered by the buildings for years following excavation, prevent the modern visitor from fully appreciating one of the nicest and most interesting parts of Pompeii.

INSULA OCCIDENTALIS

The Insula Occidentalis is the area of town located to the west of Via Consolare, Via del Farmacista and Vico dei Soprastanti, as far as the Marine Gate. It consists of a long row of detached houses, running from the Herculaneum Gate to the Marine Gate. Their entrances are situated to the east, on the town roads, and they are built on terraces (usually three) sloping down toward the sea, endowing them with wonderful views. The multi-level construction and the organisation of the architectural volumes in order to fully exploit the scenic aspects, suggests that these houses were urban villas rather than townhouses. The extensions of these houses to the west did not take place all at the same time; the oldest nucleus of buildings probably dates from around the second half of the first century BC. At that time, the houses did not extend beyond the city walls, which defended this side of the town. After Sulla's conquest (80 BC), when the city

walls lost their significance, and more especially in the age of Augustus (late first century BC to early first century AD), with the advent of the *Pax Romana*, the houses were extended beyond the walls, generally by constructing large gardens and peristyles below the sloping terraces. It is easy to imagine the wonderful view of the sea from this part of the town, and it was probably this view that inspired the numerous landscapes portraying what are known as 'seaside villas'. It is believed that these buildings were influenced by the experience of many Italic merchants and

158 top This magnificent head, with its idealised features and long, thick hair, is part of the statue of an Ephebe found in the house of Fabius Rufus VII-16-22.

158 bottom This small painting of two heads crowned with vine shoots, set against a red background, decorated the centre of the west wall of the oecus. Note the use of different shades on the two vaults to differentiate the perspectival planes.

158-159 The back wall of the oecus in the House of the Golden Bracelet VI-17-42 portrays a

magnificent imaginary garden containing a variety of plants, flowers and birds. At the top, oscilli hang against the blue background of the sky.

159 top right The House of Fabius Rufus VII-16-22 commanded a magnificent view over the Gulf of Naples thanks to the terrace and the apsidal exedra with its large windows. This façade was built above the city walls.

Fabius family because a bronze seal and graffiti were found in a number of the rooms. After the earthquake of AD 62, the house's last owner combined a number of smaller dwellings to create a single large complex over four floors. The view from the west is spectacular: the lower half consists of the stout city walls surmounted by two large, rectangular *avant-corps* flanking a series of arched niches framing windows. In the centre is a large apsidal drawing room with two rows of three wide windows. Above this level is a porticoed area from which the beautiful view could be enjoyed.

businessmen in the Orient, to show their assimilation of the Greek culture. The builders who worked on these houses had fine technical skills, and the architects were successful in interpreting the specifications drawn from buildings seen in distant countries.

In the section corresponding to Via Consolare (VI-17), neighbouring houses nos. 41 and 42 are of special interest. House VI-17-41 was identified in 1759, when it was explored, but only to remove the most interesting-looking paintings. Two walls, decorated in the 2nd style, are now in the Archaeological Museum in Naples; on one, a hare hangs from a red partition against which a Dionysian mask rests (no. 9847); on the other, fish and game hang from two partitions flanking a central *aedicule* which leads to an unroofed area with a *tholos* and a colonnaded building (no. 6594). *Exedra* (no. 18) is also decorated in the 2nd style, with a tall podium surmounted by two porticoed *alae* at the sides and an apsidal *aedicule* in the centre, in which a crowned poet stands, wearing a short toga with a red border over a short-sleeved tunic. House VI-17-42 is known as the House of the Golden Bracelet, because the body of a bejewelled woman with a child and a casket full of coins was found there. The building is laid out on three sloping terraces. The most fascinating part is at garden-level,

where a magnificent *nymphaeum* stands, decorated with a glass paste mosaic, to which a swimming pool and a triclinium are connected. The side rooms are frescoed with an imaginary garden, with fountains, statues and small paintings supported by *hermae*.

In the section corresponding to Via del Farmacista and Vico dei Soprastanti (VII-16), there are two houses of note. The first, house no. 15, was owned by U. Umbricius Sciaurus, as demonstrated by the inscription set in an unusual floor mosaic around the *impluvium*; four of the small amphoras used to store *garum* are displayed in the corners, together with the owner's name and business. The second is the large House of Fabius Rufus (VII-16-22), magnificently frescoed with paintings of the 2nd, 3rd and 4th styles. The house has been attributed to the

*159 bottom right
This decoration, from the* exedra *of House VI-17-41, portrays a tall podium surmounted by a*

porticoed ala *on either side, and an apsidal* aedicule *in the middle, in which a crowned poet wearing a short toga stands.*

A *House VI-17-42*
B *The House of the Golden Bracelet VI-17-22*
C *The House of Fabius Rufus VII-16-22*
D *The House of Umbricius Sciaurus VII-16-15*

THE SUBURBAN BATHS

In the area to the north of the road leading to the Marine Gate, further downhill from the city walls, a grandiose multi-storey baths complex was built, brilliantly constructed by the architect on an irregular, steep slope. The main entrance was located on the north side of the porticoed road that climbed upwards to the town; it consisted of a vestibule with the façade framed by two half-columns, which gave onto a triangular porticoed area paved with blocks of tuff. All the usual bathing rooms were situated on the ground floor. Bathers first entered the changing room, frescoed in the 4th style with numbered erotic paintings in the upper section. They would then go into the magnificent *frigidarium* with its floor of marble slabs, and columns at the sides supporting a corbel and a complex vault decorated with stucco reliefs. At the end was a large swimming pool, whose walls were frescoed with seascapes, *naumachiae* and scenes of the Nile. The pool was filled by a pretty *nymphaeum* with a cascading fountain covered with glass paste mosaics; at the point where the

160-161 The Suburban Baths complex is situated in the area between the city walls and the road that led down to the Marine Gate.

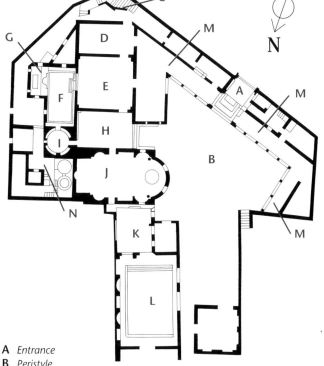

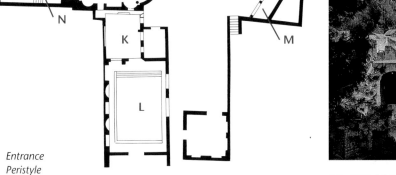

A Entrance
B Peristyle
C Staircase
  to top floor
D Changing room
E Frigidarium
F Balneum
G Nymphaeum
H Tepidarium
I Laconicum
J Calidarium
K Anteroom
L Hot pool
M Porticoes
N Praefurnium

*160 bottom right
The* nymphaeum *above the cold swimming pool was formed by a distyle niche from which water cascaded down a small staircase to fill the pool. The coloured mosaic decoration in the niche portrays Mars and two cherubs.*

161 left This detail, showing a cherub wielding a sword, is part of the mosaic that decorated the niche of the nymphaeum *above the cold swimming pool.*

161 top right The area in front of the baths is an unusual trapezoid shape with two porticoed sides, which must have provided bathers with shade from the sun.

161 bottom right The imitation 1st-style decoration of the façade must have been visible from the sea. The area in front of it was paved with blocks of grey tuff.

160 bottom left A room on the top floor of the baths, which was frescoed in the 4th style. It was reached via a wide staircase at the end of the south portico; the rooms, possibly used by prostitutes, overlooked the magnificent scenery of the Gulf.

water gushed out, Mars was portrayed with cupids bringing his weapons.

On the left of the *frigidarium* is the *tepidarium*, the raised floor of which was supported on *suspensurae* and the walls were lined with *tegulae mammatae*. To the left of the back wall is the classic, circular *laconicum*, which has four apses set into its walls. Immediately after this comes the large *calidarium*, which also had a floor supported on *suspensurae* and *tegulae mammatae* walls, which were ornamented with niches and apses where marble statues must have stood. The view from the windowed apse in the west wall, overlooking the porticoed courtyard would have been magnificent. After the *calidarium* came another heated antechamber which led to a heated swimming pool; here the sides of the pool were stepped and, again, the walls were decorated with apses and niches. A winding passage

162-163 *This magnificent stucco relief of a cherub riding a triton decorated one of the panels in the vault of the* frigidarium.

162 bottom left The top part of the changing room walls was decorated with numbered panels, each portraying an erotic scene; this decoration has been interpreted as a catalogue of services offered by the brothel on the top floor.

162 bottom right This relief decoration portrays a standing cherub with a cloak, looking right towards the swimming pool. The whole frigidarium *is exquisitely decorated with stucco in the 4th style.*

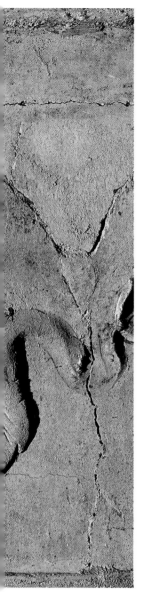

from the south-eastern corner of the complex led to the service rooms, which were situated behind the bathing complex. The *praefurnium* consisted of ovens and boilers of an unusually large capacity in order keep the many rooms heated.

Other rooms associated with the baths led onto the outer courtyard; one of them, connected with the antechamber between the *calidarium* and the swimming pool, is magnificently frescoed in the 4th style

earthquake of AD 62, and was closed at the time of the eruption, although the repair work was well under way. After the eruption, the area was raided repeatedly, and towards the end of the first millennium, was probably inhabited, as demonstrated by finds dating from the middle ages. Although the complex was identified in the nineteenth century, it was not completely excavated and philologically restored until quite recently (1987–1992).

163 top This painting, of outstanding craftsmanship, shows a small cart drawn by two billy-goats, which contains a comedy mask, a cornucopia and a thyrsus. The scene decorated the vault of the frigidarium.

163 bottom A flying stork in an arch supported by fluted pillars. The arch is framed at the top and bottom by an ovolo cornice. This decoration is situated in the frigidarium.

with stucco relief decorations. A small marble *labrum* that provided fresh running water stood here. Another room in the north-west corner had four large windows, one on each wall, which afforded magnificent views over the Gulf. From the south side, a wide masonry staircase led to the upper storey, where a number of chambers faced onto the west side, with other service rooms and a kitchen behind them. It is probable that the services depicted in the changing room were supplied by girls in these chambers, which is why they were numbered.

The complex, which was probably built in the late first century BC, was badly damaged in the

THE MARINE GATE

The paved road leading into Pompeii from the Marine Gate is so steep that it is unlikely to have been used by carts. All goods entering the town from this side were probably carried by capable porters or by mules, and the quantities involved must have been vast, since ships' cargoes were conveyed into the town along this route from the nearby harbour. The road was flanked to the south by a low wall and to the north, by a wide pavement porticoed with square pillars and paved with *opus signinum*. Various shops and the entrance to the Suburban Baths gave onto the porticoes. A large wharf-like area, with rings of stone arranged at regular intervals along the vertical wall, could also be reached from here; these elements suggest that there was a canal or harbour here, where ships anchored, but the experts do not all agree with this theory.

During the recent restoration work another inscription was found relating to the magistrate Suedius Clemens, who was sent to Pompeii after the earthquake of AD 62 to restore order to the town's properties, occupied illegally by private citizens (*see also* The Nuceria Gate and the Necropolis). This gate is certainly one of the most recent in the town. It has as a large *avant-corps* with a square tower standing apart from the line of the walls. The gate has a large barrel-vaulted gallery divided into two parts;

the larger opening on the right served for goods and animals, and the smaller, more convenient one on the left, for pedestrians. Both openings were closed with double doors, as suggested by the marks in the ground. This is the entrance now used by most visitors to the ancient town.

THE TEMPLE OF VENUS

Following the eruption of AD 79, the structures of this temple, which must have been one of the loveliest in Pompeii, were pillaged to such a devastating extent, that it is now difficult to imagine what it must have looked like. Unfortunately, as it stood to the south-west, on a terrace overhanging the valley between the Marine Gate and the Basilica, the temple was partly visible and thus identifiable by raiders.

The cult of Venus had ancient origins in Pompeii, although it originally related to Venus Physica, a goddess who ruled over life and death, and therefore both a celestial deity and a deity of the underworld. It was the dictator Sulla who introduced the cult of Venus as the goddess of love and

beauty; in fact, the colony he founded in Pompeii was called Colonia Cornelia Veneria Pompeianorum, and the temple at the Marine Gate was dedicated to Venus. As demonstrated by recent stratigraphic surveys, the earlier buildings on the site were expropriated.

In the early first century AD, the temple was entirely rebuilt, almost completely in marble; it would have stood on a tall podium with the front, probably of the Corinthian order, facing south. It stood in the middle of a huge site and was porticoed on at least three sides. No traces of the stylobate or the channel used to drain off rainwater have been found on the south side, which may have been left open, so that the temple could be seen from below by those crossing the

valley or sailing down the River Sarnus. During this second stage, the sacred area acquired the forms of an urban sanctuary and was further extended, as suggested by the south wall of *opus reticulatum*, which is built inside the southernmost third of the roadbed of Via Marina. The main entrance was in the north-eastern corner of the area, on the south pavement of the Marine Gate.

The temple was badly damaged by the earthquake of AD 62, but rebuilding work was probably at an advanced stage, as demonstrated by the finish of the few surviving elements. Very little now remains, however: the podium of the temple, made of cement and surrounded by a perimeter of large blocks of basalt stone; a beautiful, complete column with a Corinthian capital, which has been raised so that its exact position cannot be ascertained; and finally, two statue bases. The south face of the terrace was substructed on a series of vaulted rooms reached by a staircase that led down into a gallery in the south-eastern sector of the terrace; the western and eastern sides of the area probably had two rows of columns, and there may have been shops associated with the sanctuary on the end walls.

THE IMPERIAL VILLA

The Imperial Villa, as it is known, was built to the south of the road leading east to the Marine Gate, against the western walls of this section, at the end of the first century BC, when the city's defence walls lost their purpose, with the advent of the Pax Romana. This is evident from the magnificent 3rd-style decoration on the back wall of the portico. Behind the city walls (a large section of which can be seen where the pictorial decoration has been lost), a long, wide, rectangular terrace was created, bounded to the west by a low wall and, to the east, by a very long portico supported by 41 brick columns covered with fluted white stucco. The back wall of this portico is decorated in a style particular to a phase of the 3rd style, characterised by the use of paratactic ornamentation of the black background with slender *aedicules*; small paintings and figured medallions (mainly removed by eighteenth-century

excavators) were alternated in the centre of the *aedicules*.

The area in front of the portico was laid out as a hanging garden. The ancient town ring road ran alongside it, and further on, crossed Via di Porta Marina, which was abolished when the villa was built. A grandiose, tall drawing room, magnificently decorated in the 4th style, gives onto the portico in a roughly central position. Much of the floor, decorated with an exquisite

pattern of marble hexagons edged by a white strip, has sadly been lost, and it is assumed that the room was being restored, and it had not yet been laid. The frescoed walls are divided into panels painted with the precious vermilion colour (Pompeiian red), and feature three large paintings of good quality, inspired by the Cretan cycle. The painting on the east wall portrays Theseus after the slaying of the Minotaur, the one on the north wall Theseus abandoning Ariadne asleep on Naxos, and the one on the south wall, Daedalus flying and Icarus lying on the ground. The upper part of the walls features *trompe l'œil* open windows, through which can be seen female figures and poets, such as Sappho and Alcaeus.

164 left The Marine Gate, at the top of the road leading up from the sea, consists of a wide archway for goods traffic and a narrower, more convenient pedestrian passageway.

164 top right This magnificent athlete's head, with short curly hair tied with a fillet, was found in the southern part of the Temple of Venus; it may be a Hellenistic original dating from the second century BC

164 bottom right The temple occupies the far south-west corner of the town, in a position overlooking the Gulf and the Sarnus Valley. It was destroyed by the earthquake of AD 62, and never reopened.

165 left The 4th-style painting in the large drawing room of the villa portrays the death of Icarus under the horrified gaze of his father Daedalus and a muse sitting on a rock.

165 top right The villa portico, which gave onto a terrace overlooking the Gulf, could be reached directly from the road leading up from the Marine Gate; the end wall was magnificently decorated in the 3rd style.

165 bottom right The large drawing room in the centre of the portico is finely decorated in the 4th style with mythological paintings of fine craftsmanship.

GLOSSARY

AEDICULE: An architectural structure in the form of a small temple containing a statue.

AGATHODEMONE: 'Which bears good fruit'; said of serpents that approach the altars in domestic *lararia*.

AGGER: The ramparts behind the inner city walls.

ALA: A waiting room in the atrium, near the *tablinum*, with an entrance almost as wide as the whole room.

ANTEFIXA: An earthenware ornament placed at the ends of the curved tiles of pitched roofs; usually decorated with palmettes or the head of a Silenus or Gorgon.

APODYTERIUM: The changing room in the baths.

APSIDAL VAULT: The apse-shaped end wall of the *calidarium* containing a fresh-water basin.

ARA: Altar used for sacrifices and libations.

ARULA: A small mobile domestic altar, usually made of terracotta.

AUGUSTALES: The college of priests who honoured the memory of the Emperors.

BICLINIUM: A rest room containing two couches.

BISELLIUM: An honorary two-seater chair, used for one person.

CALIDARIUM: The room in the baths used for hot baths.

CAPITOLINE TRIAD: Jupiter, Juno and Minerva, the most important gods to the Romans, worshipped on the Capitol (Capitolium).

CAPITOLIUM: The temple dedicated to the Capitoline Triad: Jupiter, Juno and Minerva.

CARDO (CARDINES): A secondary road running north-south.

CASTELLUM PLUMBEUM: A lead pillar 1-1.5 metres square and 6 metres tall.

CAUPONA: Inn where hot meals were served to diners seated around a table.

CAVEA: The area reserved for spectators in the theatre and amphitheatre, usually divided into three tiers: the *ima* (bottom) *cavea*, *media* (middle) *cavea* and *summa* (top) *cavea*.

CHALCIDICUM: The area in front of the entrance to the Basilica.

CLIENS (CLIENTES): An inhabitant with very limited rights; they devoted themselves to the service of a patron, who took them under his protection.

COLONY: A town founded by citizens of a state who were forced to leave their home town for military, political or economic reasons and settle elsewhere. For the Romans, this was the means of penetrating and dominating conquered territories.

COLUMELLA: A grave marker made of volcanic stone or marble, in the form of a highly stylised bust of the deceased.

COMPLUVIUM: An opening in the middle of the atrium roof of houses which conveyed rainwater to the impluvium.

CRUSTA: A marble element used to decorate *opus signinum* floors or in monochrome mosaics.

CRYPTOPORTICUS: An underground corridor illuminated by window slits, used as a cellar and store for amphoras, often corresponding to the colonnaded porticoes at ground level.

CUBICULUM: A small bedroom containing only one bed.

CURIA: The hall where the *decurions*, who represented the town's Senate, met.

DECUMANUS: A main road which ran east-west.

DECURIONS: Members of the town's Senate, usually former magistrates, who met in the *curia*.

DOLIUM: A large, spherical terracotta wine container with a wide mouth, usually embedded in the floor.

DUUMVIRI: The most important town magistrates; two were elected every year, and subsequently entered the *curia*.

EMBLEMA: A figured representation or geometrical mosaic pattern.

EURIPUS: Ornamental pool with fountains and cascades, which often had garden statuettes along its edges.

EXEDRA: A large living and dining room, usually well lit, situated next to the peristyle or in a panoramic position in suburban villas.

FAUCES: Part of the entrance to the house, usually the initial part.

FREEDMAN: An emancipated slave, whose children became free citizens.

FRIGIDARIUM: The room in the baths used for cold baths.

FULLONICA: A laundry where clothes and fabrics were washed and dyed.

GARUM: A sauce made from fermented fish innards, used to flavour food.

HERM: A marble or bronze bust or head supported by inverted truncated-pyramid shaped elements.

HORTUS: A cultivated garden.

IMAGINES MAIORUM: Portraits of illustrious ancestors.

IMPLUVIUM: A low, square basin in the middle of the atrium floor into which rainwater flowed from the roof via the *compluvium*; the water was conveyed from the *impluvium* into cisterns through channels underneath it.

INSULA: A rectangular block of buildings in a town, bounded by four roads.

LABRUM: A circular basin, usually on a stand, which supplied running water; generally located in the apsidal vault of the *calidarium* in the baths.

LACONICUM: The room of the baths resembling a sauna, in which heat was provided by braziers or the hypocaust.

LARARIUM: A niche or apse containing statuettes of the household gods, lares and penates.

LAVA CEMENT: Flooring made of crushed Vesuvius lava mixed with mortar.

LAVAPESTA: See page 31.

NICHE: A rectangular recess in a wall, which often housed a statue.

NYMPHAEUM: A monumental fountain.

ODEON: A roofed building used for musical recitals.

OECUS: A reception room.

OPUS AFRICANUM: See page 25.

OPUS INCERTUM: See page 25.

OPUS LATERICIUM: See page 25.

OPUS QUADRATUM: See page 24.

OPUS QUASI RETICULATUM: See page 25.

OPUS RETICULATUM: See page 25.

OPUS SECTILE: See page 31.

OPUS SIGNINUM: Flooring consisting of crushed earthenware vessels mixed with mortar (see page 31).

OPUS TESSELLATUM: See page 31.

OPUS VERMICULATUM: See page 31.

OPUS VITTATUM: See page 25.

OPUS VITTATUM MIXTUM: See page 25.

OSCILLUM: A disc- or shield-shaped marble ornament decorated on both sides, hung in atria and peristyles.

PALMENTUM: An *opus signinum* floor with rounded corners on which grapes were trodden.

PAN: The god of the woods, depicted with horns and hoofs.

PAPPAMONTE: Soft lava quarried in the upper part of lava flows.

PILASTER STRIP (OR LESENE): An imitation pillar, often made of stucco or carved into a tuff surface.

PISTRINUM: A bakery, where corn was ground and bread baked.

PLUTEUS: A low wall closing the space between columns.

POMOERIUM: Sacred, inviolable public land behind the outer walls, usually 100 feet wide.

PRAEFURNIUM: A furnace producing the heat required by the baths.

PRIAPUS: Son of Dionysus, worshipped as the god of the fields, flocks and, above all, of vegetable gardens.

REGIO: A district of a town, bounded by major roads.

ROSTRUM: A beam with metal spurs fitted in the prow of a ship and used to ram enemy ships.

SCHOLA: A semi-circular stone seat, often used for tomb architecture.

SUSPENSURA: A cavity under the floor of the baths in which heat circulated.

TABERNA: A shop.

TABLINUM: The room of the house situated between the atrium and the peristyle, on the same axis as the longitudinal part of the house, in which the owner conducted business and received *clientes*.

TEGULAE MAMMATAE: Quadrangular tiles with four peduncles, laid on the walls of the baths to create a cavity inside which heat circulated.

TEPIDARIUM: The room of the baths used for massages after the hot bath and sauna, which allowed the bather to acclimatise gradually to the different temperatures of the adjacent rooms.

THEMENOS: A sacred wall surrounding a sanctuary.

THERMOPOLIUM: A place where hot and cold food was sold, usually located along the roads and consisting of an L-shaped masonry counter which contained large terracotta vessels.

THOLOS: A circular temple.

TORCULARIUM: The room in which grapes were pressed with the *torculum*.

TORCULUM: A beam with a pressing system used to press grapes on the *palmentum*.

TRIGLYPH: A rectangular slab with three vertical grooves which separated the metopes in Doric temples.

VELARIUM: An awning over theatre seats, to provide spectators with shade.

VIRIDARIUM: The pleasure garden of the peristyle at the end of the house.

WAXED TABLET: Rectangular writing tablets with filleted edges; wax was applied to them and the words engraved with a stylus.

WEDGE: A wedge-shaped sector of the theatre containing tiers of seats which gradually narrowed from the highest to the lowest.

BIBLIOGRAPHY

-F.Furccheim, *Bibliografia di Pompei, Ercolano e Stabia*, Napoli 1891

-H.B. Van der Poel, *Corpus Topographicum Pompeianum*. Pars IV: 'Bibliography', Roma 1977

-V.Kockel, *Archaeologische Funde und Forschungen in den Vesuvstaedten I-II*, in 'Archaeologischer Anzeigen', 1985, 1986.

-AA.VV., *Pompeiana. Raccolta di Studi per il secondo Centenario degli scavi di Pompei*, Napoli 1950

-A. Maiuri, *Pompei*, Roma 1961

-M. Della Corte, *Case ed abitanti di Pompei*, Napoli 1965

-R. Etienne, *La vita quotidiana a Pompei*, Milano 1973

-M. Grant, A. Mulas, *Eros a Pompei*, Milano 1974

-B. Andreae, H.Kyrieleis (edited by), *Neue Forschungen in Pompeii*, Recklinghausen 1975

-P. Castren, *Ordo Populusque Pompeianus*, Roma 1975

-A.Carandini (edited by), *L'instrumentum domesticum di Ercolano e Pompei nella prima età imperiale*, Roma 1977

-AA.VV., *Fonti documentarie per la storia degli scavi di Pompei, Ercolano e Stabia*, Napoli 1979

-W.Jashemski, *The gardens of Pompeii, Herculaneum and the villas destroyed by Vesuvius*, New York 1979

-F. Zevi (edited by), Pompei 79, Napoli 1979

-AA.VV., *La regione sotterrata dal Vesuvio. Studi e prospettive*, Napoli 1982

-A. Barbet, La peinture murale romaine, Parigi 1985

-AA.VV., *Le collezioni del Museo Nazionale di Napoli*, Roma 1986

-AA.VV., Pompei. *L'informatica al sevizio di una città antica*, I-II, Roma 1988

-L. Franchi dell'Orto (edited by), *Restaurare Pompei*, Roma 1990

-F. Zevi (edited by), *Pompei, I-II* (Banco di Napoli) 1991-1992

-S. De Caro, *Lo sviluppo urbanistico di Pompei*, in 'Atti e Memorie della Società', 3.1, 1992, pp. 67-88

-P. Zanker, *Pompei. Società, immagini urbane e forme dell'abitare*, Torino 1993

-L. Eschebach, *Gebeadeverzeichnis und Stadtplan der antiken Stadt Pompeji*, Cologne 1993

-A. Varone, *Erotica pompeiana*, Roma 1993

-L. Franchi dell'Orto (edited by), *Riscoprire Pompei*, Roma 1993

-S. De Caro, *Il Museo Archeologico Nazionale di Napoli*, Napoli 1994

-E. Furnari (edited by), *Neapolis I-II-III*, Roma 1994

-A. Wallace-Hadrill, *Houses and society in Pompeii and Herculaneum*, Princeton 1994

-E. La Rocca, M. and A. de Vos *Guida archeologica di Pompei*, Milano 1994

-H. and L. Eschebach, *Pompeji*, Cologne 1995

-AA.VV., *Archaeologie und Seismologie*, Munich 1995

-N.De Haan, G.Jansen (edited by), *Cura aquarum in Campania*, Leiden 1996

-AA.VV., *Domestic Space in the Roman world: Pompeii and Beyond*, Portsmouth 1997

-AA.VV., *Pompei. Pitture e Mosaici, I-X* in Enciclopedia Italiana Treccani, Roma 1990-1998.

SPECIALISED REVIEWS

-Rivista di Studi Pompeiani 1934–1946

-'Cronache Pompeiane' 1-5 1975–1979

-'Pompeii, Herculaneum, Stabiae' 1 1983

-'Rivista di Studi Pompeiani' I-VI 1987–1994

-'Opuscola Pompeiana' I-V 1991–1996

ILLUSTRATION CREDITS

All the photographs, apart from the following, are by **Alfredo and Pio Foglia/Archivio Fotografico Foglia S.a.s.**: *Giulio Veggi/Archivio White Star*: pages 29 top, 38 bottom right, 41 left, 41 top right, 41 centre right, 48 bottom, 51 top left, 74 bottom, 75 bottom left, 75 centre left, 79 top left, 79 centre left, 96 left, 107, 108 left, 108 right, 109 top, 109 centre, 109 bottom, 116-117, 155; **A.K.G. Photo**: pages 9, 12-13 top, 14, 15, 16-17; **Giovanni Dagli Orti**: pages 5, 86-87; **Mary Evans Picture Library**: pages 18 centre, 18-19; **Guido Alberto Rossi/The Image Bank**: 'Permission S.M.A. no. 01-337 of 3 March, 1996' pages 2-3, 20, 21 left, 21 right, 80 top, 92, 126 top right; **Archivio Scala**: pages 154-155, 157 right, 158 centre; **Roger Viollet**: pages 18 top, 18 bottom, 19 top right.
Black and white drawings are by Livio Bourbon.

168 Three sea-horses seem to spring out of the red background, conveying a feeling of liveliness and supernatural force. The artist wanted to try a subject which required great skill, because it was a view of three figures in violent movement (triclinium of the House of the Vettii).